Making Nutrition Your Business

Building a Successful Private Practice

SECOND EDITION

Ann Silver, MS, RDN, CDE, CDN

Lisa Stollman, MA, RDN, CDE, CDN

Academy of Nutrition and Dietetics
Chicago, IL

Academy of Nutrition and Dietetics
120 S. Riverside Plaza, Suite 2190
Chicago, IL 60606

Making Nutrition Your Business: Building a Successful Private Practice,
Second Edition

ISBN 978-0-88091-952-4 (print)
ISBN 978-0-88091-953-1 (eBook)
Catalog Number 440818 (print)
Catalog Number 440818e (eBook)

The views expressed in this publication are those of the authors and do not necessarily reflect policies and/or official positions of the Academy of Nutrition and Dietetics. Mention of product names in this publication does not constitute endorsement by the authors or the Academy of Nutrition and Dietetics. The Academy of Nutrition and Dietetics disclaims responsibility for the application of the information contained herein.

10   9   8   7   6   5   4   3   2   1

For more information on the Academy of Nutrition and Dietetics, visit www.eatright.org.

Library of Congress Cataloging-in-Publication Data
Names: Silver, Ann (Ann M.), author. | Stollman, Lisa, author. | Preceded by
   (work): Mitchell, Faye Berger. Making Nutrition Your Business. | Academy
   of Nutrition and Dietetics.
Title: Making Nutrition Your Business : Building a Successful Private
   Practice / Ann Silver, Lisa Stollman.
Description: Second edition. | Chicago, IL : Academy of Nutrition and
   Dietetics, [2018] | Preceded by Making Nutrition Your Business / Faye
   Berger Mitchell and Ann M. Silver. | Includes bibliographical references
   and index.
Identifiers: LCCN 2017036900 (print) | LCCN 2017037531 (ebook) | ISBN
   9780880919531 (eBook) | ISBN 9780880919524 (print)
Subjects: | MESH: Dietetics | Entrepreneurship | Private
   Practice--organization & administration | Practice
   Management--organization & administration
Classification: LCC RM218.5 (ebook) | LCC RM218.5 (print) | NLM WB 400 | DDC
   613.2068--dc23
LC record available at https://lccn.loc.gov/2017036900

Table of Contents

Preface

Welcome to the new edition of *Making Nutrition Your Business*. You have made a very wise decision to read this book as you plan to develop a private practice. What an exciting time to embark on this venture to own your own business! There is a lot to learn and understand about starting and running a prosperous business, and we'll share what we've learned firsthand about building our own successful private practices.

First, some history of this book: The very first edition, published in 2004, was titled *The American Dietetic Association Guide to Private Practice: An Introduction to Starting Your Own Business*. It was written by two trailblazers, the late Ann Selkowitz Litt and Faye Berger Mitchell, and it covered the basics of going into private practice, which was considered less traditional at that time. In 2011, the next edition of the book, coauthored by Faye Berger Mitchell and Ann Silver, modified the name to *Making Nutrition Your Business: Private Practice and Beyond*. In addition to addressing the details of starting a private practice, this edition covered other areas, such as speaking and writing, which can be additional ways to diversify a private practice and expand your revenue stream.

Due to the tremendous growth of registered dietitian nutritionists (RDNs) working with patients in a private practice, the Academy of Nutrition and Dietetics recognized the need to focus this edition of the book exclusively on building and growing a private practice in even greater detail. This book presents the essentials for starting, developing, and growing your own private practice. The following pages contain what we recommend an RDN considering this business venture needs to know:

- Find out if having your own private practice is right for you. You may have the skills to see patients, but having an entrepreneurial temperament is a separate issue to consider.

- Discover the fundamentals of being in business, including identifying your target market, business name, and your niche.

- Understand what's involved in setting up a private practice, from the legal aspects of creating a business to finding your office and setting up the necessary forms and tools you need for billing and for becoming an insurance provider, which are all crucial for getting paid.

- Explore the many options for getting the word out by marketing your business in your community and on various social media platforms, setting up a website, and more.

- Get inspired with real-life stories and suggestions for succeeding in your business from trendsetting private practice RDNs.

- Learn where to go for more information; we provide a list of other resources that we recommend to support your efforts to establish and build your practice.

Since the last edition of the book, we've seen many more RDNs use their entrepreneurial spirit and drive to become their own bosses and hang out their shingles. As the medical community and the public continue to realize that nutrition is the cornerstone of optimal health, the need for RDNs in private practice is at an all-time high. In addition to having freestanding offices, RDNs are delving into telehealth and setting up virtual offices where they can counsel patients from any location using Wi-Fi access. Insurance coverage has expanded for nutrition, but it has also become more complex; this edition now offers more guidance on setting up third-party reimbursement and helps answer the many questions you may have on becoming an insurance provider. Depending on your office location and your practice specialty, you'll learn that being an insurance provider may help you see more patients. Note that throughout the book, we refer to either *patient* or *client* interchangeably. In your practice, you will choose the term that you feel appropriately refers to the individuals you treat.

Keep in mind that this book is not intended to replace valuable advice from accountants, lawyers, and other business professionals. Seek out these professionals when you feel you need them. You may read this book cover to cover, or you may jump around to learn about a specific aspect of private practice. Keep this book on your bookshelf for future reference even once you are in your dream practice. You never know when you will need to refer back to it.

We have both been fortunate to have successful private practices, and we are thrilled that you have decided to make nutrition your business as well. You can read more about how our practices developed and thrived in chapter 10, along with other successful private practitioners. We hope that this book will provide the support you need to find your office, open up your business, and enjoy the journey as your business grows. Having your own business is like having a baby—you need to nurture it constantly if you want it to grow.

We wish you the very best as you set out to make nutrition your business.

Ann Silver, MS, RDN, CDE, CDN
Lisa Stollman, MA, RDN, CDE, CDN

Reviewers

Rebecca Bitzer, MS, RD, LD, CEDRD
President, Rebecca Bitzer & Associates, Inc
Annapolis, MD

Mara Bujnowski, MAEd, RD
Manager, Advocacy & Communications, Nutrition Services Coverage
Academy of Nutrition and Dietetics
Chicago, IL

Jennifer McGurk, RDN, CDN, CDE, CEDRD
Owner/Registered Dietitian Nutritionist, Eat With Knowledge
Nyack, NY

Marsha Schofield, MS, RD, LD, FAND
Senior Director, Governance and Nutrition Services Coverage
Academy of Nutrition and Dietetics
Chicago, IL

Reba Sloan, MPH, LDN, FAED
Nutrition Therapist, Private Practice
Nashville, TN

Therese S. Waterhous, PhD, RDN, CEDRD
Owner/President, Willamette Nutrition Source, LLC
Corvallis, OR

Acknowledgments

This book would not have been possible without the support of many people. Thank you to:

- our editors at the Academy of Nutrition and Dietetics, who with their skillful expertise and nurturing style made the book writing and editing process easier and actually pleasant.

- the department of Publications, Resources, and Products at the Academy of Nutrition and Dietetics for their patience and willingness to listen.

- Marsha Schofield, Senior Director of Governance and Nutrition Services Coverage at the Academy of Nutrition and Dietetics, who shared her vast knowledge and insight on third-party reimbursement, both current and for the future.

- our fabulous colleagues from the Nutrition Entrepreneurs Dietetic Practice Group, who were willing to share their personal success stories, as well as marketing and networking strategies to help this book come to fruition.

We extend a special thanks to our many RDN friends who helped answer our questions and provided assistance as needed: Aarti Batavia, Maria Bella, Lesli Bitel, Rebecca Bitzer, Chere Bork, Jill Castle, Patsy Catsos, Andrea Chernus, Nancy Clark, Marci Evans, Bonnie Giller, Joey Gochnour, Digna Cassens Irizzary, Molly Kellogg, Cathy Leman, Dana Magee, Linda Eck Mills, Lisa Musician, Jennifer Neily, Jill Nussinow, Jan Patenaude, Dee Pratt, Yvette Quantz, Judy Simon, Felicia Stoler, Lori Auerbach Sullivan, Evelyn Tribole, Susan Weiner, Penny Wilson, Lisa Young, and Tanya Zuckerbrot.

1 | Private Practice: Is It Right for You?

Bravo! You are at that point in your nutrition career where you're thinking about starting your own private practice. Many registered dietitian nutritionists (RDNs) have been bitten by the entrepreneurial bug and are passionate about going out on their own. Building the practice of your dreams and being your own boss are at the top of many nutrition professionals' bucket lists. But are you sure this is truly for you? This chapter will teach you about what it takes to be an entrepreneur and will help you determine if this would be a good fit for you.

Why Do You Want to Be Your Own Boss?

The very first question you need to ask yourself is: *What is your motivation for wanting to start your own private practice?* Do you want to spend more time with your patients? Do you want to have more creativity in your work? Do you want to have a more flexible work schedule that accommodates traveling and, perhaps, your family life? Do you want to make more money? These are all valid reasons for wanting to be your own boss, and they are all realities of running your own business. However, not everyone is cut out to be an entrepreneur.[1] Before taking the giant leap out on your own, it is important to know what it takes to be a successful entrepreneur. There are personal and profes-sional characteristics and traits typical of those who are successful. It is not necessary (or likely) that you naturally possess all these traits. Most entrepreneurs don't. What is important is the ability to evaluate your strengths and weaknesses honestly and to seek help when you aren't capable of doing it all. You can always find people to help you shine as an entrepreneur, whether it's to help you with social media, create your website, or write a weekly blog. Read through the questions in the box below to see if you have what it takes to be an entrepreneur, and then we'll explore some of these important personality traits in greater detail.

Do You Have What It Takes to Be an Entrepreneur?

- Do you dream of being your own boss?
- Are you a risk taker?
- Are you a leader?
- Are you self-confident?
- Can you live with the ups and downs of owning a business?
- Do you have determination and follow-through?
- Are you creative?
- Are you disciplined?
- Can you make your own deadlines and stick to them?
- Do you have common sense?
- Do you have a solid foundation of nutrition and diets?
- Can you multitask?
- Are you organized?
- Are you passionate about nutrition?
- Do you like working alone?
- Are you good at networking?
- Are you able to hear constructive criticism?
- Are you ready for self-reflection?

Adapted with permission from Ann Silver and Lisa Stollman.

Some skills that lend themselves to entrepreneurship can be learned. But for the most part they are inherent to your persona. If you answered **no** to three or more of these questions and aren't sure these are areas you want to work on, being your own boss may not be for you—at least not right away. No worries—this book will still benefit you. You may find that you need more time to develop the skills and confidence to be an entrepreneur. Perhaps starting out you are better off working for an RDN who has his or her own practice. You can learn the ins and outs of private practice from another RDN and in time go out on your own.

Personality Traits of Successful Entrepreneurs

Many RDNs have mastered the necessary educational, clinical, and food-service skills to be effective in their employed positions. Understanding what makes a successful RDN provides some insight into the traits of a successful nutrition entrepreneur.[2-4] However, in addition to expanding upon the skills of a successful RDN and learning new skills that are necessary to become a successful private practice owner, it is also recommended for those going solo to have the following personality traits.

Being a Risk Taker

It is risky to leave a dependable job, steady paycheck, benefits package, and sense of performance expectations. Questions you never had to think about as an employee will loom large when you are in private practice. How will you establish yourself in your local community and on social media? How will you structure your day? How will you make money? What are your additional revenue streams (if needed)? When do you hire employees or take on a partner? You likely never considered these questions as an employee, but they will weigh heavily on you as a private practice owner.

Taking that first step requires confidence and self-determination, along with the ability to handle stress and the unknown. The Small Business Association (SBA) estimates that one-third of small businesses fail due to inadequate finances within the first two years.[5] You need to be willing to take the inherent risk that comes from moving from an employee to a private practice owner, but you can minimize your risk and increase your chances for success by being prepared. Seek the advice of business advisers, such as other RDNs who have gone into private practice and friends who are business owners. Do your research and evaluate the environment to determine whether your business idea is viable.

To lessen the financial risk, investigate the possibility of part-time employment or consulting while you develop your private practice. If part-time employment isn't an option, build your practice outside of your usual work hours. You can start by seeing patients in the evenings or on weekends. Eventually, if you choose to enter the world of private practice on a full-time basis, you will need to leave the world as an employee, but it's important to wait until you feel confident and financially prepared.

An RDN will encounter many risks in private practice. That first step is just the beginning. As risk taking eventually becomes part of your job description, you will learn to tolerate risk and see it as energizing rather than frightening.

Being Passionate

Most successful entrepreneurs will tell you that they are fueled by a passion for their business. They thrive on having the opportunity to solve a problem and make life easier and better for others.[4] You should be passionate about your business idea if you want to be successful. Having a deep love for the work you do will keep you motivated and inspired to nurture your practice and help it grow. Having a true passion for your work is felt not only by those who work with you but also by your patients and referrers. If you ever come to a time in your practice when you aren't feeling excited and driven, it may be time to tweak what you are doing so you don't get in a rut. That is one of the great perks of being your own boss. You can regularly make changes to keep yourself motivated by your work. You have the ability to build a practice that is inspired by the areas of nutrition you are truly interested in. If you aren't passionate about your work, you may not see your vision through to completion and just give up. Now that you are taking the time to think about starting your private practice, take a pad of paper and jot down what you love to do and what you are passionate about.

Being Disciplined

To work on your own, you need to be disciplined. You won't need to punch a clock, tell anyone where you are going in the middle of the day, or ask your boss for a day off. Without discipline, it may be tempting to not "go to work" because you aren't accountable to anyone but yourself and your clients.

By establishing workdays and hours when you will see patients, posting on social media, writing blogs, or marketing your practice in other ways, you will impose discipline and structure based on when you are most productive. Determine when you will do paperwork, return phone calls, read your email, and network. Creating a work schedule will force you to be more organized. Don't worry if your schedule doesn't exactly follow traditional hours—remember that one of the perks of private practice is the ability to have a flexible schedule that works for you.

Disciplined practitioners will also need to plan events and schedule opportunities to stay current. As an employee, you may have been able to attend grand rounds, join journal clubs, or benefit from professional dialogue with colleagues. On your own, you will need to make the effort to keep your skills current. You may have to take time out of your schedule to attend a meeting. You will also need to set aside time to stay current by tracking issues online, listening to webinars, or subscribing to and reading many different publications. You might also want to make it a point to network with colleagues on a regular basis just to stay connected.

Make sure to include free time in your schedule, too. It's extremely important to take care of yourself and plan self-care. Practice what you preach! You need to be disciplined enough to take time off to attend a child's field trip, get a workout in, go on vacation, or just give yourself a mental health day. If you're not disciplined, you might find yourself doing paperwork long after the traditional workday has ended. All work and no play will not make a productive entrepreneur and can lead to eventual burnout.

Having Confidence

Some individuals are born confident, and others need to find their confidence. If you are going to be successful, you will need to develop confidence and act as if it were always there. The more successful experiences you have in practice, the easier this becomes.

Confidence will help you promote yourself 24/7. According to James Robinson of entrepreneur.com, self-promotion is one of the most beneficial yet most underused marketing tools that the majority of business owners have at their immediate disposal.[6] No one really feels comfortable relentlessly self-promoting, but being confident can help. Be sure to assess the environment and determine when it is appropriate and when it just doesn't feel right to sell yourself. Always have business cards on hand, just in case.

Confidence also means you are able to admit deficiencies and look for ways to correct them. A confident RDN will readily refer a patient to someone more experienced in another area, send a reporter to an RDN who might have more expertise in a particular subject, or call upon a web designer to create a website if he or she lacks this skill. Assessing your skills and determining what you are capable of handling and what should be delegated are also signs of confidence.

Being Adaptable

Being in business requires you to be a visionary. You must be able to spot nutrition trends in the marketplace and adapt your practice as appropriate. You don't need to be a trendsetter or compromise your beliefs, but you do need to be open-minded enough to see the existing trends and recognize that your clients may want information on topics you don't agree with.

Being adaptable means knowing when to let go of an idea that isn't going to fly, regardless of how much you like that idea. Moving on and getting over a failed project or an idea that isn't feasible now is part of being an adaptable entrepreneur. Perhaps your idea to have weekly group nutrition classes for teens in your office is not doable now. But hang on to your idea, as it may become worthwhile in the future.

You will meet many personality types in private practice. Although you are not required to become best friends with clients, referral sources, or others you may encounter while doing business, being kind and having a flexible personality will enable you to keep many people on your side—an important asset in private practice. People will not remember you because you are smart or attractive; people will remember you because you are kind and easy to work with.

Another important aspect of adaptability is having a backup plan for days that do not go as scheduled. If you have a canceled appointment or meeting, you can still be productive. You can use the time to send letters to physicians, update your social media pages, or write a new blog post. Always have a to-do list that you can work on to keep your private practice successful.

Being Tenacious

Entrepreneurs are driven self-starters who never give up. They don't necessarily act impulsively, but they tend to grab opportunities and take advantage of them. An entrepreneur will always see the glass as half full instead of half empty. You may make many mistakes, but learning how to turn disappointments into learning experiences is an important lesson for anyone in business.[7]

Owning a private practice is demanding, exhausting, and exhilarating. To realize the exhilaration, you will need to be strong to endure the emotional and physical demands placed on a private practitioner. It may be difficult at times to remember why you even wanted to be your own boss. Although your tenacity and drive will help you accomplish your goals, it's also important to know when to take time to reenergize and recharge. Make sure to write a to-do list at the beginning of each week and check off completed tasks when they are finished. Set boundaries for your time so you get things done but still have time to enjoy life.

Professional Skills of Successful Entrepreneurs

Unless you had a successful business career before you became an RDN, you will need to develop a new set of professional skills. Most dietetics programs provide limited business training. Although many RDNs are very comfortable with their clinical expertise, professional skills beyond clinical training are needed to run a private practice. Gaining real-world experience will be helpful before you go out on your own. Subscribe to business publications and listen to webinars and podcasts that can help you obtain business skills. Learn how to use accounting software such as QuickBooks so you can manage your money. Most important will be your ability to assess what you can and can't manage on your own as a private practice owner.[7]

Being Business Savvy

Being an entrepreneur requires a transition in thinking from being an employee to being a business owner. You likely got into this profession to help people, and while you will never leave the helping profession, you will need to expand your thinking to include how to reach out to your target market and provide quality goods and services that offer consumer value. This expansion in thinking helps you become a more skilled private practice owner. What counts in private practice is the bottom line.

How you price your services is only one factor in determining your bottom line. Learning how to control costs, when to cut corners, and where to invest valuable dollars requires a business mind. If you are unsure, solicit input from colleagues already established in a private practice, other allied health professionals in practice in the community, and business organizations such as the SBA. This topic is covered in more detail in chapter 2.

To promote your services, you may initially have to do some volunteer work, such as providing free lectures and volunteering at health fairs. However, you need to determine where you draw the line—after all, you need to earn a living.

You will also need to become comfortable with determining appropriate fees for your services. Chapter 3 covers this topic in more detail.

A wise business owner learns to make decisions under pressure. In nutrition, you make decisions about patient care, so the foundation for decision making is in your training. Private practice situations may be unfamiliar, and you might have only your gut instincts to guide you at times. Thinking like a business owner is a work in progress.

1

Being Organized

Knowing how to delegate, organize, and multitask are tremendous skills. A private practitioner will be required to plan, organize, and implement everything related to his or her practice. You may not have the luxury of hiring information technology (IT) support to help you create a presentation, an assistant to schedule your appointments, or a custodian to clean your office. You will need to determine what you can and can't do. If cost is an issue, consider hiring a nutrition student or intern to help you out.

Planning is an important aspect of organization. In private practice, be sure to plan for administrative tasks such as scheduling appointments, contacting other health care providers on the treatment team, sending follow-up letters, and spending time on billing and accounting activities.

You will need to multitask, but be careful when doing so. In some cases, you may not be as productive while multitasking. Carefully evaluate what you need to get done and determine whether you can do the tasks simultaneously or whether certain tasks need your full attention. For example, tasks that lend themselves well to multitasking are sending a fax while checking emails and being on hold with an insurance company over the phone. Avoid multitasking when you are doing a task that requires your complete attention. A good rule of thumb: Always recheck your work for typos.

Communicating Effectively

Excellent communication skills are important in everything you do in life. In private practice, you must be able to communicate in a confident, positive way. You need to put a positive spin on your practice as you communicate to the public. Being a good communicator means being a good listener, too. Whether you are communicating with a patient, a reporter, or an audience, you need to be comfortable with the give-and-take of conversation.

The first introduction to your services may be an initial telephone call to schedule an appointment or hook a client. You need to be persuasive without making promises that can't be kept. Learn how to speak succinctly and effectively. It is also quite possible that the first introduction to your services is a written inquiry through email. Make sure that your written communication skills are polished, and consider having a few blurbs available to explain your services to a potential client. You can save these in a document to then cut and paste into an email.

There are many excellent resources available on communication. If you are not a natural communicator, effective communication is one practice skill you will need to develop to be successful.

Being Professional

Remember that first impressions do count. Your appearance makes a statement about you and the quality of your work. Putting your best foot forward will help market your practice. It is particularly important to dress for success. If you are seeing patients or speaking in public, dress appropriately. Avoid jeans, rumpled clothes, or excess scented products, makeup, and jewelry. Dress conservatively in clothes that fit well. You may even dress differently depending on the situation. For example, if you are seeing patients, you may dress in formal work attire, such as blazers, tailored shirts, ties, trousers, dresses, or skirts. If you are teaching a nutrition class to a group of teen athletes, you may feel more comfortable dressing more casually.

In addition to having a professional appearance, you must be aware of how you conduct yourself in your phone and email communications. It is always important to treat others with respect and maintain diplomacy, even when dealing with difficult situations.

Being an Expert

Experience in clinical practice is a good foundation for private practice. A clinical position in a hospital, clinic, or corporation can provide you with some business-related skills, which can be a stepping stone to opening your own private practice.

If you plan to have a medical nutrition therapy (MNT) practice, it's essential to have a strong clinical background and hospital-based work experience. The experience you gain and contacts you make while practicing in a traditional role are irreplaceable. Having clinical expertise can also help you develop your niche. See chapter 4 for more in-depth advice on finding your niche. If you plan to practice primarily in the areas not commonly classified as MNT—such as sports nutrition, wellness, or general nutrition—you might find your clinical skills to be less important. However, if you don't have a strong knowledge base in MNT, this will limit the types of patients you can see in your private practice.

The Advantages of Going Solo

Starting a private practice is appealing for many reasons. You may be excited to transition from being an employee to being your own boss. There's a thrill and prestige in being on your own. Having creative freedom, the potential for unlimited income, and the flexibility to make your own schedule are three huge selling points for RDNs to start their own private practices. The following sections highlight some of the specific benefits a private practitioner can enjoy.

Ability to Control Your Schedule

One of the biggest draws to owning your own private practice is the ability to control your schedule. When you set your own office hours, the days you work and when you take vacation are dictated by you. You can also select an office location that's convenient for you. Take advantage of this flexibility by structuring your day around when you are most productive. You must keep in mind that your office hours need to work for your clients, but if you are a morning person, you can try to set up early office hours or do most of your work at that time. If you want to take vacation time during the busy winter holiday season, block out that time from your schedule. Many private practices are slow during this time of year, so have fun and enjoy it, too. As your practice grows, you will be able to see patients during the hours that are ideal for you.

Private practice offers the luxury of flexibility. A private practice should allow you to practice when, where, and how much you want. You might be able to choose the hours when you see patients and select an office location that is convenient for you. However, be prepared to work more than you did as an employee—in addition to counseling clients, you might need to put in long hours managing your books and paying bills. The difference is that you will decide when you will put in those long hours to have a profitable private practice.

Balanced Life

Going solo appeals to many people looking to find the perfect balance between work and personal time. A home-based office or a private office close to home may seem like ideal places to work. The reality is that starting a private practice is extremely demanding. The days of working 9 to 5 are gone. However, you will find that you can schedule in your workouts and time off without answering to anyone else. Depending on the type of practice you have, you can work when and where you want. The flexibility and ability to have unlimited freedom is an appealing advantage to anyone seeking more control over his or her personal life.

Potential Earnings

An RDN in private practice can earn more than an RDN working as an employee.[8] However, starting a private practice, like starting any other business, is not a get-rich-quick scheme. Financial rewards take time. It is estimated that a new private practice takes three to five years to realize a profit.[5] Starting your own practice carries risks, but the benefits should include making more money than when you were an employee. Keep in mind that some of the income boost can come from the many potential tax advantages that private practitioners are afforded.

The earning power of a private practice is not limitless. Money is made by billing patients as well as third-party payers, and there are only so many billable hours in a week. You may increase your earning potential by branching out into other types of consulting. Oftentimes, you can realize more profits by having additional revenue streams, which may include writing, public speaking, online classes, or webinars.

Expressing Your Own Style

Your private practice will be a personal extension of you. What you say, how you say it, and to whom you say it should reflect your style. You are the boss. You only have to answer to your professional code of ethics and yourself, not the clinical nutrition manager of the hospital or facility that employs you.

Regardless of where you work, you need to maintain a professional image, as discussed previously. However, you can always make small tweaks to your work attire based on your personality or the specific event you are attending.

Professional Pride

One of the most gratifying aspects of private practice is pride in knowing that you work hard for your personal and professional fulfillment. It is thrilling to see your patients improve their health and to see your practice grow. Success will be self-perpetuating. You need to be passionate about what you do and sell that passion along with your services.

The Disadvantages of Going Solo

Of course, you need to think about the disadvantages as well as the advantages of your new potential venture. Anyone in private practice can speak to the pros and cons of going solo. Listen carefully. There are risks and struggles involved in being on your own. Those of us who are successful private practitioners can see the cons, but the pros far outweigh them.

Doing It All by Yourself

Nutrition counseling or coaching may be the main focus of your private practice, but you will be wearing all the hats to make your practice work. When the fax machine breaks, electronic health records need to be updated, or bills need to be sent out, you will be the one responsible. The challenges of learning many new things will seem overwhelming at times.

One of the downsides to having your own practice is the pull to always be working. Work demands can put strains on personal relationships. Try to focus on the flexibility you have as a private practitioner. Be careful not to overextend yourself. There are times you will have to say no, and that can be frustrating. Remember your priorities when it comes to outside obligations, such as family vs work. You must prioritize the demands on your time. To accomplish this, keep in mind that you will often feel that there is still work to be done. Keep a schedule and a to-do list so you don't get stressed.

You will carry all the responsibilities on your shoulders. You will take all the blame when things don't work out. This can be draining, both emotionally and physically. Recognizing you can't please everyone is a reality of private practice. Going solo means just that: You are on your own.

You must make an effort to network with others. There are ways to avoid feeling isolated, but it is up to you to make that happen. Make a point of connecting with other professionals regularly. Join relevant electronic mailing lists (EMLs), meet colleagues for lunch or dinner, or just go out for an afternoon with a friend. You will need to recharge to stay motivated.

GETTING HELP: HAVING A BUSINESS PARTNER

Although many RDNs decide to go it alone, at least initially, taking on a business partner or hiring other RDNs to join you can help you build and expand your private practice more quickly. Working with someone of equal stature can help you join forces as you build your nutrition practice together. You can bounce ideas off each other and provide inspiration for new projects. Having a partner can bring new skill sets to your business. Perhaps your expertise is in working with adult clients who require weight management. Maybe your partner(s) or RDN employees specialize in sports nutrition. By teaming up, you can expand your client base. Working together can also bring in more income. You can also share in all expenses, which can reduce your overhead. Many RDNs today are joining forces with other like-minded nutrition colleagues to establish a joint practice. This is a great option for those who don't like to work alone and want to share the workload.

Financial Concerns

There will always be financial risk involved in owning a private practice. Cash flow may be a problem. To keep your business afloat, you may need to consider having additional revenue streams. You can develop webinars and online classes that can bring in additional income. If money is tight, you might need to invest your own savings, take a part-time consulting job (so you have some steady income), or obtain a business loan to stay solvent. In any situation, the financial arrangements may create stress in your life.

If you have advanced skills in a specialty nutrition area, are well known locally or in the media, and have many years of experience, make sure that your fees are in line with your skill set. Never undersell yourself! Refer to chapter 3 for more information on setting fees.

Financial issues ultimately affect those dependent on you as well. It is important to have the moral support of your family when you take on the risk of having your own practice. They may need to feel that the initial sacrifice is worth it for you to succeed.

Financial concerns can become more intense should you become ill or need to take time off for other reasons. Whether you are ill, want to take a day off to attend a conference, or have to cancel patient appointments due to inclement weather, these are all situations that will affect your bottom line. If you are financially independent, you may want to consider getting disability insurance in case you need to be out of work for an extended period of time.

Last, be aware that your income will be erratic. Eventually you will come to know the normal fluctuations and patterns. Pace yourself by learning which months are busy and which are slow. Try to schedule vacations when your patient population seems more likely to be taking time off as well or when your workload is a bit lighter.

Is Private Practice Right for You?: A Summary

Here are the key takeaway points from this chapter:

- The personality traits of successful private practitioners include being a risk taker, having passion, being disciplined, having confidence, being adaptable, and being tenacious. You may not possess all these traits, but you need to identify your strengths and weaknesses and reach out for professional help as needed.

- Professional skills needed for stepping out on your own include being business savvy, having good organizational skills, being an effective communicator, being professional, and possessing expertise in some area of nutrition.

- There are pros and cons to being your own boss. Be honest with yourself and look at the whole picture before you jump into building your own private practice. If you feel you need more guidance

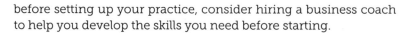

before setting up your practice, consider hiring a business coach to help you develop the skills you need before starting.

- If you don't want to work solo, you can take on a partner or hire other RDNs to work for you.

- As RDNs consider private practice, they must carefully assess the environment and their own commitment. There is nothing more gratifying than building your own successful business. Being a successful entrepreneur should be financially rewarding as well as professionally and personally fulfilling.

References

1. Strauss S. *The Small Business Bible*. Hoboken, NJ: John Wiley & Sons, Inc; 2012.

2. Tyson E, Schell J. *Small Business for Dummies*. New York, NY: John Wiley & Sons, Inc; 2011.

3. Guillebeau C. *The $100 Startup: Reinvent the Way You Make a Living, Do What You Love, and Create a New Future*. New York, NY: Crown Business; 2012.

4. Costa J. Common traits of successful entrepreneurs. *Huffington Post*. December 10, 2014. www.huffingtonpost.com/jose-costa/traits-of-successful -entrepreneurs_b_6303992.html. Accessed May 10, 2017.

5. Frequently asked questions. SBA Office of Advocacy website. www.sba.gov /sites/default/files/FAQ_Sept_2012.pdf. Published September 2012. Accessed May 10, 2017.

6. Robinson J. The 7 traits of successful entrepreneurs. *Entrepreneur*. January 10, 2014. www.entrepreneur.com/article/230350. Accessed May 10, 2017.

7. Johnson K. *The Entrepreneur Mind: 100 Essential Beliefs, Characteristics, and Habits of Elite Entrepreneurs*. Atlanta, GA; Johnson Media Inc; 2013.

8. Rogers D. Compensation and benefits survey 2015. *J Acad Nutr Diet*. 2016;116(3):370388. https://doi.org/10.1016/j.jand.2016.01.002. Accessed June 7, 2017.

2 | First Steps: Business Essentials

One of the many reasons you are going into private practice is to make money, right? Now you will be stepping into the world of business: your own business. What do you know or not know about being in business? Perhaps you took a business course in college. Great! You have some background. Or maybe you never took a business course and hated anything having to do with accounting. Don't worry. This chapter will help you understand what you need to build your private practice from a business perspective. Setting up the structure of your business, maintaining your financials—commonly referred to as your books—writing a business plan, and choosing good advisers will build a foundation for your success. In addition, your success as an entrepreneur will depend on how well you meet your legal obligations and insure yourself and your business.

Transitioning to Self-Employment

As you move from being an employee to being self-employed, you will need to choose a title to describe yourself. Are you a registered dietitian nutritionist (RDN) in private practice, a nutrition therapist, or a nutrition consultant? Possibly you will use one or more of these titles or other titles, and sometimes you will use your titles simultaneously.

The title(s) you designate for yourself in business is not the title the Internal Revenue Service (IRS) will use for tax purposes. The IRS will want to know if you are an independent contractor (meaning self-employed) or an employee.[1] These distinctions are critical to determine your federal tax obligations, your Social Security and Medicare payments, and how and when to file your tax returns.[2] There are three categories the IRS uses to determine that you are an independent contractor/self-employed; these are listed in the box below. One single factor does not determine your status. You must comply with all the criteria. An independent contractor is exactly what it means—independent. You decide when, where, and how you will work, with some exceptions. For example, you may sublease an office on only certain days of the week, but you can still be self-employed as long as no one else is actually controlling your work. If you are an employee, someone else is telling you how to work. RDNs who plan to work in a setting like a physician's office, where everything is controlled by the physician's staff,

Internal Revenue Service Criteria to Determine Whether You Are an Independent Contractor[2]

Behavioral control: You do not receive direction about your work.

- Instructions
  - You are not told where, when, or how to perform work.
  - You are not told what tools to use.

- Training
  - You are not trained on policies and procedures for how to conduct your work.

Financial control

- Significant investment: You have a financial stake in your business.
- Expenses: You are not reimbursed for some or all of your expenses.
- Opportunity for profit or loss: You can make money or lose money.

Relationships of the parties

- Employee benefits: You do not receive employee benefits, such as insurance, pension, or paid leave.
- Written contracts: These may or may not establish you as being self-employed.

may not be considered independent contractors but rather be considered employees. An accountant can help you determine whether you are an independent contractor or employee. All aspects of your situation have to be taken into consideration.

As you launch your private practice, you may decide to maintain your status as an employee with your current employer, perhaps part time, while you begin building your practice. This is an important decision to make from the outset because having a steady stream of income can be crucial during your transition to self-employment. You will then be both an employee and an independent contractor. Here are some suggestions as you make the transition to self-employment:

- Seek professional advice from an accountant to determine your correct employment status because this is not always clear-cut.

- Check with your employer to see if you have a noncompete agreement in place before stepping out on your own. A noncompete agreement is a contract between an employer and an employee that states that the employee will not be in competition for a certain amount of time or within a specified distance from the employer. For example, if you work as an outpatient dietitian at a hospital, the hospital noncompete contract may not allow you to open a private practice within a 2-mile radius of the hospital for three years. A noncompete agreement may affect your ability to work both for your employer and for yourself.

Choosing an Appropriate Business Structure

Business structure is not a static concept. You might operate under more than one type of structure at the same time. What you may find to be an appropriate structure when you start your practice may change as your practice develops and grows. How you structure your private practice will determine which items you are entitled to deduct as business expenses; how and when you file your taxes; how you can protect your assets; and which, if any, business licenses you are required to have.

There are essentially two business structures to choose from: incorporated and unincorporated. Sole proprietorships and partnerships are unincorporated businesses. C corporations, S corporations, and limited liability corporations (LLCs) are examples of incorporated business options. The difference in the business structure determines how you will file and pay your taxes, the amount of legal paperwork you are required to complete to operate your business, how you will be able to raise money for your business, and your personal liability.[3] An accountant or attorney can advise you on which business structure is right for your practice.

2

Sole Proprietorships: Going It Alone

A sole proprietorship is the most common type of business structure in the United States. Most businesses start out as sole proprietorships, as do many private practice RDNs.[4] There is a good reason for this: It is the easiest and least costly way to operate a business. Should you decide to open your practice tomorrow, you could essentially do so as a sole proprietor.

As a sole proprietor, you can operate under your own name or choose a fictitious name. (See the section on Naming Your Business later in this chapter. There is also more about naming your practice in chapter 4.) As a sole proprietor, you are the boss. You make all decisions about your practice. You pay for all your expenses, you are responsible for all your debt, and you reap all the profits. Should you choose to stop practicing and close your doors, you can quite literally shut the door behind you and call yourself retired (or out of business).

Your business is not a taxable entity as a sole proprietor. However, you are responsible for paying a self-employment tax in addition to your other tax obligations.

For tax purposes, your business expenses, profits, and losses are recorded on either a Schedule C, Profit or Loss from Business form or a Schedule C-EZ, Net Profit from Business form. These are then included with your annual individual tax return (Form 1040) and filed annually with your personal taxes. Depending on your profitability and your total household income, this structure could benefit you because your business losses can offset the income you have from other sources, lowering the amount of your net taxes. For further information on filing taxes, ask an accountant or refer to the Small Business Association (SBA) website (www.sba.gov).

Being a sole proprietor has advantages and disadvantages. To determine if a sole proprietorship is right for you, see the box on the next page.

Partnerships: A Match Made in Heaven?

If you are joining forces with another individual, you will likely want to form a partnership. There are two types of partnerships: a general partnership and a limited partnership. The type of partnership you choose will depend on the roles of the partners.

A general partnership is an arrangement in which two or more people own and operate a business. The partners are equal. In a limited partnership, there are two different types of partners who are not equal. Both types of partnerships will be discussed in the following sections. Most RDNs who form a partnership choose to form a general partnership.

Advantages and Disadvantages of Sole Proprietorship

Advantages	Disadvantages
Sole proprietorships are easy to form and dissolve. Few, if any, legal documents are required to set up shop. When you are ready to close the business, you simply cease to operate.	Personal liability is unlimited. You and your business are viewed as one entity by the legal system. If your business incurs debts or if you are sued, your personal assets, such as your car or your house, may be seized to satisfy a legal claim or business debt. You should have insurance to protect your assets, but it may not be enough to completely protect you.
This is the least expensive form of business to start.	
Paperwork is minimal. Your state may or may not require you to register your business and obtain a business license.	Funding your business can be difficult. Banks may be less likely to lend to sole proprietorships than they are to corporations. Funding may depend on your personal credit history.
You are taxed as an individual.[a] Your business expenses and profits or losses from your business are recorded on a Schedule C and filed annually with your personal tax forms.	
You are the boss. You make all the decisions related to your business. You don't answer to anyone else. You retain total control.	It gets lonely at the top. Being a sole proprietor can be isolating because you work alone. You need to make an effort to interact with and get input from others.
The big bucks are yours. Once your business is profitable, you are entitled to all the profits!	Your business will lack continuity. When you stop practicing, your business ends unless it is sold.

[a] As a sole proprietor, you must file a Schedule SE and pay self-employment tax.

GENERAL PARTNERSHIPS

Like a sole proprietorship, a general partnership is relatively easy to start. There are no required legal documents, although your state may require a business license. This makes this type of partnership appealing and can be beneficial to RDNs starting a new practice. Partnerships allow you and your fellow RDN(s) to pool your resources, talents, and expenses. If you are just starting out, that means one scale, one set of food models, and one rented office.

A general partnership can bring your talents together in a cooperative way. Perhaps one RDN is a diabetes expert and the other has strong organizational skills because of her work as a clinical nutrition manager at a large teaching hospital. Combining these strengths can be very effective.

Reporting your income as a partnership is not as straightforward as reporting it as a sole proprietor. The partnership is not taxed, but each partner is required to report his or her share of the partnership income and deductions on IRS Form 1065, Schedule K-1. Many new entrepreneurs may require the assistance of an accountant to compile this information.

As with all business structures, there is a downside to general partnerships. Partners expect a great deal from one another. It is important to honestly assess and evaluate your partner as a business partner, not as a friend. You must understand one another's work ethic and share common goals and visions for the partnership. You must be explicit in determining what you expect from one another. If those expectations are not clearly defined at the beginning of the partnership, there is a greater chance for disappointment or disagreement, and the partnership will suffer.

Although you are not governed by legal documents, when forming a general partnership (even with a close friend) it is highly recommended that you spell out all details pertaining to the partnership in a legal agreement.[5] A lawyer should be consulted when writing the agreement. A partnership agreement should address the following:

- the name of the partnership,

- the purpose of the partnership,

- the expectations of each partner,

- how you will make business decisions,

- how profits and losses will be distributed,

- how money and time will be contributed,

- how disputes will be resolved,

- how new partners will be added, if needed, and

- how you will terminate the business in the event of a partner's death, disability, illness, or desire to leave.

Like a sole proprietorship, a partnership faces unlimited legal and financial liability. This means that each partner is responsible for 100% of the debts. If one partner incurs debt, the other partner's assets can be used to cover the joint debt. And regardless of your partnership agreement, a creditor may collect from the partner from whom it is easiest to collect. If one partner is sued, both are vulnerable.

When a partnership is terminated, as when a marriage ends, you must clearly identify who is entitled to what. This can get very sticky if an agreement has not already been put in writing. For more information, see the box on the next page.

Advantages and Disadvantages of General Partnerships

Advantages	Disadvantages
General partnerships are easy to form. Some states may require a business license to operate.	When you decide to split the partnership, it can be difficult to dissolve. Assets and debts must be divided.
You will have pooled resources and talent. Two heads are better than one.	Like a sole proprietor, partners are personally responsible for all debts. If one partner is sued, both are responsible. The partner with more assets stands to lose more.
Little capital is required to start a partnership, and your borrowing ability is greater than in a sole proprietorship.	
Partners are taxed as individuals rather than as a business.	
Partners have a broader management base than sole proprietors.	

LIMITED PARTNERSHIPS

Imagine having someone give you the money to start your practice along with full responsibility for running the practice. Sound great? This is a limited partnership. A limited partnership includes both a limited partner and a general partner. A limited partner is an investor and is not involved in managing or operating the business. The limited partner has limited liability up to the amount of his or her investment in the practice.[3,5] The general partner—the RDN—is responsible for the day-to-day operations and assumes all liability.[3,5] The partnership does not pay income tax. However, profits and losses are proportional to the partners, and they are responsible for their own taxes.[3] According to the SBA, this type of partnership suits investors of short-term projects.[6] It is best to have a business adviser help you determine which type of partnership is most appropriate for you to form for your private practice.

Corporations: Not Just for Big Companies

When small business owners think about corporations, visions of Microsoft, General Motors, or Walmart may come to mind. However, even a single RDN may become a corporation! In fact, many individual RDNs do incorporate because of the distinct advantages.

Corporations are legal business structures. Although they involve more complex and potentially expensive documentation and rules for operating, many RDNs think that the advantages far outweigh the complexities. Unlike a sole proprietorship or a partnership, a corporation is legally separate from the people who own it. That means that your personal assets may be protected from your practice assets in the event you are sued.

As a legal business entity, a corporation is governed by state laws. To be in accordance with such laws, paperwork must be filed and fees must be paid in order to conduct business. Generally, it is best to hire an attorney to assist you in complying with the paperwork needed to incorporate.

Once you incorporate, you will pay yourself a salary from the revenue you bring into the practice. As with any business structure, this means that you will need to establish business checking and savings accounts under the name of your corporation to keep your personal and business funds separate. Corporations pay taxes separate from the individuals who run the business. For these reasons, corporate finances may become time consuming. Such business matters can also be costly, especially if you pay an accountant to handle them.

A standard corporation is known as a C corporation. Although C corporations are usually large, publicly traded businesses, this does not mean that a private practice cannot be one as well. C corporations have shareholders. When it comes to taxes, C corporations have a big disadvantage, especially for small businesses. C corporations' profits are taxed twice—once for the corporation's income and again for the shareholders when the profits are paid.[5] Work with a lawyer and an accountant—they will be able to tell you if choosing to form a C corporation will be beneficial for your private practice.

There are options available that make incorporating more feasible for small businesses. The S corporation (or subchapter corporation) and LLC are two examples of corporations suitable for private practice. These types of entities protect an individual's personal assets, but their tax structures are similar to that of a sole proprietorship or partnership.

An S corporation is more appealing than a C corporation from a tax standpoint.[3,5] Profits and losses for an S corporation are paid on the shareholder's (your) income tax returns. S corporations can also provide limited personal liability.[3]

An LLC, or limited liability corporation, is a hybrid entity that combines the best features of a general partnership and a corporation into one business structure.[3] It provides the business owner protection from personal liability similar to a corporation, but it can offer a tax structure similar to that of a general partnership, where each partner reports his or her share of the income and deductions on his or her tax returns. Many

Advantages and Disadvantages of Incorporation

Advantages	Disadvantages
A corporation is a separate legal entity, so shareholders are generally protected from corporate liability.	Corporations can be difficult and more complex to manage because they are highly regulated by the government. The paperwork adds to your workload.
Ownership can be transferable.	
A corporation may be considered more legitimate than a sole proprietorship and has greater ability to raise or borrow money.	Corporations can be expensive and time consuming to form and maintain.
	Incorporating may result in higher overall taxes.

states allow you to complete LLC forms online on your own, which can save money. Discuss setting up an LLC with a lawyer, and ask your lawyer to review your application before you file any paperwork. For more details about forming an LLC, visit the SBA website (www.sba.gov) and refer to the resources in chapter 11.

Some states also allow professionals to form a professional corporation (PC) or a professional association (PA). PCs and PAs were created for lawyers, doctors, and other professionals and may be appropriate for RDNs in some states. The main advantage of PCs or PAs is that the professionals in the corporation are not liable for malpractice committed by others in the corporation.

There are no simple answers about who should or should not incorporate or what type of corporation is appropriate. This is an important business issue to discuss with your accountant, attorney, or business adviser. For further information on incorporating, see the box above.

The Business Plan: Planning for Success

Whether you are driving from Miami to Dallas, cooking a Thanksgiving dinner, or planting your vegetable garden, you have a map, recipe, or plan to guide you. Without a plan, you don't know where you are going or how to get to the finish line. The same is true with your business.

Purpose

Your business plan is a blueprint for success. Writing your vision on paper doesn't make it a reality, but it does force you to focus on the vital information needed to run your practice: who your target market is, what your philosophy is, how you will fund your business, what you will charge, and how you will market your business.

It is not only a good idea to write a business plan, it is essential, especially if you seek financial help. Whether you seek a loan from your family or friends or from the bank, they will want to know more about what they are investing in. You will need to describe your practice, your plans for managing the practice, and your plans for how the borrowed money will be used.

Don't be intimidated. Writing a business plan should not be an obstacle to starting a practice. It does not need to be a 400-page tome. It may be a simple, informal document that helps you formulate your vision and pave the way to making this vision a reality. To get started, begin by jotting down your business ideas. As your practice evolves, so will your business plan. There are many models and guides available, including free online templates, so it is not necessary to start from scratch.[3,5,7-9]

What to Include

What you choose to include in your business plan is not mandated. Include in your business plan what will be important to your practice. The depth and detail of your business plan will be dictated by how you plan to use it. Most formal business plans include the following information: cover sheet, executive summary, table of contents, organizational plan, marketing plan and analysis, financial plan, and supporting documentation.

- Cover sheet: The cover sheet is a title page that includes your practice name, address, telephone number(s), and contact information. A simple promotional description of your practice should appear here, too.

- Executive summary: The executive summary appears at the beginning of the plan, but it will probably be the last thing you write because it will be an overview of the business plan. It is the most important part of your plan. No more than one page in length, it should succinctly describe your business structure, the goals of your practice, what makes your practice special or unique, your expertise, and your financial needs. It should express the excitement and enthusiasm you have for your practice and encourage the reader to read on, especially if you are presenting your plan in an effort to borrow money.

- Table of contents: Like the table of contents in a book, this lists the information contained in your business plan and the corresponding page numbers. It is included to aid the reader.

- Organizational plan: This section outlines your business structure, where your practice is or will be located (if you have not secured a location), and the equipment and resources you need to run your practice. It also outlines what your services are, who will use your services, and why your services are important to the user. You could also include an overview of your practice that identifies your goals and objectives and explains why you are or want to be in business.

- Marketing plan and analysis: The marketing plan and analysis section is where you evaluate and define your market. (Marketing plans are discussed in detail in chapter 8.) You should include information about trends in the marketplace and how your services are affected by those trends. Pricing of your services should be included in this section. You will assess the competition, detailing who they are, how you are different, and why consumers should choose you. When looking at the competition, do not limit this to RDNs; think about others who could be considered competitors, such as other health professionals or the local health food store. You should also include your marketing strategy, which outlines the tools, resources, and techniques you plan to use to make your target market aware of your services.

- Financial plan: This section is critical to your business plan. Here, you determine the cash requirements for your practice, such as what equipment is essential for starting out. You will also project income and create a cash flow analysis. Your accountant and the SBA can help. If you are just starting out, this section should be based on projected costs and income. It will be important to speak to other RDNs in private practice to get data for compiling this information, especially about insurance reimbursement rates if you will be accepting third-party payments.

- Supporting documents: The final section of your business plan should include supporting documents such as your resume, contracts or leases, articles of incorporation, partnership agreements, and personal financial statements.

Basic Requirements for Starting Your Business

The requirements for running a business vary from state to state. The following is a summary of the general considerations and questions you will need answered before opening your practice. Your city hall, county courthouse, or state revenue department may have a comprehensive listing of requirements in your area. The local office of the SBA or the public library may have information and offer classes specific to doing business in your area.

Naming Your Business

If you are operating as a sole proprietorship or partnership, you can use your own name(s) or choose a fictitious business name. Fictitious business names are referred to as DBA, or "doing business as." The process for naming your business varies from state to state.

Before naming your practice, you may want to secure the domain name for your website and account name for social media, especially if you want your practice name to be the same for the different outlets. Check whether the domain name is available. Chapter 8 can provide guidance on this.

Naming your practice protects your name locally, but it does not prevent someone in another locale from using the same name. It is necessary to register your business name both to protect that name from others using it and to use that name legally on your bank account.[10]

Generally, if you are going to name your business, you must register that name with the county clerk or other local government agencies and ensure that no one else in your community is using that name. Another way to register your DBA is to publish your fictitious name in a general circulation paper in the county where your business is located. There are specific rules on doing this, so check with your local government for additional information.

If you are a corporation, naming your business is a formal process. When you begin the process of establishing your corporation and complete the required paperwork, the procedure for naming your business will be part of the documentation you will need to complete.

There are advantages and disadvantages to naming your private practice. Using your own name lends itself to better name recognition. If you are already established, this may be an advantage. Should you appear on television or get quoted in the newspaper, it is your name people will remember, not your business name. On the other hand, having a business name may give more credibility to your business in the public's eyes.

Tax Identification Number

In identifying your practice for tax purposes or other situations where you are requested to use a Tax Identification Number (TIN), you can use your Social Security number only if your business operates as a sole proprietorship. With the rise in identity theft, even sole proprietors (with no employees) should not use their Social Security numbers in business; if you do so, your Social Security number will be used as an identifier. Your TIN will be printed on your superbill, you will have to provide it when you communicate with a third-party payer, and it will appear on the explanations of benefits clients receive to explain how their insurance paid the claim. This will make your Social Security number vulnerable.

It's best to apply for a federal TIN, also referred to as an Employer Identification Number (EIN). The application (Form SS-4, "Application for Employer Identification Number [EIN]") is available from the IRS website. When you apply, you will be provided with an EIN easily and quickly.[11]

Licenses and Zoning

Licensing for RDNs varies from state to state. Consult your state department of education, your professional licensing board, or the Academy of Nutrition and Dietetics website (www.eatrightPRO.org) to determine whether the state in which you are conducting business is a state that licenses RDNs. If you are operating a practice in a state that requires RDNs to be licensed, it will be necessary for you to be licensed in that state even if you do not reside there. The purpose of licensure is to protect consumers—in this case, your clients.

Before you set up your practice in your home, make sure that you have checked out all the zoning and code ordinances for your neighborhood with an attorney and that you acquire any permits or licenses needed to run a business from your home. You would not need to do this if you were writing a book from your home. But when you conduct a business in a residential area with clients coming and going, there are laws to protect the integrity of the neighborhood and its residents. It may be perfectly fine to operate your practice out of your home, but if you are out of compliance with local ordinances and laws, you can be fined.

Insurance

As an employee, you might not have given much thought to the insurance your employer carried. As a business owner, you must consider several different types of insurance. There are many types of insurance policies. It may seem prudent to buy all of them, but the reality is you probably don't need to. Sit down with your business adviser or insurance agent and investigate what is essential for you to have as you start out. A brief overview of the common types of insurance policies used by most small businesses follows.

PROFESSIONAL LIABILITY INSURANCE

As a private practice RDN, you should obtain professional liability insurance (also known as malpractice insurance).[12] Although you may not ever expect legal trouble, when you are in business, there is a chance that you will be sued. Because you are the "nutrition expert," if someone feels that you have not lived up to what he or she expected, the person can initiate a lawsuit.[13] Professional liability insurance can protect you financially in a lawsuit. Professional liability insurance may or may not cover all of your nutrition-related activities beyond your private practice. If you are also an author, writer, consultant, or speaker, you will want to consider specialized insurance for that scope of work.

You can purchase the minimum amount of liability coverage; however, many third-party payers will dictate the amount of coverage required to be an in-network provider. This is usually greater than the minimum. Read through (or have a lawyer read through) your policy. To find professional liability insurance carriers, you can look on the Academy of Nutrition and Dietetics website (www.eatrightPRO.org) or ask colleagues who they use.

GENERAL LIABILITY AND PROPERTY INSURANCE

You will want to obtain an insurance policy to cover the contents of your office in the event they are damaged in a fire or flood or are stolen. In addition, general liability insurance should be purchased to cover you if someone is injured in your office. Be sure to ask your insurance agent about any other policies he or she may deem necessary.

HEALTH INSURANCE

If you've had the luxury of having someone else pay for your health insurance, be prepared when you need to purchase it on your own. Health insurance is expensive! There are options available for the self-employed. One resource is the insurance available through the National Association for the Self-Employed.[14] You can also search the internet, explore options from the federal government or your state, ask family and friends, and inquire with other affiliations that offer group plans for health insurance where you may be able to obtain premiums that are more competitive.

When you leave an employment situation with health insurance to start out on your own, you may be entitled to coverage through the Consolidated Omnibus Budget Reconciliation Act (COBRA). If you've been employed in an organization with 20 or more employees and you meet the eligibility requirements, your previous employer must give you the option to extend your health insurance for 18 months, for which you are required to pay the full premium. For eligibility requirements, consult the COBRA website (www.dol.gov/agencies/ebsa/laws-and-regulations /laws/cobra).[15]

LIFE INSURANCE AND DISABILITY INSURANCE

If you have dependents who rely on your income, it is a wise idea to investigate disability and life insurance policies. Disability insurance protects your earnings in the event that you cannot work by providing a percentage of your earnings on a monthly basis for a specified amount of time. Life insurance provides your beneficiaries with a payment in the event of your death.

If you have had policies with a previous employer, it may be possible to take over the payments to continue coverage with those policies. Insurance policies are also available through many professional organizations, including the Academy of Nutrition and Dietetics.

Contracts

A contract is commonly defined as a binding agreement between two or more persons or parties, especially one that is legally enforceable.[16] As an RDN in business, you will likely be presented with a written contract, or you may choose to have your own contracts for the various types of work you do. Examples of these are a lease, an agreement to rent space in a physician's office, an agreement to become a provider for an insurance company, or an agreement to give a presentation. You want to have a clear understanding with the other party as to the work you are to perform, the compensation you will receive, and the time frame or deadline.

Many RDNs question whether they should hire an attorney to write or review their contracts. If you are presented with a written contract, it is likely that an attorney for the organization prepared it. If you don't understand the contract, you should seek advice from legal counsel.[17] Even if you have decided to draw up your own contract, consult an attorney. He or she will have your best interests in mind.

Business Advisers

There are many types of business advisers available to help you do what you cannot do, do not want to do, or should not do. As most of us have been trained as RDNs and not as entrepreneurs, it is important to know when to seek help. Spending money on an adviser who knows about small businesses will be a wise investment in your future. If funds are limited, offer to barter for professional services.

The following is a list of people and brief explanations of how they might assist you in the business world. You can also explore online resources for business advice, but you may still need the advice of a professional.

Accountants

An accountant can advise you on your taxes, including legitimate business deductions, a suitable business structure, and record keeping. As your business grows, an accountant can also advise you on investments. It is best to work with an accountant who is familiar with small businesses. Be aware, however, that fees vary significantly. Try to obtain a recommendation for an accountant from those you know. You can also search online for an accountant, but you should always request references.

Attorneys

It is advisable to consult an attorney before making any decision with legal implications, such as determining your business structure or drawing up a partnership agreement. You might also consult an attorney before signing a lease, negotiating a bank loan, copyrighting written material, or drafting or signing a contract of any variety. Be sure to hire an attorney who is familiar with small businesses and has fees in line with what you can afford.[17-18]

Bankers

Establish a relationship with a friendly banker. Even if you don't plan to take out a loan, a banker can often advise you on the best accounts for your business, lead you to credit cards with the most attractive interest rates, and even help guide you on how to accept credit cards in your practice. Open a checking account and obtain a credit card to be used exclusively for your business. This will make it easier to track your business finances and help keep them separate from your personal expenses. A banker can also provide you with information on setting up individual retirement accounts (IRAs) for small businesses. Best of all, the advice from bankers is free.

Business Consultants

A business consultant can serve as a general adviser to your business. He or she may be able to guide you to an ideal office location, help you project a professional image in the community, or offer ideas for establishing your business priorities. The best way to find an adviser is by speaking to others who have started a business. The SBA may also keep lists of people who are available in your community; this information can be accessed through the SBA website (www.sba.gov).[19] Valuable business services are also available through the Service Corps of Retired Executives (SCORE). SCORE services are free.[20] You can find out more about SCORE on the organization's website (www.score.org).

Marketing Consultants and Public Relations Advisers

As your business grows, consulting a marketing person or a public relations adviser might take you to the next level. These consultants can also help you name your business, design your logo, develop business cards and a website, identify media contacts, or create marketing and social media campaigns. They are probably more helpful once your business is off the ground and running. Fees vary significantly. Shop around and be sure to get references from individuals with similar business goals.

Technology Consultants

A computer will be an essential tool in your nutrition business. A technology consultant or computer specialist can assist you with identifying your computer needs, help you when you have computer problems, and guide you in terms of your presence on the internet and on social media. Chapter 5 discusses the selection of computer equipment and office- and nutrition-related software, whereas chapter 8 explores the internet and social media technology.

Coaches

A coach—also referred to as a life coach, executive coach, or career coach—can empower you to understand the right business path for you. The coaching process focuses on helping you discover the gap between where you are now in your business and life and where you want to be and how to close the gap. A coach will ask powerful questions and listen rather than simply giving advice. Coaching can help you find what you thought was impossible. Many RDNs work with a coach when starting out or transitioning their practices. There are RDNs who specialize as coaches and can help you in your business endeavor. You can find a coach by asking for recommendations from colleagues, posting on a dietetic practice group (DPG) LISTSERV, or checking on the Nutrition Entrepreneurs DPG website (www.nedpg.org).

Mentors

A mentor can be a valuable resource. A mentor with experience in private practice or business can provide guidance and suggestions based on his or her own experience of what to do and what not to do in starting your practice. Finding a mentor can be challenging. A successful colleague you extol and want to emulate but who does not know you may not be willing or able to invest time in working with you. There are options to find a mentor. You can develop rapport with a colleague you admire on social media by sharing his or her tweets, blog, and posts on LinkedIn. SCORE offers a mentor service, as does the Academy of Nutrition and Dietetics eMentoring Program.[20,21] Many of the Academy of Nutrition and Dietetics DPGs and member interest groups (abbreviated as MIGs) provide mentoring as a member service.

First Steps: A Summary

Here are the main points you should take away from this chapter:

- You can structure your private practice as a sole proprietorship, a partnership, or a corporation. Each business structure has advantages and disadvantages. It may be a wise investment to discuss your business with an attorney, an accountant, or a business adviser to determine the most appropriate structure for your practice.

- You should write a business plan to determine your target market, organize your business structure and funding, and state the goals of your practice and how you hope to achieve those goals. A business plan is necessary to borrow money from a bank. There are many tools available to write a business plan.

- To conduct business, you need to explore the pros and cons of naming your practice and the steps to obtain a business name, the licenses and permits you need to be in business, and the necessary insurance policies.

- You may be presented with a contract, or you may want to present a contract for your services. Depending on the specifics, hiring an attorney might be prudent.

- Advisers to your business may include attorneys, accountants, bankers, general business consultants, marketing consultants, public relations advisers, technology consultants, coaches, and mentors. When inquiring about the services of these consultants, be sure that they are familiar with small business issues and that their fees are in accordance with your budget. It is best to get referrals from colleagues who are in private practice.

References

1. Self-employed individuals tax center. US Department of the Treasury Internal Revenue Service website. www.irs.gov/individuals/self-employed. Accessed May 10, 2017.

2. Independent contractor or employee? US Department of the Treasury Internal Revenue Service website. Publication 1779 (Rev. 3-2012). www.irs.gov/pub/irs -pdf/p1779.pdf. Accessed May 10, 2017.

3. Staff of Entrepreneur Media, Inc. *Start Your Own Business: The Only Startup Book You'll Ever Need*. 6th ed. Irvine, CA: Entrepreneur Press; 2015.

4. Allen KR. *Starting a Business All-In-One for Dummies*. Hoboken, NJ: John Wiley & Sons, Inc; 2015.

5. Strauss SD. *The Small Business Bible: Everything You Need to Know to Succeed in Your Small Business*. 3rd ed. Hoboken, NJ: John Wiley & Sons, Inc; 2012.

6. Choose your business structure. US Small Business Administration website. www.sba.gov/starting-business/choose-your-business-structure. Accessed May 10, 2017.

7. Shelton H. *The Secrets to Writing a Successful Business Plan*. Rockville, MD: Summit Valley Press; 2014.

8. Brown, C. Do you need a business plan for your startup? Black Enterprise website. July 23, 2014. www.blackenterprise.com/small-business/do-you -need-business-plan-for-your-start-up/. Accessed May 10, 2017.

9. Price B. Creating a business and marketing plan—10 steps to success. *Today's Dietitian*. 2009;11(5):22. www.todaysdietitian.com/newarchives/050409p22 .shtml. Accessed May 10, 2017.

10. Business name registration (doing business as). Business.usa.gov website. https://business.usa.gov/knowledgebase/register-your-business-name. Accessed May 10, 2017.

11. How to apply for an EIN. US Department of the Treasury Internal Revenue Service website. www.irs.gov/businesses/small-businesses-self-employed/ how-to-apply-for-an-ein. Accessed May 10, 2017.

12. Busey JC. Do food and nutrition professionals really need liability insurance? *J Am Diet Assoc*. 2007;107(9):1480.

13. Do I need professional liability insurance? Insurance Information Institute website. www.iii.org/individuals/business/optional/professionalliability. Accessed May 10, 2017.

14. National Association for the Self-Employed website. www.nase.org. Accessed May 10, 2017.

15. Health plans & benefits: Continuation of health coverage—COBRA. US Department of Labor website. www.dol.gov/general/topic/health-plans/cobra. Accessed May 10, 2017.

16. Simple definition of contract. Merriam-Webster website. www.merriam-webster .com/dictionary/contract. Accessed May 10, 2017.

17. Busey JC. When do you need a lawyer? *J Am Diet Assoc*. 2007;107(5):733-735.

18. Busey JC. Are all lawyers the same? *J Am Diet Assoc*. 2007;107(6):915-917.

19. US Small Business Administration website. www.sba.gov. Accessed May 10, 2017.

20. Service Corps of Retired Executives (SCORE) website. www.score.org/. Accessed May 10, 2017.

21. eMentoring and Mentoring Resources. eatRIGHT.org website. www. eatrightPRO.org/resource/career/career-development/mentoring-networking-and-volunteering/ementoring-and-mentoring-resources. Accessed May 10, 2017.

3 | Show Me the Money: Setting Up Your Business

This chapter explores the essentials of money management. The skills required to work as a registered dietitian nutritionist (RDN) are not necessarily the same skills you need to run your own business. Traditional nutrition and dietetics programs do not require very much in terms of business classes. To be successful in your own practice, however, you must start thinking and acting like a businessperson. You may have fantastic ideas and be excellent at what you do, but before you officially launch your business and see your first client in your practice, you must have all your business systems in place. You need to be constantly aware of the bottom line. You must feel comfortable with being paid and not be afraid to ask for money!

Setting Fees

A common burning question from aspiring private practice RDNs is *How much should I charge a client?* Many RDNs turn to colleagues in private practice to ask what they charge. Do not do this. It is a potential violation of federal antitrust laws to discuss fees for professional services with other RDNs because this could be construed as price fixing.[1,2] You want to base your fee schedule on your situation. Even if you plan on accepting insurance payments—also referred to as third-party payments—you will still need to have a fee schedule. Remember. The fee you set now does not have to be the fee you charge forever. As you gain experience, you will be able to charge a higher fee.

Factors to Consider

Many factors must be considered when setting fees. There are no hard-and-fast rules on establishing your fees. Basing your fees on actual (or even projected) numbers will help you arrive at a fee schedule that can work for you to make a profit. The formula shown here can facilitate setting your hourly fee.

$$\text{Hourly fee} = \frac{\textit{Desired annual salary} + \textit{Expenses}}{\textit{Number of working hours}}$$

This formula will help you develop a basis for your hourly fee. Think of it as a starting point. You can then adjust your hourly fee accordingly. Let's look at each component of this formula.

DESIRED ANNUAL SALARY

How much do you want to earn? Determine your desired annual income before income taxes (it is important to be realistic) as a starting point. Do you want to earn about the same amount of money that you earned in your previous job and reap the benefits of being self-employed? Or is your goal to earn more than you previously earned?

EXPENSES

What are your expenses? To earn a salary, you must set fees that cover your expenses and provide a sufficient profit. Therefore, one of the first things you must do when setting fees is to project your annual expenses. There are different expenses you will incur in your practice.

Business and Office Expenses Business and office expenses are often referred to as overhead costs. These will include both fixed and variable costs.

Fixed costs are expenses you have regardless of the number of clients you see. These are consistent expenses you may incur on a weekly, monthly, quarterly, or annual basis. The box on the next page lists some of the potential fixed expenses you may have.

Variable costs, on the other hand, are costs directly associated with the actual services provided to clients. Your variable costs may increase as you see more clients, and these will depend on the services and materials you use with each client. Variable costs can be brochures or booklets you purchase to provide to clients for a specific diagnosis or condition, or they can be single-use items needed to perform a specialized service, such as the mouthpiece for measuring indirect calorimetry or credit card fees for each transaction. You will want to build many of these variable costs into your fees when seeing a client, but you may also separately charge the client for some variable costs. Keep this in mind when looking at your potential expenses.

Fixed Costs

Rent	Insurance
	• Professional liability
Utilities:	• General liability
• Telephone	
• Internet	Professional dues
• Electric	and licenses
• Gas/oil	
	Subscriptions
Office supplies	
	Taxes
Postage	
	Employee expenses
Bank fees	• Salary
	• Insurance
Website fees and other	• Taxes
marketing expenses	
Electronic health records (EHRs)	

You will have the greatest amount of expenses when first starting out and setting up your practice. Some of these expenses will be one-time expenditures. These can include furniture, equipment, supplies, a security deposit, and legal fees. You should be somewhat frugal to keep your expenses down but not so strict that you neglect to purchase the necessary supplies and equipment you need to properly do your job. In the future when you have a higher profit from your practice, you can purchase those top-of-the-line or expensive items you wanted for your practice. For a complete listing of the necessary office supplies and equipment you will need, refer to chapters 5 and 6.

Benefits Factor in the cost of benefits when setting your fees. Benefits are usually provided by employers include health insurance, life insurance, disability insurance, and other forms of insurance, as well as 401(k), profit sharing, or pension plans. You will now have to pay for these benefits.

Taxes Whether your business is a corporation or a sole proprietorship, you will need to pay employee taxes, and these can be a substantial expense. Being self-employed, you must pay both the employer and employee portions of the Federal Insurance Contributions Act (FICA) tax. The FICA tax is imposed at a single flat rate. Currently, the Social Security tax rate for employees is 6.2% and the Medicare tax rate is 1.45%, which account for 7.65% of your gross income. Because the employer is required to match this tax, a self-employed person is considered both employer and employee. The 6.2% becomes 12.4%, and the 1.45%

becomes 2.9%. As a self-employed person, you now pay 15.3% of your income in FICA taxes to the federal government.[3]

You will still be required to pay income taxes. The amount of your tax bill will depend on your income after business-related expenses or whether you give yourself a salary. Unfortunately, it will be difficult to build your personal tax responsibility into your hourly fee. Get into the habit of regularly setting aside monies specifically for your taxes. Keep in mind that taxes are federal, but you may also need to pay state and local taxes depending on where you live. Estimated taxes are paid quarterly. Your actual tax bill will be determined when you complete your tax forms for the calendar year. Your accountant can provide guidance on taxes and how to prepare for them.

NUMBER OF WORKING HOURS

In addition to the salary you'd like to earn and your business expenses, you also need to factor in your time when setting your fees. One of the many benefits of being in private practice is that you determine how many days a week you will work and how many hours you will work in a day.

In private practice, you are billing for your time. There are many things to consider. Determine your salable time—how many hours can you really work or, more specifically, how many hours will you actually be paid for? Again, it is important to be realistic in your estimates. Build vacation time, sick days, holidays, and personal time into your formula. Figure out how many weeks of each year you want.

Consider your nonbillable time, which always seems to amount to more than you may think. This is the time spent on administrative work, such as returning and making phone calls, writing letters, checking and writing emails, paying bills, sending bills, and other accounting. Think also about how much time you will be spending on marketing, network-

Example of Formula to Determine Hourly Fee Based on Annual Projected Numbers

Your desired salary is $100,000 annually. You project your annual expenses at $35,000. You only want to work three days per week for eight billable hours each day. Considering your vacation time, personal time, sick time, and attendance at conferences, you will work 45 weeks each year.

Using the previous formula:

$$\frac{(\$100,000 + \$35,000)}{(8 \text{ hours} \times 3 \text{ days} \times 45 \text{ weeks})} = \frac{\$135,000}{1080 \text{ hours}} = \$125.00 \text{ per hour fee}$$

ing, and continuing education, whether this means attending seminars, doing research in your office, or catching up by reading journal articles. This should all be accounted for in your hourly fee.

Now that you're aware of all the factors you must take into consideration, refer to the box on the previous page for an example of using the formula to determine your hourly fee.

Consider the following:

- How many hours a day do you want to work?

- How many days a week do you want to work?

- How many weeks in a year do you plan to work?

Creating Effective Financial Policies and Procedures

Before you open your doors for business, it is important to institute your office policies and procedures. Establishing your office accounting procedures, other administrative tasks, and payment policies will keep you organized, consistent, and on top of your practice. Initially, if you are starting your business on a small scale, you may think that you can just wing it. This is not recommended. You need to have policies in writing and systems in place.

Where will you keep and how will you maintain your expenses, payments you receive, and other crucial information? Contracts, lease agreements, and other legal papers; employee paperwork (if applicable); and licenses all must be made available as well.

All successful businesses have good bookkeeping and record-keeping systems in place. It is imperative to keep detailed records for the following reasons[4]:

- To monitor and track the performance of your practice: To understand which expenses are necessary and which can be reduced or eliminated, you must constantly monitor your practice. Ultimately, this will tell you whether you are making money and assist you in making sound business decisions.

- To determine your salary: To know how much to pay yourself, you must know how much you have. It is as simple as that!

- To track tax obligations: If you maintain up-to-date and accurate financial records, it is much easier to gather accurate data for filing taxes and other returns or paying quarterly taxes. It will also decrease your accounting bills if you present these detailed records to your accountant when it comes time to prepare your tax returns.

- To obtain a loan from the bank: If you want to borrow money, banks request very detailed financial records.

- To monitor client accounts receivable: You want to stay on top of payments received and those client accounts with a balance, whether the client is paying or you are receiving payment from a third-party insurance provider.

- To maintain a database of your clients: Keep a list of your clients' names, addresses, phone numbers, email addresses, and other important information. This can be managed on a spreadsheet or on an electronic health record (EHR), as discussed in chapter 7. You never know when you may need this list for when you move your office location or want to send out a newsletter.

With written policies and procedures in place, your practice will run smoothly.

Managing Your Bookkeeping

You will have to manage your bookkeeping on some level, whether you do it yourself or hire an accountant or bookkeeper. Organizing your financial information will make it easier and less frustrating in the long run.

Many accounting software packages are available to make detailed record keeping quite simple for small businesses. However, regardless of the computer software program, you still need to download or manually enter the data and categorize the information. Information that needs to be tracked includes cash receipts (the money coming in) and cash disbursements (the money going out).

To keep your finances straight, you will need to set up your system to record and track your income and expenses (accounts payable). This information will be used when filing your income taxes and to determine your profits. The system you set up will also help manage your accounts receivable (payments received) and allow you to send invoices out to clients who owe you money.

INCOME TRACKING

All payments you receive must be recorded. You will be reporting this as your practice income. The form in which you receive payments depends on what you decide is best for your practice. You may accept cash, checks, credit and debit cards, or electronic fund transfers directly into your checking account. This is discussed later in this chapter.

TRACKING EXPENSES

There are numerous expenditures you will have in private practice. Each expenditure or transaction should be recorded and assigned to a category, such as office supplies, rent, and advertising. Setting up categories properly can make it easier for tax preparation each year. Following

Suggested Record-Keeping Categories

Income: Track all payments—checks, electronic fund transfers, credit cards, PayPal, cash, etc. If you accept insurance, you may want to categorize by payer. It's a good idea to keep your business income separate from your personal bank accounts.

Advertising: Website design and hosting, business cards, signs, promotional items

Car and truck expenses: Car expenses related to your practice, but not daily commuting. Going from one office or client to another qualifies. Be sure to record your mileage and related car expenses.

Commissions and fees: Your state license, other fees related to your practice

Contract labor: Electrician, plumber, virtual assistant

Employee benefit programs: Employee benefits you provide, such as health insurance, profit sharing, or 401(k) plans

Insurance (other than health): Professional liability (malpractice), general liability

Interest: Interest on loans or credit cards related to your practice

Legal and professional services: Legal, accounting, and bookkeeping expenses

Office expenses: Paper, printer toner, envelopes, pens, staplers, folders, postage, hand soap, toilet paper, paper towels, etc; cleaning service and snow removal

Pension and profit-sharing plans for your employees

Rent or lease:

- **Vehicles, machinery, and equipment**
- **Other business property:** Rent for your space, fees for storage space (if applicable)

Repairs and maintenance: Repairs to equipment such as your computer and printer, scale calibration

Taxes and licenses: Related to your practice, not your income taxes

Travel, meals, and entertainment: Travel costs and deductible meals and entertainment

Utilities: Telephone, electric, gas/oil

Wages: Employee salaries, Medicare and Social Security payroll taxes

Other expenses: Expenses that don't fit in another category but are related to your practice

the format on the Internal Revenue Service (IRS) form Schedule C (Form 1040), Profit or Loss from Business for categories can be helpful. The box on the previous page lists suggested record-keeping categories based on the IRS Schedule C, Form 1040. Consult an accountant or bookkeeper for assistance with setting up your categories.

If each transaction is accurately recorded, the cash balance from the software package will equal the cash balance in your practice checking account. This is known as a balanced set of books. Obviously, this is desirable.

TRACKING ACCOUNTS RECEIVABLE

Although you will be tracking your income, which is payments, you will also have to keep track of client accounts. Do any of your clients owe money? This should not be an issue if you do not accept third-party payments because you should have the client pay you at the time of the appointment. It is different when you accept third-party payments. You need to track if you were paid or not paid by the insurance company and if the client is responsible for any payment. This can be for a copayment, for meeting a deductible, or for situations when the insurance claim is denied by the third party. Using an electronic billing program for billing third-party payers or a spreadsheet to track payments can help you monitor the status of your accounts receivable. This is discussed in more detail in chapter 7.

Choosing Accounting Software

Software programs can perform all the necessary accounting and bookkeeping functions you will need for your practice. There are many programs available on the market.[5] They all offer similar functions, but some programs are easier to use than others. Choosing the right system for your practice is very important.[6] You may want to ask other private-practice RDNs what accounting software they use. You should also ask your accountant which program he or she recommends.

To help you narrow down your choices, consider which functions you want the system to perform. For example, you may want software that provides profit-and-loss statements, writes checks, and sends monthly bills. Again, your accountant can certainly advise you. You can also check the internet for additional resources. The box on the next page lists criteria you may want to consider before purchasing accounting software for your business.[7]

Hiring an Accountant or Bookkeeper

If you are not very good at money management, you may consider hiring someone to do your accounting and bookkeeping. You can hire an accountant or bookkeeper to set up a bookkeeping system for you to manage. If you prefer to spend your time on other aspects of running

Factors to Consider When Choosing Accounting Software[7]

Do you...

- Need something very basic or a program with versatility?
- Want to track accounts receivable?
- Need payroll/have employees?
- Want to write checks?
- Want to do bookkeeping for taxes?
- Need to send invoices, whether faxed or emailed?
- Want online banking access?
- Need customized reports?
- Accept credit cards?

your business, then consider hiring an accountant or bookkeeper to manage your books on a monthly basis. This does not necessarily have to come at a huge cost to you. For example, if you can bill $120 per hour for your time and pay a bookkeeper $50 per hour, you come out ahead. From a cost-benefit standpoint, you may be better off spending your time on providing services, developing your business, and marketing while leaving the administrative tasks to someone else.

The downside of hiring someone to manage your business finances, particularly when you are first starting out, is that initially, most RDNs going into business prefer to keep costs as low as possible. Also, when you are first getting started, it may be beneficial to have a better understanding of the financial aspect of the business. When you do the billing and accounting and perform other financial administrative tasks, you get a clear picture of what it actually costs to run your practice and understand what is involved on the administrative end. As your business expands, you can then hire someone as an office administrator or even a part-time bookkeeper, depending on your needs. Weigh the options and decide which approach is best for you.

Saving Financial Documents

You may not want to think *What if?*, but what if the IRS audits your practice? You want to make sure that you have all the necessary documentation that supports what you claimed as business income and expenses. The IRS works on the honor system. What you said you did is what you did, and if you are audited, you have to provide proof. To be prepared for the what if, save all supporting paperwork for your income and expenses. These items may include bank deposit slips, copies of checks, credit card receipts, credit card statements, canceled checks, bank account statements, invoices, and receipts for all expenses.

Having merely a credit card statement for a purchase or payment as proof of an expense is inadequate documentation for a transaction. It does not explain what was purchased or paid for in the transaction. For each and every transaction, save the actual paper or electronic receipt. To save electronic receipts, set up folders on your computer, as suggested in the box on page 41, to duplicate your bookkeeping categories. For paper receipts, you can scan the receipt, save it as a document, and file it under the appropriate category. Back up or copy your receipts. Save all your documentation by calendar year, as it's particularly important should the IRS ever audit you. Keep it for at least seven years. Some states can look back farther than the IRS. Review your state guidelines to determine how long tax documents should be kept.

Office Payment Policies

Before you begin to see clients, you need to establish your payment policies. Payment policies explain to the client the rules of your practice regarding payment and clients' financial responsibility. You will need to inform new clients of your office payment policies. Present your policies in writing either before or during a client's first appointment. You can also post your payment policy on your website with your new client forms.

Each new client should sign a form stating that he or she has read and understands your office policies, including responsibility for payment. Inform the client that payment is collected at the time of the visit unless you will be billing his or her insurer. Clients then know what to expect, and there are no surprises. See the Making Your Business box on the next page for a sample statement.

HOW WILL YOUR CLIENTS PAY YOU?

In determining your office policies, you need to decide *how* your clients will be able to pay you. Will you only accept checks and cash? Or do you also want to accept credit and debit cards?

Cash When you accept cash, there are no additional costs (such as when you process debit or credit cards). Of the different forms of payment, cash is the easiest to accept and the most desirable. You do not have to deposit the cash into a bank account, but you do have to account for cash as income. Always provide a receipt to your client when accepting cash. You can use a superbill or a Form CMS-1500, as discussed in chapter 7. A cash receipt form from an office supply store or one developed on your computer word-processing program can also be used for proof of payment. Be sure to credit a client's account. It is easy to lose track of who paid once the cash is in your hand.

Making Your Business:
Sample Payment Policy Statement

Payment Policy Statement

Payment for services is due at the time services are rendered, unless other arrangements have been made in advance. I accept MasterCard, Visa, American Express, cash, and checks. I will be happy to help you with an insurance claim form for reimbursement if I am not a provider of your insurance. Assignment is accepted only from those insurance companies for which I am a provider. However, if your insurance company denies coverage, you are financially responsible for the payment.

Reprinted with permission from Ann Silver.

Checks Checks are not as popular these days, but you can still receive them as payment. You will not incur any additional expenses by accepting checks. However, your bank will assess fees if they bounce. You can take precautions to safeguard yourself from bounced checks. If a check lacks a printed name or has a low number (such as 101), assume the account is new. You may want to inquire about such accounts with the client.[8] If you have doubts about the validity of the check, it would be wise not to have another appointment with the client until the check has cleared.

Consider having a policy in place for handling returned checks. Determine what your bank charges you for returned checks. You will want to pass this added expense on to the client. It is important to include this information in your office payment policy and post a sign in the waiting room. One way to avoid returned checks and overdue accounts is to accept credit cards.

Credit and Debit Cards Accepting credit and debit cards can have many advantages, such as helping you collect payments efficiently and attracting clients. The disadvantage of accepting "plastic" is the added expense. You must pay fees to the credit card companies. The fees affiliated with credit and debit cards can include a percentage-per-transaction fee, a monthly fee, a processing equipment charge, and set-up fees. Some RDNs charge a "convenience fee" to cover the added cost of accepting credit cards. Check the credit card policy and your state and local laws regarding passing along the fee to the client. It may be prohibited. You cannot impose fees for debit cards.

The same equipment you use to accept a credit card can also accept a debit card. This means that you can also accept debit cards for health savings accounts and flexible spending accounts. Even though debit cards are connected to a bank account, they are not processed like a check and will incur a fee like other credit cards. Do some research to

Criteria to Consider When Choosing a Credit Card Processing Company

Will you purchase or lease equipment?

How is the transaction transmitted—through phone or internet?

Is there a monthly minimum charge?

Is there a monthly statement fee?

Is there an enrollment or application fee?

Is there a setup fee?

What is the transaction fee? Is that fee fixed per transaction, or is it calculated as a percentage of the transaction?

Are there any additional fees for not swiping the credit card and manually entering the credit card or debit card information?

How long is the contract?

How long does it take for payment to be deposited into your bank account?

determine whether accepting credit and debit cards is a viable option for your practice. You have options for accepting credit cards, and the associated fees can significantly vary, so it is best to shop around to figure out what will work best for your practice.

One way to accept credit cards is by going through a bank or a credit card processing company. Oftentimes the credit card company will ask you to provide an estimate of your expected monthly charges before quoting rates. A higher sales volume will generally provide you with lower monthly fees. The processing terminal to process the credit card charge will entail an added cost as either a one-time purchase or a monthly lease. Depending on the type of terminal, you will need to have a separate landline phone number or a wired or wireless internet connection to transmit the transaction. A processing terminal is not easy to move around if you plan on having more than one practice location.

Another credit card processing option used by many private practice RDNs is a mobile credit card reader. These small devices connect to a smartphone or a tablet through the headphone jack. They generally do not involve a monthly fee; however, there may be a small one-time investment for the mobile reader plus the fees for each transaction. Mobile credit card readers, as the name implies, can be used wherever you go.

Online payment systems, such as PayPal, are another option available for accepting credit cards. Some accounting software programs and electronic health records also provide online payment options. Other than transaction fees, there are usually no additional costs. Clients can pay online at their appointment or even before their appointment. You can also have a *pay here* button to link to online payments on your website. The box on the previous page lists the options to evaluate before deciding which credit card processing company to use.

BILLING CLIENTS

There may be situations when you have to send an invoice to a client. When properly maintained, your accounts receivable, mentioned earlier in this chapter, will reveal when a client has an outstanding balance. Should you have to bill a client for your services, do so in a timely manner. Try to send an invoice to the client within a month of the date of service. With insurance, bill the client as soon as you learn that the insurance claim indicates that the client has a financial responsibility. As shown on the invoice in the Making Your Business box below, indicate the client's name, date of service, details about the amount due, and method of pay-

Making Your Business: **Sample Invoice**

Your Name, RDN
Registered Dietitian Nutritionist

INVOICE

Address
City, State Zip code
Phone #
Email address:
Website:

Date: 11/20/2017

For:
Nutritional services

Patient Name
Address
City, State Zip code

DATE of SERVICE	DESCRIPTION	FEE	INSURANCE PAYMENT	PATIENT PAYMENT	ADJUSTMENT	BALANCE DUE
10/02/2017	MNT Initial 97802	XXX.00	ZZZ.00	0	(KK.00)	JJ.00
10/06/2017	No Show Fee	MM.00		0		MM.00

Balance due 12/18/2017 $BBB.00

Payment options:
Mail a check payable to [RDN name] at [complete address].
PayPal on my website at [website address].

Thank you!

Reprinted with permission from Ann Silver.

ment (eg, check, credit card, on your website). Specify a due date for the payment. Follow up if payment is not received.

To minimize the need for billing and to save you time and postage, establish a routine of collecting payment at each visit. There will be exceptions. For example, it is often difficult to obtain payment after visits from teenagers and young adults whose parents are paying the bills.

COLLECTING UNPAID BALANCES

You must have a collections policy in place in the event that you are not paid. The policy can specify that patients with an outstanding balance will not be seen. The first step is to send an invoice indicating that the client has a balance due. When a client has not paid once the due date has passed, your next step is to send another invoice indicating that the account is past due. If you still do not receive payment, place a friendly phone call to the client. Ask the client if he or she received the invoice and when you can expect payment. If these approaches are unsuccessful, send a letter stating that payment is due by a certain date or further action will be taken, and specify the action. Usually the letter will prompt payment. If not, you may want to use the services of a collection agency, but this will depend on the amount of the debt. Agencies charge a percentage of the total sum collected or a flat fee for each satisfied account. The additional fees can be added to the client's outstanding balance depending on your state laws. Include this in your payment policies. Ask colleagues and others in business for recommendations of a reputable collection agency.

MISSED APPOINTMENTS

Many practitioners have a 24- or 48-hour cancellation policy. They inform clients in advance that the client will be charged for missed appointments or cancellations on short notice. Include this in writing as part of your payment policy. This way, you can collect for missed appointments (although you usually cannot enforce this policy for first-time appointments). A statement such as "Forty-eight (48) hour notice is required for cancellation of appointments or a $XX.00 fee will apply" can be added to your new client forms. Some RDNs charge the full amount for a session when the appointment is canceled with inadequate notification or when the client is a no-show.

Note that you cannot bill third-party payers—including private insurance companies, Medicare, and Medicaid—if services were not rendered. However, you may be able to bill the client a fee for a missed appointment.[9] Confirm this with each third-party payer.

If you accept credit cards, you can keep each client's credit card number on file and bill for missed appointments. This policy should be printed on your client information sheet and presented in writing along with your other payment policies during the first visit. Some practitioners find it helpful to have their policy printed on the bottom of appointment cards.

Putting Your Office Payment Policies in Writing

Once you figure out your office policies, it's crucial to put them in writing. Share the written copy with each new client. Have the client sign the policy acknowledging that he or she has read and received it. Keep a signed copy in your records for each patient and also provide the patient with a copy of the policy. The Making Your Business box below provides an example of an office's payment policies, which can be modified to fit your practice.

Making Your Business:
Sample Payment Policy Statement

Office Payment Policies

1. Payment for services, including copays, is due at the time services are rendered.

2. Assignment is accepted only from those insurance companies for which we are a provider.

3. You are responsible for obtaining a referral if your insurance policy requires one. You will not be seen if you do not have a referral. If you want to be seen without a referral, then you agree to self-pay for the visit at $ [   ] for an initial visit and $ [   ] for a follow-up visit.

4. If your insurance company denies coverage or payment, you are financially responsible for the visit.

5. If we are not a provider of your insurance, a superbill will be provided to you. You can submit the superbill to your insurance company for you to be reimbursed.

6. Payments can be made via cash, check, MasterCard, Visa, American Express, or PayPal.

7. There is a $ [   ] fee for any returned/bounced checks.

8. You will be responsible for the full fee of the appointment if you do not provide the office with twenty-four (24) hour notice to cancel or change the appointment or if you do not show up for your appointment.

9. You will not be seen if you have an outstanding balance.

10. Outstanding balances after 60 days will be sent to collection. When an account is sent for collection, you are responsible for an additional [   ] % fee on the balance.

I have read, understand, and agree to these policies

Signature: Date:

Reprinted with permission from Ann Silver.

Show Me the Money: A Summary

Here are the main points you should take away from this chapter:

- When setting fees, factor in your desired salary, the cost of benefits, business and office expenses, and the amount of time you want to work.

- Closely monitoring your finances is extremely important—this will assist you in determining the viability of your practice and in paying taxes. Choosing the right accounting software will help.

- You must have policies in place for billing, collecting past-due accounts, and returned checks. Have patients acknowledge your written payment policies with their signature.

References

1. Price fixing. Federal Trade Commission website. www.ftc.gov/tips-advice /competition-guidance/guide-antitrust-laws/dealings-competitors/price -fixing. Accessed May 10, 2017.

2. Setting Fees. eatrightPRO.org website. www.eatrightPRO.org/resource /practice/getting-paid/smart-business-practice-and-management/setting -fees. Accessed May 22, 2017.

3. Social Security and Medicare tax. Social Security Administration website. www.ssa.gov/news/press/factsheets/colafacts2017.pdf. Accessed May 10, 2017.

4. Marks G, ed. *Streetwise Small Business Book of Lists.* Avon, MA: Adams Media; 2006.

5. Strauss SD. *The Small Business Bible: Everything You Need to Know to Succeed in Your Small Business.* 3rd ed. Hoboken, NJ: John Wiley & Sons; 2012

6. Wasserman E. How to choose business accounting software. Inc website. www.inc.com/guides/choosing-accounting-software.html. Accessed May 10, 2017.

7. Service Corps of Retired Executives. How to choose accounting software. SCORE website. www.score.org/resource/how-choose-accounting-software. Accessed May 10, 2017.

8. Pritchard J. Avoid taking a bad check. The Balance website. http://banking .about.com/od/businessbanking/fl/Avoid-Taking-a-Bad-Check.htm. Accessed May 10, 2017.

9. Centers for Medicare and Medicaid Services. Charges for missed appointments. Transmittal 1279. Pub 100-04: Medicare Claims Processing. www.cms.gov/Regulations-and-Guidance/Guidance/Transmittals /downloads/r1279cp.pdf. Published June 29, 2007. Accessed May 10, 2017.

4 | What's Your Business Name and Who's Your Target?

Now that you've learned about some of the logistical things you need to keep in mind while developing your practice, it's time to think more about what exactly you plan to do and who you plan to reach. In addition to deciding where to locate your office, you need to think about what types of patients or clients you want to work with. You also need to spend some time determining what is unique about you to help build your brand and stand out from the rest of the pack. What do you do that is different from other registered dietitian nutritionists (RDNs)? Do you have an outgoing personality? Are you able to connect with people easily? These are all assets that can be very beneficial in attracting patients and having them market your services to others.

This chapter will help you determine your practice name, create your brand, find your target, and create the tools to help market your practice.

What Type of Nutrition Practice Will You Have?

You should think this through. The first question you'll want to ask yourself is *Do I want to see patients in an office, or do I want to work virtually?* You can always do both initially. You can see patients in an office where you rent space and also have a virtual practice, where you can work from anywhere you desire (with available Wi-Fi and Skype). It is important to know that if you accept insurance, you may need to see patients face-to-face to bill insurance unless you live in a rural area. If you live in a rural area, check with your insurance providers to see if you can bill for telehealth visits, which are typically done over the phone, via Vimeo (a platform compliant with the Health Insurance Portability and Accountability Act), or over email. In time, some insurance providers may start to reimburse for nutrition visits via telehealth within your state, so stay informed on your state insurance policies regarding telehealth. If you will be counseling patients virtually in a state where you are licensed and the patient does not have telehealth coverage for nutrition services, the patient must pay you directly. If you are not licensed in a state, you should be able to do coaching. Coaching is not the same as individualized medical nutrition therapy (MNT). Check with your state licensing bureau to see what is within your scope of practice when working virtually and to make sure that if you are coaching that you are not actually providing MNT. Again, patients must pay you directly, as coaching is not reimbursed by health insurance. Please refer to chapter 9 for more information on coaching versus MNT.

Will You Be a General or Specialized Nutrition Practitioner?

You are probably asking yourself *Where do I begin?* The field of nutrition is extremely vast and provides RDNs with so many areas to choose from. Truly, the possibilities are endless. You may want to start out as a general nutrition practitioner, which will allow you to see a variety of people. Over time, you can decide what types of patients you would like to work with. In the beginning stages of starting your practice, you will most likely see many patients who have weight issues, elevated lipid levels, or diabetes.

Having a general practice will allow you to build up your patient and referral base. A general practice is a practice where a variety of medical diagnoses, as well as wellness, may be seen. Typical medical problems seen in a general nutrition practice include weight management, gastrointestinal disorders, diabetes, and hyperlipidemia. You may also have patients calling you who want help with following a vegetarian or vegan diet. New moms may want nutrition guidance for breastfeeding. To help brand and market your services, first determine whether you want to have a general nutrition practice or a specialized nutrition practice from the get-go. What are you passionate about in the field of nutrition? This is a good starting point to determine how you want to plan out your services initially.

GENERAL NUTRITION PRACTICE

A general nutrition practice will allow you to see a wide range of clients. Generalists need to be current and informed about current trends in addition to being able to work with a variety of patients with long-term conditions, such as diabetes, obesity, and coronary heart disease. Generalists will rarely find their work stale or boring. If you don't have a specific area of interest or if you enjoy the challenge of keeping current with a broader base of nutrition specialties, creating a more flexible generalist practice may be a good fit for you. As an RDN generalist, you need to be confident that you have the expertise to see a wide variety of patients. The box below lists some pros and cons of having a general nutrition practice.

Pros and Cons of a General Nutrition Practice

Pros

- Your work will never be boring; you can be creative by working in many different areas of practice.

- Your business can constantly evolve as new opportunities come along.

- Having a wide area of expertise allows you to see a variety of clients.

Cons

- It may be a challenge to stay current in a variety of nutrition specialty areas.

- You may not always feel prepared when a client has an issue you aren't familiar with.

- Even if you have prior experience, you will need to enhance your clinical skills.

- There may be several registered dietitian nutritionists in general practice in your area, which increases competition.

SPECIALIZED NUTRITION PRACTICE

A specialized practice makes complete sense if you have a passion for or a strong background in a specific area of nutrition, such as diabetes or oncology. However, be aware that this can limit how fast your practice grows. Quite often, a person with a specialized medical condition may already have a full medical team, which could include an RDN, that they see either in a hospital setting or in a group practice. This is more common in large urban areas. Perhaps you could team up with several private practice physicians who also specialize in the area you are interested in. Just remember: You can always start out as a generalist and, as your practice grows, you can limit your practice to the specialty area that you are most passionate about. That's what makes private practice so great: freedom and flexibility! Let's look a little closer at the pros and cons of having a specialty practice, which are listed in the box below. This may help you decide what is better for you.

Pros and Cons of a Specialty Nutrition Practice

Pros

- If you specialize in one or two areas you are passionate about, you can focus on developing your expertise with these particular types of patients.

- You have a greater depth of knowledge in a specific area than the vast majority of other registered dietitian nutritionists (RDNs).

- If you practice in a community with other RDNs in private practice, a specialty practice will make you stand out from the competition.

- Specialists can usually charge more than generalists.

- Specialists draw from a larger geographic area, as people will travel a greater distance to see a specialist or will be more eager to consult you via Skype or phone if travel is an issue.

Cons

- There may not be sufficient need for your practice specialty to create a full-time practice.

- Your knowledge in other areas of nutrition can become outdated very quickly. For example, if your patient with diabetes is diagnosed with celiac disease and you are not well versed in the latest research on celiac nutrition, you may need to refer the patient elsewhere.

Even if you specialize in a certain area, you may need to see a variety of patients when you first start your private practice to build up your client base. Try working with as many populations as you have experience with and feel comfortable with. You may find that you enjoy working with pediatric patients or patients with weight management issues. As your private practice grows and you feel that you can financially limit your practice to one specific specialty, or as a specific passion begins to emerge, you can consider specializing in one area. The box on the next page lists potential areas you may want to consider specializing in.

Whichever specialty you choose, be aware of the training necessary to truly excel at that specialty, for the good of your clients. Many specialties may require additional credentialing in order to counsel clients, which is important to keep in mind when you are building your practice. Check in with the Academy of Nutrition and Dietetics Commission on Dietetic Registration to see what credentials your specialization may require. Additionally, become familiar with the outside organizations that are considered the best for a specialty area and join those organizations, read their publications, and go to their conferences. Specialty certification will not only benefit you and increase your level of expertise—it will also help further the profession of nutrition and dietetics.

Potential Specialty Areas of Nutrition Practice

Diabetes	Gastrointestinal issues	Eating disorders
Cancer prevention	Brain/mood	Bariatric nutrition
Wellness	Dental health	Drug addiction
Weight management	Pediatrics	Oncology
Plant-based nutrition	Sports nutrition	Pregnancy nutrition
Heart disease	Wedding nutrition	Fertility

Choosing Your Practice Name

Once you know how you would initially like to begin your practice, deciding on your practice name is quite often the first step in branding your practice (the process of naming your business was discussed from a logistical standpoint in chapter 2). You have so many options. Many RDNs use their name for their practice. It can make it easier for people to remember you if your practice title includes your name. If you are quoted in the press, people will be able to find you easier and remember your name. If your practice name is different, they may not be able to link the two. The more often the public or the media hears your name, the more likely they will be to seek you out when they need an RDN.

You can also choose a name that is consistent with your brand if you would like. If you work mainly with people who have diabetes and your last name is Smith, you might call your practice "Smith Diabetes Associates." Another option is to name your practice after the town you're in, such as "Oak Park Nutrition." This is another brainstorming project for you to work on. Just as your brand will evolve, so can your name. You can always change your practice name in the future. Sometimes starting out with your name as your practice name is a simple way to get going and open your doors. If you think that another name would be more appropriate down the road, make a change. The great thing about having your own private practice is that it's all up to you!

Creating Your Brand

What are you passionate about? What do you love to do? What types of clients do you want to have? What do you want to be known for? Are you the vegetarian dietitian who loves to teach your patients how to enjoy more plant-based foods? Or the pediatric nutritionist who makes home visits and teaches families how to create healthy meals? Your brand is what makes your business unique.[1] Your brand is your business identity.

Your brand should reflect your business name, logo, website, and social media handles. But you can start out without a brand and let it evolve as you grow your business. It's good to keep brand planning on your mind as you plan the logistics of your private practice. Do you love working with people with prediabetes and diabetes? Do you love to take your clients grocery shopping and teach them how to cook? You can take a pad of paper and write down everything you're interested in. Then you will have a better idea of what you want to be known for. Once you have decided on your brand, you can plan ways to market yourself. Having a logo is another way to help build your brand. The following section provides some ideas on how to choose and design your logo.

Logos

As your business grows and as your budget permits, consider developing a logo for your business cards and other materials. A well-designed logo creates a lasting impression and definitely contributes to name recognition. You may want to hire a graphic artist to design your logo. There are also online logo creators. Some are free or low in cost. Whatever you decide you can afford, just make sure that it is what you want to portray your image. What image do you want to portray? Are you more traditional or contemporary? Do certain colors appeal to you? Do you want two-color printing? If so, note that it will cost you more but may differentiate you from the crowd.

Once you design your logo, keep in mind that you can use it on all your forms and marketing materials, including business cards, invoices, letterhead, labels, and any other forms you develop. Your logo can also be added to the home page of your website.

Keep in mind that as your practice continues to grow and evolve over time, the same principle applies to your logo. The image you create today may not be the one you will use in the future, and that's not unusual in the business world. The Words of Wisdom box on the next page includes samples of some logos used by RDNs who have their own businesses. They have also included why their particular logo resonates with their brand.

Words of Wisdom

Choosing a Logo

Melissa Joy Dobbins, MS, RDN, CDE
My logo is an essential part of my business and my brand—it's a visual representation of what I stand for. My business name (Sound Bites) and tagline (sound science, smart nutrition, good food) convey food, nutrition, and communications. My mother, a graphic artist, helped me design the logo, and my web designer tweaked it a couple of years later. Because the words *sound bites* can have many different meanings, I used a fork to represent food and nutrition. Because my business also has a focus on communications, I liked the play on words and used a play button. Another graphic artist strongly discouraged me from using two images in the logo (both the fork and the play button), but I felt it was important to have both images to convey the meaning of food, nutrition, and communications. My tagline enhances the logo and helps pull everything together.

Chere Bork, MS, RDN
I am a life coach for registered dietitian nutritionists. I infuse them with energy and inspire them to live their life to the fullest. The word I always hear after my keynotes is *energy*, and my clients often call me a life-changer. Red represents my natural excitement and bold approach in living life to the fullest. The sparkles represent the spark I bring to people's lives: the spark to change lives forever. I credit Stephanie Hofhenke from String Marketing (www.stringmarketing.net) with discovering my true essence and bringing it alive!

Cassandra Golden, MS, RDN, LD
When I was looking to launch my private practice, the very first task I created for myself was to revamp my logo. I had just decided it was time for everything to be streamlined in

(Continued on next page)

Words of Wisdom (continued)

order to build a brand. I contacted an acquaintance who had created the logo for my sister's business. I sent her some descriptions about myself that I thought would be helpful. I wanted the logo to reflect food, obviously, and the fact that I am a nutrition consultant. From there I drew out many options on paper with my own hand. I was trying to search on the internet for what I was picturing in my mind, but I found that drawing it myself was the best way to communicate my vision to the logo designer. I'm glad I did draw out the vision (literally) because the graphic designer picked up on it right away. The hard part was deciding which one to choose! I feel that this logo is fresh, crisp, and modern and is somehow able to portray me and my small business perfectly!

Determining Your Target Market

Who needs or will use your services or products? Marketing your services or products requires you to be specific and objective. To identify your target market, you will need to identify characteristics of the population you wish to reach as well as those of your competition and how your services or products are priced in the marketplace.[1] You must also find out about trends in the marketplace and answer how (or if) your target market is presently having its needs met.

Your research will help you learn about the population you wish to reach. What is their socioeconomic profile? Where are they now turning for the services or products you hope to offer them? How much are they paying? This research will help you conclude where your business is most needed or will most likely succeed.

Conducting an analysis of the marketplace will help you identify what nutrition services are being provided and what is missing. If other local RDNs are already providing the same or similar services that you wish to pursue, assess which needs are not being met. You may uncover a practice area that has not yet been tapped. This allows you to position your business advantageously. Also, keep in mind that if you plan to work virtually and provide telehealth, you don't have to worry about other nutrition practices in your local community. When working virtually, your community is now the entire globe. Just remember that you can only provide MNT in a state where you are licensed. Otherwise, you are doing health coaching.

To find out which services are most needed, you need to track consumer trends. Read annual reports from trade organizations, professional publications, and government publications. Immediate information on trends is available simply by reading newspapers and magazines. They can provide insights into issues such as what readers think is hot, which foods they are purchasing, and current diet fads. Although you may not agree with the efficacy of every diet trend, you do need to be informed to provide credible, science-based feedback to your clients.

Formal marketing research can be daunting and quite costly, especially for a new RDN who is just getting started. Be creative to find the information you need without spending your entire marketing budget. You don't need to rely on sophisticated market surveys. To keep expenses down and methods manageable, you can use some creative resources that are readily available to you. Online searches can be a good place to start.

For many reasons, it might be necessary to be open to all aspects of practice when you first start. As your practice grows, you might find that the population you wanted to work with was not what you expected. Be open to everything, but remember that you don't have to *do* everything. What you love will emerge, and it will most likely be what you are good at.

In addition to gaining patients through physician referrals, you will want to market directly to potential patients and clients. Start by thinking about who your clients or patients will be. Do they belong to a particular age group, or do they have a specific diagnosis, such as diabetes? Once you have identified the population you want to concentrate on, learn everything you can about these potential patients or clients.[2] Understanding all aspects of your target population will assist you in marketing to them. What are the demographics of this group? What are their socioeconomic backgrounds? Where do they go for medical services? For example, if you want to specialize in pediatrics, your marketing plan will be more directed toward parents but should also appeal to children, pediatricians, and family practitioners.

What will you call the people who receive your services: clients or patients? These terms can affect your marketing and signal to individuals whether you are the right nutrition professional for them. You may choose to use *clients* if your practice is wellness based or specializes in eating disorders. *Patients* is a preferable term for RDNs who provide MNT.

Who Is Your Competition?

Many RDNs view their competition as the enemy. This is a shortsighted analysis. In fact, other food and nutrition professionals can be your greatest referral source if you market yourself properly. Be a courteous and kind colleague. Do not step on toes. Review the population statistics where you'd like to practice. Will you be in a large city or a small rural area? Will you work virtually from your home office? Colleagues working together to ensure that certain niches are covered in a geographic area will present a more unified professional image. Do your research and see what types of nutrition specialties are needed in your locale or online.

Competitor Profile

	Competitor #1	Competitor #2	Competitor #3
Name: Location:			
Products and/or services Products/services: Pricing comparison:			
Background and overview of company Background: Current overview:			
Estimated market share Target market served: Market share: Demographic/ psychographics of customers:			
General marketing strategy Advertising: Promotion: Community involvement:			
Strengths and weaknesses Strengths: Weaknesses:			
Additional notes			

Adapted with permission from Linda Pinton.[3]

A careful analysis of your own strengths and weaknesses will allow you to refer clients to other RDNs when you cannot fulfill a need. This not only allows you to assist your clients but may also result in reciprocal referrals from other RDNs.

Thorough marketing research should reveal information about your competition. Your competitors can include noncredentialed nutritionists and wellness coaches. Your goal in assessing the competition is to determine how your services will meet a client's needs in a way that the competition does not.

Analyze the competition by assessing their strengths and weakness (see the Competitor Profile chart on the previous page).[2] Compare them to your own. To set yourself apart from the competition, ask yourself what is special, unusual, or different about your experiences or services. How well are your competitors performing? Is there an area of the marketplace that has not yet been addressed?

Tools for obtaining information about your competition can range from a formal mailed survey to an online survey tool that targets your identified audience. Gathering information can also be as simple as sending an email. Depending on your practice, information gathering may entail learning what commercial programs and local hospitals offer, purchasing books or products from your competition, exploring the websites of your competition, or even contacting other food and nutrition professionals.

What Is Your Niche?

Developing a niche and marketing to that niche can be beneficial. Your niche could be a specific aspect of nutrition, such as diabetes, food allergies, or vegetarianism. Or it could be a certain age group, such as elderly persons or children. Or it might be based on special skills you possess, such as your fluency in Spanish, your geographic location, or your willingness to travel to the client. A niche can even be providing high-quality services that surpass those of the competition. However, it's not the niche that will determine the success of your practice, but how you run the practice.[1]

Marketing to a niche can help focus your marketing efforts.[3] Your market may be individuals who are overweight. However, a focus on a particular segment of that population will help you with more specific marketing. The tools you might use to market to overweight middle-aged executives, for example, will be quite different from the tools used to market to overweight teenagers.

When developing a niche, think of where and how you can be connected with these possible clients. A practice limited to sports nutrition for women could market to health clubs (especially those exclusively for women), physical therapists, massage therapists, gynecologists, and orthopedists. Send letters to these potential referral sources introducing you and the services you provide, and include business cards and

Registered Dietitian Nutritionists Who Have a Particular Niche	
Nancy Clark, MS, RDN, CSSD	Sports nutrition
Maria Bella, MS, RDN, CDN	Lipids
Patsy Catsos, MS, RDN, LD	FODMAP
Susan Weiner, MS, RDN, CDE, CDN	Diabetes
Jill Castle, MS, RDN	Childhood nutrition

brochures. Write articles for a local newspaper's sports page and other health and sports publications, leave brochures at sporting goods stores, or present at a local Road Runners Club meeting. See the box above for a list of RDNs who have developed a particular niche.

Developing a Mission Statement

Once you have created a niche for your business, you're ready to create a mission statement (see the box on the next page). A mission statement includes, in a few succinct sentences, your practice goals and the philosophies underlying them. Equally important, the mission statement reveals what your practice is all about to your patients (both current and prospective) and the community. If you don't have a mission statement, create one by writing a one-sentence explanation of the purpose of your business. Once you have your mission statement, you will need to periodically review and possibly revise it to make sure that it accurately reflects your goals as your practice grows. To do this, simply ask yourself if the statement still correctly describes what you're doing.

In your mission statement, include who you are, how you can help your patients, and a brief summary of your philosophy. Once complete, who you are will become clearer to your target population. This will also highlight how you are unique among your competition. Be honest and up-front about your philosophy. Don't hide behind your philosophy, regardless of how unconventional it might be.[4] Just be sure that your statement reflects you—this is what will separate you from the pack. A good mission statement will also help keep you focused when marketing to your clients.[5] It will also help shape your brand. A great place to post your mission statement is on the home page of your website.

Creating Your Mission Statement

People form impressions of others within the first 20 to 30 seconds. It is wise to have a mission statement that reflects what your practice does, its goals, and its philosophy. Plan what you will say, write it down, and memorize it. Your preparation will help you gain better results in all your marketing activities. You can also include your mission statement on the home page of your website.

Using a pad of paper or your computer, in 20 words or less, describe who you are, what you do (be creative), and how your services benefit your clients.

The next box includes examples of mission statements from three successful RDNs.

Examples of Registered Dietitian Nutritionist Mission Statements

Digna Irizarry-Cassens, MHA, RDN, CLT:
Improving the quality of your life one bite at a time.

Lisa Musician, RD, LDN: To provide education and alternative solutions for a safer environment while maintaining optimal health for those managing food allergies.

Jill Nussinow, MS, RD: Teaching people how to eat and cook healthier, faster and tastier "real" foods so that they live healthier, happier and more productive lives, no matter what their age.

Developing a Powerful Elevator Speech

Your first impression should be a lasting impression. You want to tell someone what you do, not who you are. That's where writing your elevator speech comes into play. What's the difference between a mission statement and an elevator speech? A mission statement is a brief statement that explains what your practice does, its goals, and its philosophy. You can include your mission statement on the home page of your website so your prospective clients can see what you can provide to them.

An elevator speech is a one-sentence personal statement that you can use to quickly respond to someone asking *What do you do?* It's your first introduction to selling *you*. Are you ready to write your elevator speech?

Get a notepad and jot down some ideas of what you could say when a new acquaintance asks *What do you do?* Go through all of your ideas and formulate one sentence that will have an impact and that people will remember.[5] The keys to creating a self-introduction that people will remember include:

- Make it simple so people will know and remember what you do.

- Keep it short: Say it in 7 to 10 seconds.

- Make it distinct and professional.

- Use layperson terms so that the listener can relate.

- Connect with your listener. Your words, tone, eye contact, and body language have an impact.

It's important to develop your elevator speech early—if you are able to easily pull this together, it shows that *you* truly understand your brand, mission, and target market. If you are stumped, you might need to go back and revisit those ideas and come up with a clearer vision for your business. Once you develop the elevator speech, make sure you practice it. Memorize it so you are prepared when asked.[6] One example of an elevator speech is "I help people with diabetes improve the quality of their lives with optimal nutrition." See the box for ideas on how to develop your elevator speech.

Write Your Elevator Speech

In 20 words or less, compile your elevator speech. Say it over and over so you memorize it. Have it ready the next time someone asks, *What do you do?*

What's Your Business Name and Who's Your Target?: A Summary

Here are the main points you should take away from this chapter:

- Once you've decided to start your private practice, determining your practice name and the type of practice you will have (general vs specialized) are two major steps to contemplate. But remember: They are not written in stone. You can change your practice name and specialty as your practice evolves and as you feel more confident in a specific specialty area(s).

- Once you determine your name and practice type, you are ready to design the practice of your dreams. You can now create your brand and logo, and from there, plan who you will market your services to.

- Creating your brand will also help you write your mission statement and elevator speech. You will then have greater clarity in what you want to achieve. And you will also be able to quickly respond to someone who asks *What do you do?*

References

1. Strauss S. *The Small Business Bible*. New York, NY: John Wiley & Sons Inc; 2012.

2. Tyson E, Schell J. *Small Business for Dummies*. 4th ed. New York, NY: John Wiley & Sons Inc; 2012.

3. Pinson L. *Steps to Small Business Start-up*. Tustin, CA: Out of Your Mind...and Into the Marketplace Publishing; 2014.

4. Guillebeau C. *The $100 Startup: Reinvent the Way You Make a Living, Do What You Love, and Create a New Future*. New York, NY: Crown Business; 2013.

5. Smith D. 5 tips for a useful mission statement. Inc website. www.inc.com/ss/5-tips-on-developing-an-effective-mission-statement. Accessed May 10, 2017.

6. Koszyk S. Who Are You? Know Your Elevator Pitch & Build Your Personal Brand. NEDPG website. https://nedpg.org/sites/default/files/Members/Toolkit/2012%20Marketing/KnowYourElevatorPitch.pdf. Published 2014. Accessed June 8, 2017.

5 | Where to Set Up Shop

Now that you have decided to launch your private practice, you must determine where to see patients. If you plan to have your own office space, you may need to think about the computer and equipment you will need as well as the office supplies you will use. This chapter focuses on specific issues pertaining to setting up a private practice in an office space or when working virtually and the supplies and materials that a registered dietitian nutritionist (RDN) in private practice needs.

Where Will Your Office Be?

Before you determine what equipment and supplies you need, you should decide where your practice will be located. You have many choices. You can see patients in a variety of settings, which may include an office, virtually, in your patient's home, in a fitness center, or in another location. In private practice, unless you will be working completely remotely, finding office space is a top priority, and the decisions you make directly affect your clientele and your image.

Before you begin your search, ask yourself the following questions[1]:

- Can I work from home?

- Can I work virtually and not require an office?

- How much space do I need?

- How many hours per week do I need office space?

- Can I share space?

- Do I want to be accessible by public transportation?

- How much storage space do I need?

- Is it necessary for me to be in a traditional setting, such as an office building?

- Is subletting an option?

It is wise to keep business costs as low as possible when you are first starting out, but don't make decisions based solely on economics. Keep the future in mind as you make your decisions. If you anticipate growth, make sure the space can accommodate you in the next few years.[1,2]

As you think about office space options, consider evaluating where you should have office space. For example, if you are leaving a clinical position in a hospital to start a private practice and plan to receive referrals from the physicians you worked with in that hospital, your office should be in close proximity to that setting. You could also inquire if you can rent space from one of the physicians. (If this is your plan, make sure you have not signed a noncompete agreement with your current employer before you select a location.)

Once you have determined the general location for your office, you then need to begin to consider other variables. If you are looking at a space outside your home, refer to the box on the next page for issues to consider before deciding where to have an office.

Private Office Space

RENTING

Renting is the most traditional way to obtain office space. Check with commercial realtors and in newspaper advertisements or ask around to learn about available space.

Renting office space can be costly. You will be asked to sign a lease, usually for at least a year, and a security deposit is usually required. If you sign a lease for longer than one year, you could prevent rent increases for the duration of the lease. If changes to the space are needed, such as painting or reconfiguration, you can negotiate with the landlord. In some cases, such changes may be your responsibility. Remember that everything in the lease is negotiable, so if you want changes, it's worth asking for them.[3]

COLEASING

Still considered renting, coleasing is basically sharing office space. Two or more professionals join forces, allowing them to share rent and many

Issues to Investigate Before Deciding
Where to Have an Office

Signage: Can you place your name in the directory, on a nameplate at the entrance to the office, or at the entrance to your individual office? Who pays for signage?

Security: What type of security does the office provide? Is there a security person in front of the building or a code for access, or must visitors be announced? Appropriate security is particularly important if you will be counseling or consulting after regular business hours.

Snow removal and grounds keeping: Who is responsible for the grounds around the office?

Cleaning: Does the rent include a cleaning service? Utilities: Does the rent include utilities?

Kitchen area: Do you want a small kitchen area in your office? If you will be there for long periods of time, you may want to have a place where you can make coffee or tea, refrigerate items, or place a microwave.

Parking: Is parking available for you and your clients? Is there a parking fee? If so, will this deter patients?

Bathroom access: Will there be a bathroom in your suite or in the hall? Do clients need a key to access the bathroom?

Other fees: Are you responsible for paying a share of the building taxes or insurance?

Handicap accessibility: Is the building in compliance with the Americans with Disabilities Act?

Elevator access: If not on the first floor, are stairs the only option or is there an elevator? Many people without a disability still have difficulty climbing stairs.

Furniture: Is the furniture you see in the office now available for your use? (This is more applicable if you are subleasing.)

other expenses while they take turns using the space. You can still expect to sign a lease, but you each have an equal voice in making decisions.

It is important that you define all the parameters in writing before you enter into this type of agreement. The office must accommodate the needs of both professionals, and you must divide the available time evenly. Your schedules must mesh. Should you need to switch days, you may not have that option. Even if you and your partner are extremely compatible, you should have separate phone lines because if you decide in time that you want to move, you may be able to use the same phone number in your new location.

Coleasing can be a great arrangement for two private practitioners. Consider pairing up with another RDN whose skills and expertise complement yours. For example, perhaps you specialize in weight management and eating disorders. Consider sharing office space with someone who is a certified diabetes educator. You then have an automatic referral system.

SUBLEASING

Subleasing is an option that works well for many professionals. Again, you are still renting space but with a slightly different type of arrangement. It is often possible to find another professional with an office that is available certain days of the week or specific times during the day. You may even find a vacant room within an office that is available to sublet by the month.

Subleasing space in a physician's office can be an ideal situation for private practitioners. Many physicians have available office space at least one day per week and would welcome some extra revenue. There may be unused space within the office, or the physician may offer you the use of his or her office. Although there may be no room for personalization, it is a great option if you don't see patients full time.

Another option is to sublet extra office space or an available room within a professional office suite or health club. When subleasing, keep in mind that you may not be dealing directly with the owner of the space, so there are limitations.

Potential office payment options include paying a set fee for the space by the hour, day, week, or month. Another possibility for RDNs in private practice is for the physician's practice to pay the RDN a consulting fee for seeing patients. Physicians consider this a value-added service to their practice. In return, the physician's practice benefits from the ability to offer patients more comprehensive medical care within the office.

Questions to Consider When Subleasing

Who will do the scheduling?

Will the office receptionist greet patients and provide them with forms to complete?

Who will do the billing?

Can you use the fax machine, copy machine, and phone lines?

Will business cards be provided?

Who pays for educational materials?

Who will take care of cleaning the space if it is subleased?

Are office supplies (such as paper goods, pens, and sticky notes) included?

Is furniture included, or do you need to supply your own?

Who makes decisions on décor?

It also saves the physician valuable time by taking care of patients' nutrition concerns. The physician's office staff may also handle your patient billing.

Consider the questions in the box on the previous page when you are thinking about subleasing.

You can also consider subleasing office space from psychotherapists, social workers, or other mental health professionals. Their offices are often available during their downtimes, and many of these professionals are used to subletting their space. Because you may be sharing space, this puts a natural limit on your available hours. It will require you to set regular office hours, thus limiting your flexibility.

When subleasing, you still may be required to sign a lease or at least have an agreement in writing. Some sublet situations will require a one-year lease. If possible, consider negotiating a month-to-month lease, with the stipulation of a two-month notice period if either party wants to change the lease terms. This will allow you to assess whether the arrangement is working for both parties.

Investigate who you are subletting from. Be careful about associating with someone who may not have the best reputation. This can negatively affect your professional image.

Other Office Space Possibilities

There are many places to find office space. Think about allied health professionals and the fitness industry, and don't forget to think outside the box for other possibilities. There are so many places for RDNs to set up shop. You just have to decide what will work best for you. The box below provides some suggestions for your search.

Possibilities for Office Space

Home office	Physician's office
Physical therapist's office	Occupational therapist's office
Traveling office	Psychotherapist's office
Massage therapist's office	Cooperative work space
Executive office suite	Physician's office
Chiropractor's office	Gym
Virtual office	Psychotherapist's office
Dental office	Day spa

HOME OFFICE

A home office is likely the most affordable option for office space and the one that presents the lowest financial risk. However, some professionals find it difficult to stay on track when working at home.

If you choose to use a home office, make sure your office space is private if you will be seeing patients or clients there. Ideally, you should have a separate office in your home. Some professionals have been successful in creating home office space by partitioning off a section of a common room.

Consider how comfortable you feel having strangers come to your home. Do you have a separate entrance? Will patients, clients, or customers enter through your front door? What about a reception area—will it be your living room? Can you keep your house neat and quiet enough to receive clients in a professional manner? Some clients may feel comfortable coming to your home; others may not.

If you decide to have a home office, please be aware of safety issues. If you see a client and let them know you can't see them next week as you'll be on vacation, they will now know that your house may be vacant. Also, it's wise not to be home alone when you are seeing patients, unless you know them well.

You could also do different tasks from different locations. Some private practitioners sublet office space on a part-time basis for seeing patients and work on their administrative tasks and non-patient-related projects from their home office. This can truly be an ideal situation.

The box on the next page lists the advantages and disadvantages of working from home. Carefully review this list before you make your decision.

It is also important to set limits for yourself when working from home.[3] You can do so in the following ways:

- Try to set a work schedule and stick with it. Make sure you leave time for your personal life.

- Arrange for child care if necessary. It is very difficult to meet your clients' needs while working around kids' schedules.

- Take breaks throughout the day. Time away from your desk will ultimately increase your productivity. Get out of the office (house) at least once a day.

Having a home office may have some tax advantages. You are able to deduct the cost of your home office from your taxes if any of the following are true:

- Your home office is the principal place from which you conduct your business.

- Your home office is used for meeting with patients or clients in the normal course of doing business.

Pros and Cons of Setting Up a Home Office

Pros	Cons
• No commuting	• Potential for professional isolation or loneliness
• Greater work flexibility	• Can be hard to stay disciplined
• Lower start-up costs	• Security—especially if you are home alone
• Clients or patients relax more quickly	• Patients may feel less safe in a home setting
• You can "squeeze in" home chores	• Hard to set work-life boundaries
• Tax write-off (talk to your accountant)	• Patients may show up unexpectedly on the wrong day
	• Patients may view it as less professional
	• Possible problem with clear, healthy boundaries for some clients

Adapted with permission from the Academy of Nutrition and Dietetics.[4]

- You have a separate building on your property that you use as a home office.

Even if your home office does not meet these criteria, you may be able to claim a tax deduction for it. However, there may be limitations to the amount you can deduct. Talk to your accountant for further guidance on allowable tax deductions.

TRAVELING OFFICE

Some RDNs in private practice can avoid the hassle of finding office space by having a traveling office. They go to the patient's home, office, or a mutually agreed-upon location. Depending on the location, such as a coffee shop, there could be issues with potential violation of the Health Insurance Portability and Accountability Act (HIPAA), so it is important to look into that before choosing a space. RDNs who meet patients in the supermarket must obtain permission from the store manager and the store's corporate office. Some supermarkets do not allow others, like RDNs, to conduct business in their stores.

When you have a traveling office, you can simply gather all your necessary supplies and meet the patient. Meeting a patient at his or her home allows you to see what the patient is really eating. If your patient allows you to, you can check the refrigerator, freezer, and pantries and evaluate the kitchen. The downside is that you have to be extra vigilant in making sure that you have everything you need and that you are in a safe environment. It is also important to charge accordingly—travel time should be considered when establishing fees. When you are first starting out, a traveling office can be a smart way to begin. You may then find as your practice grows that having your own office so you don't have to travel is a better use of your time.

EXECUTIVE OFFICE SUITE

An executive office suite is an office arrangement that typically includes a receptionist, access to a conference room, and a specified day or days during the week that you have an assigned office space. Generally, you pay à la carte for each service you want. There are many companies that manage executive office space for lease with a variety of different services and amenities; therefore, it is necessary to shop around and visit different offices to determine which one is the best fit for your business. Make sure that you will have your own private space when you see patients so that you are HIPAA compliant. You also want to give your clients a private space so they can feel comfortable when they share valuable health information with you.

VIRTUAL OFFICE

Technology is helping to transform the workplace. Not too long ago, RDNs in private practice needed to set up shop either in their home or in a private office. Now virtual practitioners can grow their businesses from anywhere. You don't necessarily have to worry about paying for an expensive office in town and a large sign outside the door. You can now establish your private practice online for a low cost. You can work from home today, work from a coffee shop tomorrow, and work from a coworking space the next day. You are free to decide where to work, when to work, and how to work. However, from a payment standpoint, depending on the state, if you are providing medical nutrition therapy (MNT), you must be licensed in that particular state where your patient resides. You cannot provide MNT without a state license where you are practicing. The downside of practicing without actually seeing your clients is that you cannot weigh or measure them or take vital signs, and you might not be able to pick up on facial expressions or body language. However, providing nutrition care via telehealth can make it much easier for people to have access to RDNs as well as fit nutrition care into busy lives.

Being a Telehealth Provider Along with the growth in smartphones and apps, health care is undergoing a shift to help provide care to patients where they are. This is making health care more easily accessible. Patients don't want to take time off from work, wait a long time in an office to see a health care provider, or have to schedule an appointment several months down the road. They want to be able to access services as they need them. To meet the growing need for electronic health care, telehealth has entered the market as a valuable delivery system of medical services.

The Health Resources Services Administration defines telehealth as "the use of electronic information and telecommunications technologies to support long-distance clinical health care, patient and professional health-related education, public health and health administration."[4,5] These technologies include videoconferencing (using various HIPAA-compliant platforms), sharing imaging (such as X-rays and MRIs), streaming media, and wireless communications.

Telehealth includes a broad scope of remote health care services. This form of health care delivery consists of remote clinical services, such as MNT and nonclinical services, including provider training and continuing medical education. The Academy of Nutrition and Dietetics defines telehealth as the use of telecommunications technologies to support clinical patient care and provide health-related education using interactive, specialized equipment.[6] This may include HIPAA-compliant platforms used to provide teleconferencing (see chapter 11 for resources for telehealth), messaging with clients, and sharing documents that help provide patient care in an easily accessible and flexible format.

In the past, telehealth was carried out solely in remote or rural areas because patients may have had logistical issues getting to a provider's office or there may have been limited access to providers in that particular geographical area. Still today, telehealth for nutrition services provided to patients in a remote area may be reimbursed by various insurance providers, including Medicare. However, you must provide the service according to Medicare and private insurance telehealth policies.[7]

For RDNs who provide telehealth in urban areas, this may or may not be a reimbursable service. Patients may need to pay you directly. Many insurance providers have established policies for telehealth; however, they may not yet reimburse health care providers unless services are provided in a remote area.[8] There are many states that have signed parity laws specifying that any services that are reimbursed can be accessed via telehealth. Going forward, more third-party payers will be reimbursing providers for telehealth services.

If your patients want to use their insurance to pay for your services via telehealth, make sure that you or your patient checks with the insurance provider to see if the provider covers MNT delivered through telehealth and to determine the appropriate Current Procedural Terminology codes to use.

Telehealth is a great way for RDNs to improve the health of their patients while keeping down the costs of running a business. Plus, you can provide services from anywhere, provided that you have access to Wi-Fi.

Visualizing Your Office

As you set up your office, take some time to visualize going through your routine. In addition, you should think about your patients from the moment they step through the door until you have ended the session and it is time for them to leave. Do you want to present a medical or a counseling image? When counseling, it is recommended that you not place a desk between yourself and the patient. The preferred counseling arrangement is to sit next to or across from the client, without a barrier. This fosters communication.

Sharing your space with another health professional can raise special concerns for your private practice. For example, if you share an office with an occupational therapist, will the office accommodate the other person's equipment and still leave enough space for you? If a doctor offers an exam room for counseling, does the configuration of the medical equipment in the room lend itself to counseling patients? You must be able to visualize how that space will work in a counseling situation.

Office Essentials: Assessing Your Needs

If you are working 100% virtually, you can work from whatever location you like, so thinking about furnishing an office might not be part of your plan, and if you are subletting office space, you most likely will have a furnished office. However, if you will be seeing your patients in your own private office, you will need to think about what furniture will be required. Take some time to imagine going through a full day of work in your new office space. Visualize the entire process. What furniture will you need in your office? If you are meeting with clients, where will you greet them? What will the client do upon entering your office? Will the client need to sit in a reception area to complete some paperwork? Can the patient download your forms from your website, or will the forms be emailed to him or her when they make the initial appointment? What types of forms will they need to complete? How will you furnish the reception area? What do you want visitors to take away as their first impression? Remember: First impressions are lasting impressions. As you read through this section, jot down all the essentials that pop into your mind.

Once you have done this, you will have a better feel for all the essentials required to set up your office. Make a master list of what you will need.

The box on the next page contains the first steps in preparing your list of office essentials.

Essentials for Setting Up Your Office

Will clients be visiting often? Obviously, in private practice, the answer is yes. Consider the image you want to project and furnish accordingly.

What can your budget accommodate? Clearly, your available cash flow will determine your purchases. Set your priorities in advance, and stick with your decisions.

What equipment must you have? Decide what is essential to start with and what you can wait to purchase. For example, you must have chairs to sit on, but perhaps you can wait to purchase a copy machine and make copies at home or at the local copy shop instead.

Hiring Office Help

Another important aspect in visualizing your office is visualizing who will be doing the work. Will you be working entirely alone? Do you envision having help with various projects? You have several options for splitting up the work.

VIRTUAL ASSISTANTS

Starting out in your new business will entail many expenses. You may not be able to afford the expenditure of employing someone to assist you with your administrative tasks. On the other hand, if you spend too much of your time attending to administrative duties, you lose precious patient, networking, marketing, and development time. A virtual assistant may be the perfect compromise.

RDNs in private practice commonly use virtual assistants. This is a self-employed person who works remotely managing your business or practice performing the same services of an administrative assistant. Virtual assistants typically manage a number of clients at the same time. Hiring a virtual assistant may allow you to have the help you need and keep it affordable.

Virtual assistants typically provide support via email, internet, or phone. A working relationship with a virtual assistant can be long-term until your needs change. A virtual assistant can manage most of your administrative functions. For example, imagine that a patient who has a scheduled appointment in two hours cancels. Your virtual assistant can contact your patients and move their appointments up or squeeze in a new patient. However, a virtual assistant cannot open the door for a client, water the plants, or perform other tasks that require a physical presence.

Fees for a virtual assistant can be a retainer for a minimum amount of hours per month and then by the hour over the minimum. The costs can be similar to having someone physically present in your office, but the services of a virtual assistant may be used more efficiently.

HAVING A GROUP PRACTICE:
Hiring Other Registered Dietitian Nutritionists

Quite often, RDNs who decide to start a private practice begin by working solo. Over time as their practice grows, they may find that they are turning away patients if they don't have the time to see them. If they want to accommodate more patients, they can bring in an RDN as a partner or an employee. Some RDNs will bring in one or more RDNs with different specialties so the practice can see a greater variety of patients. If you see in time that your practice is growing and that having another RDN on board will help you expand, you can decide what will work best for you. Some RDNs continue to remain in a solo practice, as it allows them the flexibility to work when they want and take on other consulting projects as desired. But other RDNs want to have a large practice and sometimes also have more than one location. Before you decide to take on a partner or hire an RDN as an employee, make sure to do your research and see what is right for you. Maria Bella, MS, RDN, CDN, owns Top Balance Nutrition, a multispecialty private practice with three locations. Read her story in the Words of Wisdom box on the next page.

Setting Up Your Website

Whether you are planning to counsel clients virtually or face-to-face, having a website is a must if you want to have a private practice; this is an important component of your office space.

Having a presence on the internet will lend credibility to your practice. When potential new clients contact you, quite often they have already checked out your website to see if you would be a good fit for them—this means that they see your website before they ever set foot in your office. You can also have your web address (uniform resource locator [URL]) on your voice mail and business cards so potential clients can learn more about you before they make an appointment. A website is a very useful marketing tool. It is your online business card. Your website becomes a great opportunity for customers to learn more about you and your business. Your website is your opportunity to promote your brand and publicize your expertise.

PLANNING YOUR WEBSITE

You don't have to spend a lot of money to develop, maintain, and promote your website, but it can be time consuming. Take the time to plan how you want your website to look. If you feel you don't have the skills to create your own website, hire a website designer and have him or her design your site.

Words of Wisdom

Owning a Group Nutrition Practice

Maria Bella, MS, RDN, CDN, CEO
owner of Top Balance Nutrition

I am the sole owner of Top Balance Nutrition. I started my own practice, but I always knew that I wanted to expand. I made every decision from day one with that in mind. Instead of using my own name as the practice name, I used Top Balance Nutrition, Inc, to be all-inclusive for everyone who was going to be hired in the future. We have three office locations. Our headquarters are in Midtown, New York City. We have two smaller offices in Miami and San Francisco. We have five registered dietitian nutritionists in New York and one person in each other location.

I believe that one dietitian cannot be an expert in every area of nutrition, and I wanted to hire specialists in sports nutrition, eating disorders, diabetes, and other areas. There are numerous benefits to having a group practice: (1) having specialists in many areas of nutrition in the same space so there is the right match for each patient; (2) ability to hold staff meetings to discuss difficult cases and learn from each other; (3) ongoing individual supervision; (4) equal distribution of projects, such as creation of meal plans, research, and corporate consulting, which helps prevent work burnout; (5) for a person joining a group practice, no need to start from scratch, as they are entering an established infrastructure; and (6) more flexibility with scheduling vacation time.

A bigger practice requires more space, which translates to more expensive overhead. A larger practice also requires the help of a professional lawyer, accountant, and bookkeeper. Because of the larger volume, it is helpful to have full-time front desk help for scheduling and insurance preapprovals. There are also people counting on me to be a leader. We go through basic science courses and clinical rotations in school, and nobody teaches us how to manage a diverse group of employees. It is a learning curve.

Before you design your own site or connect with a web design company to set up your website, you should think through the logistics of your site.[9] As you begin to plan out your website, start by determining the purpose of your site. Will you be using your website to attract new patients? Will you be using it to showcase your business? What do you

want your website to portray for you? These questions will help influence your decisions in areas such as design, content, site organization,
and navigation. As you think about and develop your website, remember
who your target market is (discussed in chapter 4).

Choosing a Web Designer If you hire a professional to help build your
website, you can use a freelancer or a website development company.
A website company will typically be full service and can help you with
branding, marketing, search engine optimization, design, ecommerce,
updating, a content management system, a blog, or anything else you
will need. If you want to create some of the website yourself, hiring a
freelancer or a team of freelancers to do a specialized part of the project
may be your best option. Keep in mind with this option that you will
need to put together specific details on what you need the freelancers to
do, oversee them, and test out the result.

To find a website designer, get recommendations from colleagues.
Search the internet for sites you like the look and feel of. If a site appeals
to you, contact the owner of the site and ask which company he or she
used and solicit feedback. Look at the portfolio of the design company,
and ask other candidates to share their portfolios. Also, browse websites
they have designed and evaluate the following:

- Are the sites easy to navigate?

- Do all the links work?

- Is the content current?

- Does the design look clean?

- Do all the forms work?

- Do newsletter sign-ups work?

- Do the sites work in more than one browser?

Think twice before hiring your friend's nephew who does design as
a side job and is known as a computer whiz. If you are going to hire
someone, choose a professional. Get several estimates on pricing before
you make your decision.

Creating Your Own Website If you prefer to create your own website, there
are programs and websites available to assist novices. These programs allow you to develop webpages visually without having to know the technical aspects of web building and design. Designing your own site is fine
for a basic site, particularly when you are first starting out and budget is a
concern. Excellent web design programs, such as WordPress and Wix, are
available for hosting your website and blog. You can try using one of these
platforms yourself; they are easy to set up and are fully customizable.

Before you decide on web design software, look for recent reviews of each program.[10] As your practice grows, you may want to add more components to your site, such as video clips or downloadable forms. If you require more technical help at this stage, it may be worthwhile to contact a web designer for help. You can also seek input from dietetic practice group electronic mailing lists. Quite often, other RDNs can be your best resource. Many RDNs are quite tech-savvy and can point you in the right direction for either creating your own website or hiring a designer to develop a website for you.

CHOOSING A DOMAIN NAME

The domain is your web address or URL. Some RDNs prefer to use a catchy name related to nutrition, whereas others prefer to use their own name. To determine whether a domain is available, check with a domain provider, such as Network Solutions (www.networksolutions.com) or GoDaddy (www.godaddy.com). Unless you use your name as your URL, you may want to purchase the same domain name with .com, .net, and .org to protect yourself from a competitor directing your potential online traffic to its site. For a website devoted to commercial business, such as a private practice, you would use .com at the end of your domain name.

How will a prospective patient find you on the internet? If someone is searching for your services, what will he or she type into the search engine? This may help you come up with your domain name. Having a domain name that matches what people enter into their search engine can place your page higher in search results (also known as search engine optimization). For example, if someone searches for San Francisco diabetes information and your website URL is sanfranciscodiabetesinfo .com, you will have a greater chance of appearing near the top of the results list. The best domain names are easy to remember, easy to spell, and not too lengthy.

CHOOSING A HOSTING COMPANY

A web host puts your website on the internet. When choosing your hosting company, remember that cheapest is not always best. Hosting is a minimal expense, so it is worth paying extra for better service. When choosing a web host, make sure the company provides the following services:

- 24/7 support

- daily backups of your site

- website traffic reports

Look for a reputable company that offers a full ecommerce system that is transferable from host to host, provides support, and has been around for several years. This last factor is important because many companies go out of business. When you choose a hosting company, make sure they are keeping up with advances in technology, which will provide assurance that the company should be around for a while.

ESSENTIAL WEBSITE FEATURES

Regardless of who designs your website, certain features are essential. These include a home page, graphics, and navigation. The home page is your site's first impression and tells first-time visitors about what you do. This is a great spot to post your mission statement. You don't want visitors to dwell on this page; rather, you want to pull them in to browse the site. Graphics should be used to draw viewers in. They should be simple and reflect your brand. Easy navigation is also very important to users. If they cannot find what they need quickly, they will become frustrated and leave the site. Navigation helps guide visitors through a site, so it is important that the structure of the site flows well.[9]

All sites should include an about page, a contact page, and a privacy policy. The about page provides a description of who owns and is behind the site. This is also a great place to put your picture, along with a short bio. The contact page is self-explanatory—it provides a way for visitors to contact you. You can provide an email address or phone number, but consider providing both. Prospective patients should be able to email you directly from the contact page. This is also a great place to provide your office location and directions to your office. Contact information should be very easy for visitors to find when navigating your site. A privacy policy is provided for ethical reasons. The purpose of a privacy policy is to build trust online and inform visitors to your site that you will protect and respect their privacy. Your prospective patients will feel more secure if they know that any information they submit to you will only be used in ways they have authorized. There are numerous online tools available to assist with creating a privacy policy. Do an online search for *privacy policy* for websites to take advantage of free resources.

Another page to consider is a FAQs (frequently asked questions) page. Include those questions that take a significant amount of time to answer on the phone. You can use FAQs to plant questions that draw users into identifying the need for your services. For example, posting "With so much nutrition information available online, is an RDN really worth the money?" will allow you to tout the many health benefits of meeting with an RDN as well as explain why visitors to your site should schedule an appointment.

You may also want to have a testimonials page. This is where you can share your patient reviews. You can ask satisfied patients to write a review of your services, which you can then add to your website. Many prospective patients like to read positive reviews before they schedule an appointment. To protect patients' privacy, just list their first names and last initials.

You can also link your blog to your website and include it in the header. Forms that you want new patients to complete can also be on your website. If you have favorite recipes, these can also be linked. Some RDNs also have stores on their sites where they sell books and other products. Last but not least, you may also want to consider having an online appointment scheduling service, such as Zocdoc or Healthie, linked to your website. Using one of these scheduling platforms will enable visitors to your website to instantly make an appointment with you without leaving your site.

UPDATING AND ADDING CONTENT

You should develop a plan for updating content on a regular basis. This will keep visitors coming back, keep your site fresh, and increase your ranking in search engines. Daily updates are probably unrealistic, especially if you are doing everything by yourself, but consider weekly or monthly updates. New content might include recipes, blog posts, FAQs, testimonials, recent presentations, links to articles where you've been quoted, or new product reviews. Try to check your site weekly to make sure that everything is working properly.

Your website is an extension of your practice and your office. It will take time and energy to develop and maintain your website, but if you put in the effort to keep it fresh and running smoothly, it will prove to be a great asset to your practice.[11]

Equipment

Before you make any major purchases, determine what equipment you need to buy immediately. You may want to analyze how much the purchase of that particular product will increase your productivity and profitability. You may also be able to buy used equipment for a much lower price. If you have a limited budget, search online for secondhand office equipment.

BUSINESS TELEPHONE

A telephone is a business essential. Having a designated telephone number for your private practice allows you to present yourself in a professional manner. You can have either a landline or a cell phone for your business. Whichever type of phone you decide to use, make sure that it is registered with your name or business name so the correct caller ID will display when you call clients. Never use your home telephone line as your business line. Callers should always be greeted with your business name or the name of the person who is speaking.

Always answer your business telephone professionally. If you feel that it is important to have a real person answer the telephone and you cannot afford a receptionist or secretary, consider an answering service. However, be aware that answering services can mishandle calls, which results in client complaints. Carefully screen services and get recommendations from other business owners before selecting an answering service.

Voice mail provided by your local telephone company or mobile phone service provider is a good option. Voice mail allows you to set up multiple mailboxes. If you plan to do different types of consulting, you can set up a separate mailbox for each and streamline your work. A standard answering machine is also a good solution.

MOBILE DEVICES

Mobile communication devices include smartphones and tablets. In addition to these, new devices are regularly emerging in the marketplace.

The functions of mobile devices vary and overlap. When purchasing a mobile device, consider how it can best serve you in your practice and how you might foresee using it. Purchasing a mobile phone number specific for your practice can keep you in touch with your clients even when you are not in the office. When your cell phone rings, you will know that it is a professional call. You can decide whether you wish to put on your "professional hat" at that moment and answer the call or let it go to voice mail. Returning phone calls in a timely fashion can help build your practice, especially when a prospective patient or client calls. This also allows you to be a bit more flexible with office space while always maintaining the same telephone number. For example, if you decide to sublet space on a part-time basis and eventually move into full-time space, you will not have to change telephone numbers as you move. There are also a variety of phone systems that can add an office number to your existing cell phone as well as answer your office phone, thus acting like a virtual secretary.

The ability to let patients text you is another great feature of a mobile smartphone. Whether they are late for their appointments, need to make an appointment change, or want your input on a specific food, texting can be a great communication tool for your practice. Allowing texts from your patients can also further develop your relationship. It's your choice if you want to allow your patients to text you.

Mobile devices can help keep you organized. They can substitute for a laptop on the road, keep your schedule and appointments, allow you to check email, and maintain your contact list. You can add apps such as nutrient-drug interaction and nutrition analysis databases to these devices. You can also add other practice-related applications, such as those that allow you to accept credit cards and scan patient documents. RDNs typically use their devices for internet access, email, social media, phone calls, calendars, and contacts. Make sure you have a password encrypted on your phone so your data is not easily accessed. Refer to chapter 7 for further information on complying with HIPAA regulations.

COMPUTER

A computer is a necessity for managing your practice. If you are not computer-savvy and do not plan to upgrade your skills, now is the time to forge a relationship with a good computer consultant or information technology (IT) specialist. A computer consultant or IT specialist is someone who plans, develops, operates, maintains, and evaluates computer hardware, software, and telecommunications. He or she can be an invaluable resource to your business. Paying a specialist can save you time and money in the long run.

To locate a skilled consultant, ask other business owners for recommendations. Look for someone who is used to dealing with small businesses. Get references and check them carefully. The box below provides a list of questions you may want to ask your IT consultant.

Technology can save you hours of time if you choose the right tools. It can also become costly if you make mistakes. Some equipment, such as a computer, is necessary for running a successful business; some equipment, such as a fax machine or scanner, is optional. You can get a scanner app and use it to scan documents into the electronic health record (EHR) or other files on your computer. Purchase the essentials you need now and the non-essential items later as your budget allows.

If you find that you do need to purchase a computer for your business, the next section will review some basic considerations.

Questions to Ask a Computer Consultant

How do you bill?

Are you available after hours? If so, do rates increase for after-hours calls?

Can you help me determine which hardware and software I need?

Can you help me determine which new technology products will help with my productivity and are worth the investment?

Can you set up all the computer systems I need?

Computer Hardware Your first decision is whether to purchase a laptop computer or a desktop computer. If you will be traveling to different locations, will be giving presentations, or want round the clock access to your files, a laptop is the best option. If you see patients in a location other than your main office, a laptop will allow you to enter patient information and update progress reports in the EHR as well as process payments and insurance claims immediately after each visit. You can also work on other projects if you have a gap in your schedule. A laptop provides you with the freedom to do your work when and where you wish.

Your next decision will be whether to choose a Mac or a PC. Macs are known for their simplicity and ease of use, and they tend to be less susceptible to viruses than PCs. Basic PCs, on the other hand, can be much more affordable. PCs provide a greater variety of software programs. Some software is not compatible with the Mac operating system, and users must purchase additional software to make certain programs compatible.

Whether you opt for a Mac or a PC, purchase the computer with a warranty from a reputable and reliable store. If being without your computer will put you out of business, you should purchase a service contract as an insurance policy. This will allow for continued productivity in the event that your computer malfunctions and needs repair.

Data Backups One of the most essential yet often forgotten tasks you must include in your daily routine is to back up your computer files. Don't wait until you have a computer disaster to learn this important lesson. Your two main choices for backup are to use a remote server or to put the saved data on media. Remote servers are encrypted online backup systems. Backup media include CDs and external hard drives. Both options are inexpensive, so consider using both methods. Online cloud backup is also a great way to secure data, but it usually involves a subscription and can be costly.

If you are using an EHR for charting, these client records are stored on the company website server. An external hard drive is highly recommended for files you want to access but do not necessarily need to store on your computer. Backing up certain data on an external hard drive will save space on your computer. Thumb drives (also known as flash drives) are great for traveling and transferring files but not for storage. Finally, for important files, encrypted online backups are essential. Many companies, such as Carbonite, provide this service for a minimal annual fee. Keep in mind that any physical device such as an external hard drive is subject to failure. You may want to consider having your data backed up in two different ways—for example, on an external hard drive and in the cloud online. You can't be too safe.

FAX MACHINE

Medical practices are used to faxing laboratory reports, referrals, and other medical information before patient visits. HIPAA privacy regulations affect your ability to fax information. Make sure that your fax cover sheet, if you fax confidential patient information, is HIPAA compliant. It should have a HIPAA-compliant confidentiality notice at the bottom. The ability to send and receive faxes is important for any office. As with other equipment, fax machines vary in price. A basic machine may be all that you need. Another option to consider is sending and receiving faxes through your computer or through an app on your smartphone, therefore eliminating the need for an additional piece of equipment. Whatever type of fax you use, make sure it is HIPAA compliant. You can use the same email HIPAA disclosure that you use in your email signature on your fax cover sheet.

PRINTER AND COPY MACHINE

Copy machines can be quite costly yet may be necessary for conducting business on a daily basis. Do you print or photocopy ideas and notes for clients at the close of a counseling session? Do you frequently print information in preparation for a client meeting or during a counseling session to support educational concepts? Consider purchasing an all-in-one printer. These machines can print documents from the computer, make copies, scan documents and books, and send faxes. This alternative can save you money because you will be purchasing one machine rather than four. You can keep it in your house if you go to more than one office. In the office, you can scan whatever notes you wrote for the patient with an app on your cell phone and email a copy to yourself for the EHR. If you are trying to cut costs when you are just starting your practice, consider using the local copy shop until you have enough money saved up to invest in an all-in-one machine.

POST OFFICE BOX

Some consultants who work out of their homes or virtually may opt to rent a post office (PO) box for receiving mail. This helps keep business mail separate and may seem more professional, as the PO box number can be listed as a suite number.

SHARED EQUIPMENT

If you share an office suite with one or several others, often you can share the costs associated with fax machines, copiers, postage equipment, and furnishings in the waiting area. If you do this, however, make certain to designate who is responsible for handling equipment failures, maintenance, and other related situations.

Business Supplies

You cannot run a practice without certain supplies. Some basic supplies are necessary regardless of your setting or the type of consulting you perform.

BUSINESS CARDS

Your business card can be your first introduction to potential clients. A properly designed card becomes a powerful marketing tool and presents you in a professional manner. Take some time to decide what you want to have on your card. You can also use the back of the card to include a headshot as well as a list of books you have authored.

Designing Your Business Card There are many online companies, such as Vistaprint, that you can use to create your business card. It is important to always have your business cards on hand so you can give them out when requested. Your business card can be personalized to include what you like, but there are basics to consider. A professional business card should include the following:

- your name and credentials,
- your professional title or titles,
- how to reach you (your phone number and email address), and
- your website and blog URLs.

The back of your card may include a place to list the next appointment date and time. Or you can include a picture of a book you have written. You can also include your own professional picture. Adding a photo of yourself can help people remember you. Some RDNs leave the back blank—it's your call!

Making Your Business:
Sample Business Card

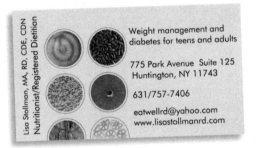

Lisa Stollman, MA, RD, CDE, CDN
Nutritionist/Registered Dietitian

Weight management and diabetes for teens and adults

775 Park Avenue Suite 125
Huntington, NY 11743

631/757-7406

eatwellrd@yahoo.com
www.lisastollmanrd.com

To give your card pizzazz, add your logo or some graphics. Determine which choices make sense for you in your situation and have fun creating a unique card. When it comes to designing business cards, there are no rules. It comes down to personal choice and affordability.[12] See the sample business card for an example.

LETTERHEAD
Your letterhead can be designed as a package with your business card. Envelopes are also usually purchased at the same time. If you have not yet developed a logo (see chapter 4), at least use the same font style and type size on your business cards, letterhead, and envelopes. Some entrepreneurs decide that they do not need printed letterhead. They use computer-generated letterhead on an as-needed basis. You can create your letterhead on your computer with unique fonts. It does not have to be fancy, but it is important to convey a professional image.

Office Supplies and Software

Remember to stock up on other miscellaneous supplies, such as pens, pencils, tape, paper clips, phone message pads, and a stapler and staples. Make sure you have all the necessary printer and fax cartridges and paper you need. Always have extra on hand.

OFFICE MANAGEMENT SOFTWARE
You can use your computer's software to enhance your business and streamline your work in numerous ways. For example, it is possible to keep records of all new clients, insurance plans, and payments received

and track how each client was referred to you by using a spreadsheet program, such as Microsoft Excel. If you want to determine who your top referral sources are, you can easily access that information.

Creating Spreadsheets Spreadsheet software such as Microsoft Excel can be used in a variety of ways. You can track your productivity by developing monthly or weekly statistics to determine the growth of your business. If you accept insurance, you can also include payment tracking to determine your reimbursement rates (how much you get paid) and when you get paid from different insurance companies. See the figure below for an example of a spreadsheet for private practice.

Making Your Business: **Sample Spreadsheet**

	A	B	C	D	E	F	G	H	I	J	K	L
1	Jun-17											
2	Date	Pt.Name	Fee	Insurance	Copay	Units	Date $ paid	Referral	Dx	ICD Code	Primary MD	
3	6/2/2017	Smith, J.	$250.00	BCBS	$20.00	6	6/16/2017	Dr. Jones	T2DM	E119	Dr. Jones	
4	6/2/2017	Fuller, B.	$150.00	Oxford	0	4	6/16/2017	Dr. Jones	HTN	401.9	Dr. Jones	
5												
6												
7												

PRESENTATION SOFTWARE
Presentation software can be used to keep the audience's attention when addressing a group or counseling a patient. For example, you could develop an educational series that can be shown to patients during their visits or create a presentation geared directly toward potential clients, patients, or referral sources. This could then be emailed to clients as an attachment or posted on your website.

VOICE RECOGNITION SOFTWARE
You can write a business proposal or follow-up letter to a referring physician without your fingers ever touching the keypad on your computer. How is that possible? Voice or speech recognition programs enable this convenience. Some computers provide this as a standard feature; you can also purchase the software separately as well as a combination headset with microphone. The beauty of using a voice recognition program is that, most likely, you can speak faster than you can type. The program will allow you to produce letters and carry out other typing functions more quickly to save time.

ACCOUNTING SOFTWARE
A good accounting software package is an asset to your business and will save you valuable time. You can keep track of all your financial data and client billing with the right program. For most small businesses, there are many good programs to handle accounting and billing. Chapter 3 provides criteria for selecting accounting software. When in doubt, you can always consult your accountant or business adviser.

Nutrition Counseling Supplies

A well-stocked nutrition counseling office is different from that of any other health practitioner. The tools required to effectively counsel patients and teach them about nutrition are unique.

NUTRIENT ANALYSIS SOFTWARE

Nutrient analysis software can aid in clinical assessment. It can help you determine the adequacy of a patient's diet and highlight specific deficiencies. In private practice, this software can be a powerful teaching tool. Providing analysis to your patients helps them visualize their nutrition goals. The printouts provide tangible evidence and feedback, which help them stay focused.

Providing nutrient analyses to your patients is a value-added service. It takes additional time to analyze a patient's diet. Determine whether you want to provide that service to your patients as an additional benefit. As an alternative, you may want to charge for the service separately as a way to generate further revenue. It can be a great marketing tool. Some RDNs offer nutrient analysis as a stand-alone service.

If you have a specific need in your practice that a general nutrient analysis software package does not meet, consider purchasing niche software. For example, if you see many patients with diabetes, you may want to purchase a specialized program that is geared toward that patient population.

RECEPTION AREA READING

Once you have all your patient counseling supplies, the last step is to stock your waiting room with reading material. Consider some health-related publications, but make sure the messages they send are consistent with your philosophy. For example, if a particular publication touts the latest low-carbohydrate diets and you do not believe in them, this may not be what you want your patients to read while they wait to see you. Good magazine choices may include *Cooking Light*, *Vegetarian Times*, and *Eating Well*. A daily newspaper and standard periodicals, such as the *New Yorker* and *Newsweek*, are usually safe choices. If you see children, consider providing a food magazine for children or coloring books and crayons.

Where to Set Up Shop: A Summary

A private practitioner's office has a unique set of requirements. Presenting a professional image is of the utmost importance. There are so many decisions you must make when setting up your office. Carefully assess the options, determine your requirements, and figure out which expenses can wait until you are more solvent. Here are some important tips to remember:

- Determine how much space you need, where you want to be located, and what type of space will work.

- Determine whether a rented, shared, or home office will meet your needs or if you would do better in an alternative location.

- Once space is secured, determine what furnishings, equipment, and supplies you need and budget accordingly. When considering furniture, make sure you have sturdy, comfortable options for larger clients. Going to see an RDN and not being able to fit into any of the chairs is not an uncommon situation.

- Utilize software programs to maximize your productivity.

- Before you decide on your location, consider a market analysis—where will your patients come from?

- Consider subleasing, sharing space, traveling to patients' homes, or having a home office to keep costs low when you are first starting out.

- As you set up your office, visualize the kind of relationship you want to have with patients and the type of experience you want them to have from start to finish of the counseling session.

- Many specialized forms, supplies, and equipment are needed to furnish your office. Choose the materials you need depending on the type of practice you hope to establish.

References

1. Strauss S. *The Small Business Bible*. 3rd ed. New York, NY: John Wiley & Sons Inc; 2012.

2. Bauer R. *The Ultimate Guide to Startup Success*. 3rd ed. ebook. RB Capital Media Group, LLC; 2016.

3. Health Care Fraud Prevention and Enforcement Action Team, Office of Inspector General. Comparison of the Anti-Kickback Statute Stark Law. Office of Inspector General website. https://oig.hhs.gov/compliance/provider-compliance-training/files/starkandakscharthandout508.pdf. Accessed May 10, 2017.

4. Leman C. Where to hang your shingle: home or rented office? NEDPG website. https://nedpg.org/sites/default/files/Members/Toolkit/2012%20Private%20Practice/Where_to_Hang_Your_Shingle.pdf .Published 2010. Accessed June 8, 2017.

5. Center for Connected Health Policy. What is telehealth? National Telehealth Policy Resource Center website. www.healthit.gov/providers-professionals /faqs/what-telehealth-how-telehealth-different-telemedicine. Accessed July 10, 2016.

6. Center for Connected Health Policy. NY state law telemedicine/telehealth definition. National Telehealth Policy Resource Center website. http://cchpca .org/ny-state-law-telemedicinetelehealth-definition. Accessed May 10, 2017.

7. Stein K. Remote nutrition counseling: considerations in a new channel for client communication. *J Acad Nutr Dietetics*. 2015;115(10):1561-1576.

8. Zanteson L. Virtual nutrition counseling. *Today's Dietitian*. April 2014:42-43.

9. Smith B. Website building checklist. MyTrainingCenter.com website. https://mytrainingcenter.com/website-building-checklist/. Accessed May 10, 2017.

10. Rockwood M. *Website Building: How to Build Your Own Website and Blog to Perfection*. CreateSpace Independent Publishing; 2015.

11. Hamilton B. How to make a website—a free tutorial. Simple Web Tutorials website. www.simplewebtutorials.com/. Accessed May 10, 2017.

12. Handley A. 8 ways to make your business cards stand out. Entrepreneur. August 29, 2012. www.entrepreneur.com/article/224000. Accessed May 10, 2017.

6 | Tools of the Nutrition Trade

To get your practice up and running, you must decide which forms, supplies, and tools you need to provide quality nutrition care to your patients. You need to think about the types of forms you will need to collect patient data in addition to the tools and supplies you will use for nutrition assessment and counseling. You will also have to decide which electronic health record (EHR) platform you will use to help run your practice. This chapter focuses on the forms you will need, the nutrition assessment tools and educational supplies you may use, and how to use the EHR in your private practice.

Forms for Patients and Registered Dietitian Nutritionists

Forms are necessary to collect and document patient information. You will need a variety of patient forms in your private practice.

You can develop, customize, and revise patient forms using your computer's word-processing program. You can create templates for several different types of forms and have copies on hand to distribute as needed. Be creative in how you use your computer software. An investment of time in developing documents can pay off in the long-term.

If creating forms does not appeal to you or you simply do not have the time, there is another option: You can purchase standardized or premade forms that you can customize for your practice and needs. Chapter 11 lists resources where you can find these products. You can also hire a more tech-savvy registered dietitian nutritionist (RDN) or dietetic intern to help you.

Patient Forms

Patient forms are forms patients will complete for you. Post your patient forms on your website. Have your patients download the forms, fill in their information, and email them back to you before or by their appointment time. In addition to saving a lot of time, it can also streamline your work. Another option is to email patients your forms (as long as you receive them by their appointment time). You can then upload the information into the patient's EHR.

You can mail your patient forms to patients who are not computer-savvy prior to their appointments if there is enough time, or you can fax the forms. If this is still not a viable option, then request that patients arrive early for appointments to complete the forms.

The following forms will help you get started with the very first patient who comes into your office. From the initial registration form to the office policy form (which is very important to make sure you get paid!), all of the basics are covered here to get your practice off to a good start. To make it easy, you can consolidate all of the forms into one document for your clients and list them as initial visit forms.

Information to Include on Patient Registration Form

Date the form is completed

Patient name

Date of birth

Contact information, including complete address, phone numbers, and email address

Insurance information

Doctor and other health professional contact information

Referral information

Reason for visit

PATIENT REGISTRATION FORMS

The first important form you will need from patients is a patient registration form. The purpose of the registration form is to obtain demographic information about your patients. This information will be needed for billing purposes or if you need to contact their physician (with their permission). The Making Your Business box here lists the information you should include on your patient registration form.

Making Your Business: **Sample Registration**

Patient Registration Form

First Name: _____ Last Name: _____ Date: _____

Address: _____ City/State/Zip Code: _____

Home Phone Number: _____ Work Phone Number: _____

Cell Phone Number: _____ E-mail Address: _____

Social Security Number: _____

Occupation: _____ Date of Birth: _____ Sex: _____

Who referred you? _____

Physician: _____

Physician Address: _____ Physician Phone Number: _____

Insurance Provider Name: _____ ID Number: _____

Group Number: _____

Do you have another plan? _____ If YES, please state which one: _____

Who is responsible for bill/copay? _____

Amount of Copay: _____

Do you need a referral for this visit? YES NO

Do you have the referral with you? YES NO

Are you covered for nutrition visits? YES NO

Have you confirmed coverage with your insurance provider? YES NO

Have you met your yearly deductible for specialists? YES NO

If visit is denied by insurance provider, you will be responsible for payment.

Reprinted with permission from Lisa Stollman.

OFFICE AND PAYMENT POLICY FORM

You will want to provide an office payment and policy form for patients to sign (see the Making Your Business box on the next page; you can find another example in chapter 3 on page 49). This will let them know your policies, what can be expected, what the patient's responsibilities are, and what will happen if insurance won't cover the cost.

Have the patient sign one copy, and be sure to scan the form into the EHR. Provide the patient with a copy for his or her records. This should help keep patients aware of your office policies, including late cancellation and no-show fees.

Making Your Business:
Sample Office and Payment Policy

Office and Payment Policy

[RDN's name]

Welcome! I look forward to helping you achieve your health and nutrition goals. Making positive changes to your lifestyle is the cornerstone of good health. This is my office and payment policy, which will help familiarize you with my practice.

Consultations

The initial visit is 60 minutes. Follow-up visits are 30 to 60 minutes. Because office visits must end on time, please arrive on time for your appointment.

Bring to the first visit, or e-mail in advance, your completed patient forms and a three-day food record. All the forms are available at [your website]. If you have had any recent lab work done, bring the results with you or have them faxed to my office (fax number:_____).

Insurance Payments

Please contact your insurance provider before we meet to ensure that you are covered for nutrition visits. If you have not met your annual deductible, be prepared to pay for the visit at the time of service. An insurance claim form will be sent to your insurance provider. If your insurance provider does not pay for the visit, you are responsible for paying for this service.

Referrals

If your insurance provider requires a referral to see a specialist, you will need one. Contact your physician for the referral and bring it with you to the initial visit.

Cancellations

If you need to cancel your visit, you must do so at least 48 hours prior to the visit. Otherwise, you will be charged $XXX.00 for the visit. The same fee applies if you do not cancel or do not show up for an appointment.

Signature: _____ Date: _____

Printed name: _____

Reprinted with permission from Lisa Stollman.

RELEASE OF INFORMATION FORM

A permission to release health information form (see the Making Your Business box on the next page) should be given to and signed by each patient. This form is provided for a couple of reasons. First, it gives you permission to communicate with the patient's health care providers or other specified persons (such as family or friends) regarding the patient's treatment. You can also gather this information on the Health Insurance Portability and Accountability Act (HIPAA) form, but some RDNs prefer to use a separate form that can be readily accessed.

Making Your Business:
Sample Permission to Release Health Information

Permission to Release Health Information

I grant the right to [RDN's name] to release and/or obtain health information about _____ [patient's name] _____to my third-party payers and the following health care providers or persons with their contact information: _____

_____

_____

Signature of person completing this form:

_____ Date: _____

Relationship to patient: _____

Print name: _____

A patient must also sign the release of health information form to have his or her signature on file for the insurance claim if you are billing a third-party payer. On the Form CMS-1500 (as addressed further in chapter 7), you will be indicating that you have the patient's signature on file. If you are writing this on the claim form, you must have the patient's signature.

There may be circumstances when a patient refuses to sign this form. This may be because he or she does not want you to contact their health care providers or you will not be submitting a Form CMS-1500 claim to an insurance provider. If a patient refuses to sign, document this fact on the form, including the date, the reason (if known), and your signature. Maintain this form in your patient's EHR.

ACKNOWLEDGMENT OF RECEIPT OF HEALTH INSURANCE PORTABILITY AND ACCOUNTABILITY ACT NOTICE OF PRIVACY PRACTICES

In order to comply with HIPAA regulations, each of your patients must receive and read a copy of your HIPAA notice of privacy practices. The patient acknowledges that he or she has received this by signing a form. HIPAA requirements are discussed in chapter 7. This signed form should be scanned and included in the patient's EHR. A complete HIPAA notice of privacy practice form is included in chapter 7.

Making Your Business:
Sample Health Insurance Portability and Accountability Act Written Acknowledgment of Receipt

Acknowledgment of Receipt of Notice of Privacy Practices

Patient name:

Date of birth:

I understand that under the Health Insurance Portability and Accountability Act of 1998, I have certain rights to privacy in regard to my protected health information (PHI). I have received, read, and understand [RDN's name] notice of privacy practices.

Signature:_____ Date: _____

Relationship to patient: _____Self _____Parent _____ Guardian

Reprinted with permission from Lisa Stollman.

PATIENT MEDICAL AND NUTRITION INFORMATION INTAKE FORMS

Patient intake forms are used to collect medical- and nutrition-related information from the patient. Information gathered from these forms is vital in formulating a patient nutrition assessment. Some practitioners have more than one form. Some may have detailed forms for specific diseases or conditions to obtain more information than can possibly be obtained in an initial appointment. Others may have shorter assessment forms and ask additional questions at the appointment. You have to determine what will be best for your practice and your patient population. When you are getting started in your own private practice, it's a good idea to begin with a medical and nutrition information intake form (see pages 99–102) and a three-day food intake form (see page 103) along with a food frequency checklist (see pages 104–105); however, you can tailor these forms to fit your needs. If you work with specific cultural populations, you may find a need to modify these forms to fit your specific clientele. All forms, after they are completed by the patient, can be scanned or downloaded and uploaded into the EHR.

Making Your Business:
Patient Medical and Nutrition Information Intake Forms

Name: _____ Date: _____

Address: _____ City/State/Zip Code: _____

Home Phone Number: _____ Work Phone Number: _____

Cell Phone Number: _____ E-mail Address: _____

Social Security Number: _____

Occupation: _____ Date of Birth: _____

Referral Source: _____ Physician Name: _____

Physician Address: _____ Physician Phone Number: _____

Insurance Provider Name: _____ Policy Number: _____

Group Number: _____ Do you have another plan? _____ If YES, please state: _____

Who is responsible for bill/copay? _____ Amount of Copay: _____

Do you need a referral for this visit? YES   NO

Do you have the referral with you? YES   NO

Are you covered for nutrition visits? YES   NO

Have you confirmed coverage with your insurance provider?   YES   NO

Have you met your yearly deductible for specialists?   YES   NO

You will be responsible for paying for today's visit if you did not confirm coverage with your insurance provider.

Major Nutrition Concern(s)_____

Height: _____ Weight: _____ Usual Weight: _____ Weight at High School Graduation: _____

Lowest/Highest Weight in Last 5 Years: _____ / _____

Medications: _____

_____

Supplements: _____

_____

Do you have a history of intestinal problems, such as bloating, excessive gas, constipation, or diarrhea? _____

_____

Do you take laxatives? _____

Do you have any food allergies or intolerances? _____

Do you smoke cigarettes? _____ If YES, how many years?_____ Number per day: _____

Making Your Business:
Patient Medical and Nutrition Information Intake Forms
(continued)

Medical History (Illnesses, Surgeries): _____

_____

Family Medical History: _____

_____

_____

Past Diet History: _____

_____

Exercise (How Often/Type/Duration): _____

Eating Information

How many meals and snacks do you eat per day? _____ Meals _____ Snacks

Do you ever skip meals? YES NO

If YES, please explain _____

Do you have times during which you eat uncontrollably? YES NO

If YES, please explain: _____

Do you ever eat because you are (please check if YES):

_____ lonely   _____ bored   _____ stressed   _____ anxious   _____ sad

_____ depressed   _____ happy   _____ tired   _____ angry

Do you eat (please check if YES):

_____ in your car   _____ in bed   _____ watching tv   _____ on the computer

_____ reading   _____ standing up   _____ sitting down   _____ when not hungry

Which do you enjoy more?

_____ Eating alone   _____ Eating with others

Do you:

_____ eat fast   _____ eat slow   _____ take big bites

_____ eat with enjoyment   _____ eat without enjoyment

Do you chew your food well before you swallow? YES NO

Do you read Nutrition Fact Labels? YES NO

If YES, what do you look for on the label? _____

Who does the cooking in your house? _____ Do you know how to cook? YES NO

Who does the grocery shopping?_____

Do you have enough money for food? YES NO

Office Policies

I look forward to helping you achieve your health and nutrition goals. Making positive changes to your lifestyle is the cornerstone of good health. These are my office policies, which will help familiarize you with my practice.

Consultations

The initial visit is 45 to 60 minutes. Follow-up visits are 30 to 60 minutes. Office visits must end on time, so please be on time.

Please bring a three-day food record with you to the visit. If you have had any recent lab work done, bring the results from that with you as well.

Referrals

If you need a referral from your physician, please bring it with you to the initial visit.

Cancellations

If you need to cancel your visit, please do so at least 48 hours prior to the visit. Otherwise, you will be charged for the visit in full.

Insurance Payments

Please contact your insurance provider before we meet to ensure that you are covered for nutrition visits. If you have *not* met your yearly deductible for specialists, you should pay for the visit at the time of service and the claim will be sent to your insurance provider.

If any fees are not covered by insurance, I understand that I am financially responsible for all accumulated charges. If I don't have a referral for this visit and require a referral, I will be responsible for paying for this visit today. All unpaid balances over 30 days will be sent to collection, which will increase fees by 35%. I will also be fully responsible for payment of any appointments that are not canceled in advance.

I have read the financial obligation clause above.

_____   _____   _____
Responsible party   Relationship   Date

Patient Acknowledgment of Notice of Privacy Practices

PATIENT: DATE OF BIRTH:

I understand that under the Health Insurance Portability and Accountability Act of 1998 I have certain rights to privacy in regard to my protected health information (PHI). I have received, read, and understand the notice of privacy practices.

The practice reserves the right to change its terms of the notice of privacy practices. I understand that the practice will provide a current notice of privacy practices upon request.

Signature:_ _____

Relationship to patient: _____ Self _____ Parent _____ Guardian

Date: _____

Permission to Release Health Information

I grant the right to [RDN's name] to release and/or obtain health information about_____
_____ (patient's name) to my third-party payers and the following health care providers or persons:

_____

_____

Signature of person completing this form: _____

Relationship to patient: _____ Self _____ Parent _____ Guardian

Print name: _____

Date: _____

Reprinted with permission from Lisa Stollman and Ann Silver.

Date	Time	Meal	Food	Amount consumed

Making Your Business:
Sample of Food Frequency Checklist

Patient Name: DOB: Date:

Weekly Food Intake

Food	Daily	4–6 times per week	3 times or less per week	Never/ Rarely
Vegetables				
Fruits				
Fruit Juice (100%)				
Smoothie				
Breads (Whole Grain or White)				
Cereals (Whole Grain or White)				
Pasta				
Rice (Brown or White)				
Potatoes and/or Corn				
Other Whole Grains (Quinoa, etc.)				
Poultry (Chicken, Turkey, Duck)				
Fish				
Shellfish (Shrimp, Lobster, Mollusks)				
Red Meat (Beef, Lamb, Pork, Veal)				
Deli Meat				
Meat Sauces, Casseroles or Stews				
Hamburgers				
Hot Dogs				
Beans, Legumes and/or Hummus				
Soy Foods (Tofu, Edamame, Tempeh)				
Veggie Burgers				
Plant-Based Meat Substitutes				
Nuts/Seeds				
Peanut Butter and other Nut Butters				
Milk (Dairy or Nondairy)				
Cream (Dairy or Nondairy)				
Cheese (Dairy: Full Fat or Low Fat))				
Cheese (Vegan)				

Food	Daily	4–6 times per week	3 times or less per week	Never/ Rarely
Yogurt (Dairy or Nondairy)				
Eggs				
Oils (indicate type)				
Butter				
Margarine				
Chocolate				
Energy Bars				
Snack Foods: Potato/Corn Chips				
Popcorn				
Sorbet and Ices				
Ice cream and/or Frozen Yogurt				
Candy				
Canned soups				
Frozen Meals				
International/Ethnic Foods				
Fast Food				
Pizza				
Take-Out Meals				
Soda Regular				
Soda Diet				
Water				
Seltzer or Club Soda				
Energy/Sports Drinks				
Alcoholic beverages				

Registered Dietitian Nutritionist Forms

GOAL-SETTING FORM

As RDNs, we want to help patients implement healthy habits that are sustainable. We also want patients to continue to work with us as they move along the continuum to better health. Using a goal-setting form is a good way to summarize at the end of each session what they will be working on until they return for the next follow-up visit. It's also good to talk about what their incentives are for working toward those particular goals. Use the form shown in the Making Your Business box below with your patient at the end of the session. Have him or her sign it, and then you can put in the next appointment date. Make a copy of the form so you have it for your records and give your patient the form.

Making Your Business: **Goal-Setting Form**

Goals to Work on

Date: _____

Patient: _____

Goals to work on for next visit:

1. _____

_____

2. _____

_____

3. _____

_____

Incentive(s) for goals:

1. _____

_____

2. _____

_____

3. _____

_____

Patient signature: _____

Next nutrition visit date: _____

FOLLOW-UP LETTER TO PHYSICIAN

Sending a follow-up letter to a physician after you see a patient is a great way to not only thank him or her for the referral but also to let the doctor know what your assessment is and the treatment plan for the patient(s). It is also an excellent way to market your services so the referring physician can see how your expertise can benefit the patients.

You can also send a follow-up letter to the physicians of self-referred patients and let them know that you saw their patient. You can include a brief summary of your assessment and treatment plan. Make sure you have your patient sign a permission to release health information form stating that you can send a letter to his or her physician. An example of a follow-up letter is shown in the Making Your Business box below.

Making Your Business:
Sample Follow-Up Letter

[Date]

[Doctor's name]

Patient name:

Address:

Date of birth:

Dear [Doctor's name],

Thank you for referring [Patient Name] for medical nutrition therapy. [Patient] came to see me for an initial visit on [date] concerning [medical concern].

[Patient] is [height in feet and inches] tall and weighs [weight in pounds]. [His or her] body mass index (BMI) is [number].

A complete nutrition assessment indicated that [findings].

I reviewed my findings with [Patient], and together we established strategies to achieve [his or her] goals for [outcome].

A follow-up appointment has been scheduled for [date]. Thank you again for referring [Patient]. Your referrals are always appreciated.

Regards,

[Your name], RDN

Reprinted with permission from Lisa Stollman.

SAMPLE EMAIL DISCLAIMER

If your practice is HIPAA compliant, as it should be, you need to have a confidentiality disclaimer attached to all of your fax and email communications. Please refer to chapter 7 for more in-depth information on HIPAA. The Making Your Business box below provides a sample for your use. Add it to your fax cover sheet and email signature.

> ## Making Your Business:
> ### Sample Email Disclaimer
>
> This e-mail message and any attached files are confidential and are intended solely for the use of the addressee named above. This communication may contain material protected by any and all privileges associated with the provision of health services. If you are not the intended recipient or person responsible for delivering this confidential communication to the intended recipient or if you have received this communication in error, then any review, use, dissemination, forwarding, printing, copying, or other distribution of this e-mail message and any attached files is strictly prohibited. If you have received this confidential communication in error, please notify the sender immediately by replying to this e-mail message. Please permanently delete the original message. If you have any questions concerning this message, please contact [RDN's name]. Thank you.

Electronic Health Record

The electronic health record (EHR), also referred to as the electronic medical record (EMR), is used by RDNs for maintaining patient records and for billing purposes. There are EHR platforms specifically developed for medical nutrition therapy (MNT) that are available to practitioners in private practice. The EHR can be adapted for your nutrition practice.

You can do an online search for EHR platforms and see which one is best suited to your practice. Office Ally is a low-cost EHR software program that can be modified to fit your practice. Healthie and KaiZenRD are both programs specifically created for RDNs. See the resource list in chapter 11 for more suggestions of EHR platforms. By maintaining patient information and progress notes on your computer, your practice can be primarily paperless. The amount of time involved in record keeping can be substantially reduced. You will no longer have to file charts at the end of the day. Although you may be in the habit of keeping paper charts, EHRs can work better for sharing information between health care providers. It is also much easier to access this information from a laptop than from a paper chart. Make sure these records are accurate and kept safe. You never know when you may need them.

Any paper received, such as referrals from physicians, laboratory test results, food records and blood glucose logs, or patient food records, can be scanned into a file, saved under the patient's name, and uploaded into the patient's EHR. Programs can accommodate the Nutrition Care Process and include billing functions as well.

Learning how to use all of the functions can be time consuming but will pay off in the end. And in time you will be able to get rid of all your file cabinets! As per the Internal Revenue Service, you should retain all of your patient files for seven years. Some state laws may dictate longer retention periods. RDNs should also check with the laws in their state to determine retention timelines.

Nutrition Counseling Supplies

A well-stocked nutrition counseling office is different from that of any other health practitioner. The tools you use to effectively counsel patients and teach them about nutrition should align with your brand. From food models and nutrient fact labels to measuring cups and spoons, the RDN's toolbox is unique to the profession. Depending on your specialty, you may also have different supplies that are needed specifically for your patient population. For example, if you see pediatric patients, you may need growth charts, or you can use an app to assess their body mass index and growth percentile.

Educational Materials

Patient education materials are crucial to imparting nutrition information to your patients. When patients walk out of the office with well-structured, clear, and pertinent educational material in hand or sent to them via email at the conclusion of the visit, they feel as though they have been well taken care of and have received their money's worth.

Many RDNs create their own nutrition handouts and tailor them to their patient population. These handouts can be saved in a folder on your computer and personalized, if needed, for your patients.

When you are first starting your practice, however, time is an issue. You need to devote your time to marketing and developing your business. Why reinvent the wheel? There are many excellent materials available, so purchase what you need. For example, the Academy of Nutrition and Dietetics publishes numerous client education items for purchase. These education items can be purchased online at the eatright store (www.eatrightSTORE.org).

Many companies and enterprising RDNs sell educational materials designed specifically for nutrition counseling. Food- and health-related companies, as well as other types of councils and agencies, such as the Dairy Council and the Food Marketing Institute, often provide free materials to RDNs. For example, many large manufacturers of calcium supplements provide educational pamphlets about calcium. Review materials before you give them to patients and make sure that the messages align with your philosophy. The material might be free, but if it promotes an idea or a product that you do not fully endorse, then the cost is too high. Chapter 11 lists selected resources for obtaining educational materials.

Food Models

Food models are a helpful visual aid for teaching patients about portion size. If you worked in a facility that provided food models, you may not realize how expensive they are. But if your counseling style depends on models, your office will not be complete without them. As these models can be expensive, research pricing and plan to work them into your budget. You don't need a lot of food models. To save on cost, start out with these three food models: a 3-ounce serving of meat, chicken, or fish; a 4-ounce glass of juice; and an 8-ounce glass of milk. The protein food model will let your patients view the standard protein size. The two glass sizes will help your patients visualize how many calories they are consuming through liquids. The 4-ounce orange juice glass is also a good visual for those with diabetes, as it shows them how much to drink if they have low blood glucose levels. The NASCO website (www.nasco .com) is an excellent resource for purchasing food models. In addition, having a set of measuring spoons and cups will help your patients visualize the portion sizes of foods they are consuming. It will also help you obtain more concise feedback from your patients on how much they are actually eating at meals.

Other Supplies

In addition to the supplies described previously, you may need others. What you need depends on the type of practice you have and the patients you counsel. Some items that you may find useful in private practice include food labels or actual food packages, a flip chart for diagramming concepts to patients, and a computer with an internet connection so you can check references and share as needed. On the other end of the spectrum, you may also want to have coffee, tea, and water available for your patients. If you plan to have an exclusive virtual practice, it's still wise to have food models and measuring cups and spoons so you can effectively educate patients virtually. All handouts can be emailed as PDFs.

Medical Equipment and Nutrition Assessment Tools

SCALES

A medical scale is a wise investment. Many medical practices are switching over from balance beam scales to digital scales, as they are also quite accurate. Digital scales are usually much lighter in weight and quite often lower in cost. When choosing a scale, think about your patient population. For example, if you counsel patients with obesity, consider purchasing a scale that accommodates greater weights. If your clientele is mostly patients with obesity, you may need to consider a balance beam digital scale, as this type of scale can weigh people up to 660 lb. Some digital scales will also accommodate greater weights, but they usually have a limit of 350 lb. RDNs who share an office or who make home visits, however, find that portable digital scales are their best option.

BODY FAT ANALYZERS

Body fat analyzers can be very helpful to RDNs in private practice. They allow patients and practitioners to measure progress in ways other than a regular scale. Patients ask RDNs to analyze their body fat, and the analysis can be expected as part of the nutrition assessment. Sports dietitians find them to be a useful tool, as do eating disorder and weight management professionals. Some of the newer digital scales can also assess body fat, so consider purchasing a scale with this option.

You need to first decide whether it makes sense to provide body fat analysis to your patients. If so, decide whether to provide it at no charge or use it as a value-added service. Some RDNs charge an additional fee for the service as a way of recouping the expense of the equipment.

If you want to incorporate technology rather than use calipers to measure body fat, there are many handheld products on the market. Also, consider scales that can measure body fat. It is important to assess their reliability and accuracy before you purchase one. Evaluate their accuracy with different patient populations—for example, individuals with anorexia who have very low body fat. Ask other professionals what they recommend and do your own research. Select the technology that works best for your practice and your patients.

CALORIMETER

Another gadget that can enhance your practice is a calorimeter. This tool measures resting metabolic rate using indirect calorimetry. It is a useful tool for RDNs working with athletes, people who diet chronically, or patients with eating disorders. Metabolic testing can add value to your practice in assessing a patient and as another source of income. As with body fat analyzers, you should research the options, ask for recommendations, and select the brand that fits your practice and patient population. Before you invest in this equipment, carefully analyze whether you need this data or if good clinical judgment can suffice.

Diabetes Management Tools

If you counsel patients with diabetes, a blood glucose monitor and insulin pump may be useful. Food models plus measuring cups and spoons are also essential to teaching carbohydrate counting as well as healthy portion sizes. Measuring cups and spoons are great to have on your desk, as they are great teaching tools for healthy eating and portion control. Contact companies that manufacture these tools and request a demonstration model to use in your office.

Tools of the Nutrition Trade: A Summary

A private practitioner's office has a unique set of requirements. Here are some key points to keep in mind:

- It is important that you consider your patient population and their needs when planning your space.

- Many specialized forms, supplies, and equipment are needed to furnish your office. Most forms can be placed on your website and downloaded by patients.

- The materials you need will depend on the type of practice you establish.

7 | Billing Options: Ways to Get Paid

In addition to wanting to help patients and clients improve and maintain their health through nutrition, you also want to be paid for the services you have rendered, right? Let's talk about making money in your practice. In the supermarket when you get to the checkout line, you must pay. It's the same in your office with your patients. At the end of each counseling session, you want to be paid.

Who Will Pay You?

A common concern of registered dietitian nutritionists (RDNs) when it comes to starting and sustaining a private practice is whether they will make enough money to generate a profit and be able to support their lifestyle. Initially, you will have to decide who will pay you.

The following are some questions to consider in making this decision:

- Do you want to exclusively be paid directly by patients and not have to deal with insurance?

- Will you accept third-party payments (insurance reimbursement)?

- Do you want your practice to make money quickly or to grow slowly and gradually?

Let's explore these and other issues to help you with this decision.

Accepting Only Self-Pay Patients or Third-Party Payers: What's Right for You?

Perhaps you have already decided to accept payment from third-party payers or only accept self-pay patients. That's great! You may be tempted to skip ahead and only read the section that pertains to your decision. Don't! You still need an understanding of both self-pay patients and third-party reimbursement, as there is overlap.

Or maybe you are undecided and in a quandary about what to do. You have heard many different stories about insurance reimbursement from other colleagues, both good and bad. The box on the next page can clarify the differences between patient self-payment and third-party reimbursement.

To assist you with making this decision, the rest of this chapter will address all aspects of reimbursement. You will also want to research as much as you can. Speak with colleagues on both sides of the fence. Identify whether accepting insurance reimbursement is feasible and something you want to do. Post your debate about accepting or not accepting insurance on dietetic practice group (DPG) electronic mailing lists (EMLs). Contact your local, state, and DPG reimbursement representatives. Be up-to-date to make an informed decision. Crunch your numbers. Compare your overhead expenses with potential income from third-party payers and self-pay patients. Make a list of the pros and cons of each.

Whether or not you choose third-party payment is completely up to you and your situation. Some RDNs do not accept insurance coverage at all. This has been a growing trend in medical practices as well. Physicians are opting out of insurance plans and seeing patients who will self-pay for services.[1] They feel they cannot practice medicine with the financial and procedural restrictions placed on them by the insurance companies. This may not be a realistic option for many private practice RDNs. They may find it necessary to accept insurance to be successful in private practice. Especially when first starting out, accepting third-party payment can quickly build your practice. Would you prefer to make less money per patient and be busier by becoming a participating provider *or* make more money per patient and work less with fewer constraints by not accepting insurance? This is a decision only you can make about what will work best for you.

Some RDNs might argue that the lack of reimbursement has kept them from being financially successful in their private practices. But RDNs *are* being reimbursed for medical nutrition therapy (MNT). Over the years, as the value of MNT in health and chronic disease manage-

Differences Between Patient Self-Payment and Third-Party Reimbursement

Question	Self-payment	Third-party reimbursement
Is there an application process?	There is no application process.	Yes. You apply to become a provider with the third party (commercial or government insurance).
When do you get paid?	Payment is due at the time of the appointment.	Payment is made after the appointment. It can take weeks.
Who pays?	The patient pays you.	The third party (insurance) pays you.
How much do you get paid?	You set your fee schedule.	The third party decides your reimbursement rate. Sometimes you can negotiate, but ultimately the third party makes the final decision on the rate.
How do you get paid?	The patient can pay by cash, check, debit card, credit card, or health savings account.	The third party will pay you. The patient may also have to make a copayment or pay to satisfy their deductible.
Is there any paperwork?	Maybe. You may have to provide the patient with a superbill for him or her to submit to the insurance carrier for reimbursement if he or she has out-of-network coverage.	Yes. You have to submit a Form CMS-1500 claim for the insurance provider to pay.

Adapted with permission from Ann Silver.

ment has been widely recognized, RDNs have seen an expansion of insurance coverage for MNT.[2]

Reimbursement policies affect how you structure your fees. Handling insurance claims increases the practice's overhead. It takes more administrative time to check on patients' eligibility and referrals, file the claims, resubmit the claims if they have been rejected, and bill the patient when denied. Usually, there is a lag time between the time of filing a claim and receiving payment. The increased administrative time required contributes to the overhead costs for handling insurance claims. Submitting claims costs you time to complete the forms and reduces the

MAKING NUTRITION YOUR BUSINESS

time you could spend providing billable nutrition services to your clients. If you decide to use someone else to submit claims, such as a biller, this will also add to your costs.

Selecting a Dietetics Practice Model

Model	Pros	Cons
Medicare clients	Stable and predictable Potential for large clientele Minimal marketing Opportunity for follow-up Recognition as a Medicare provider	Reimbursement rate may not meet salary requirements Administrative duties Medicare clients limited to diagnoses covered
Self-pay clients, third-party payers, and opting out of Medicare	Potential for higher payment rate Broader range of clients' payment rate Provider status with private plans	Requires marketing and negotiating skills May be less stable May reduce referrals Ramifications of opting out of Medicare
Medicare and third-party payers plus self-pay clients	Variety and professional satisfaction Success with Medicare generates non-Medicare referrals Maintains client flow Builds skills and confidence with billing and negotiating systems	Requires up-front work to stay organized and efficient with time Management of contracts and billing
Self-pay clients	Potential for higher payment rate Less administrative work Frequently used with highly specialized practices RDN can establish a wellness-based practice	Requires constant creative marketing May be less stable May reduce referrals

Adapted with permission from the Academy of Nutrition and Dietetics.[3]

Your decision to accept third-party payments or to only see self-pay patients may be dictated by your office location and the types of patients you will service. Take into consideration the population density and the socioeconomics of the community. Although you may want to exclusively treat self-pay patients, this is not always a viable option.

If you opt to follow the self-pay model, it is wise to have an overview of third-party reimbursement for MNT. Being knowledgeable about coverage for third-party payers will enable you to advise your patients on what their insurance might cover and help you understand how to submit a superbill for the client to be reimbursed. It can also be helpful for your own personal health insurance issues.

Let's explore in more detail the different options to aid you in making a decision about what might work best for you and your practice. The box on the previous page summarizes several practice model combinations you can consider.

Self-Pay Patients Only?

In this practice model, payment is the responsibility of the patient. The RDN is not an insurance provider for patients and does not bill third-party payers or accept what they may pay.

The RDN should inform patients when they call for an appointment that payment is expected at the time of the visit. At the end of the appointment, the patient can be provided with a superbill, which is explained later in this chapter, or a completed Form CMS-1500 to file for reimbursement with the insurance company if he or she has out-of-network coverage (see the box below for more information on out-of-network coverage). Having to self-pay may deter some potential patients from scheduling appointments. However, individuals who choose to pay for services may potentially be more serious about implementing dietary changes.

Understanding Out-of-Network Coverage

Commercial insurance plans can offer patients the option to receive services from nonparticipating providers, also known as out-of-network providers. These plans usually have a deductible that must be satisfied before the insurance company will pay. Good business practice is to have the patient pay you, provide the patient with a superbill to submit to his or her third-party payer, and for the patient to be reimbursed directly by his or her insurance. Essentially these patients are self-pay patients.

7

If you only accept self-pay patients and no third-party reimbursement, you set your own fees. Your fee schedule must be applied consistently. With less time spent on administrative duties, more time can be spent seeing patients and billing for that time. RDNs can become highly specialized in this case, and patients will seek them out for their particular specialty niches. For example, specialists in eating disorders, weight management, or functional nutrition may wish to build a self-pay practice. But choosing not to be a provider for private insurance companies has the potential to greatly reduce your client base and, unless your fees are set accordingly, possibly your income. You also must expend extra time and effort in marketing your services.

Setting Fees for Self-Pay Patients

Chapter 3 addressed the details you need to consider to set your hourly fee for your practice. It's good to start out with a base fee in mind, but over time, you may find that you need to adjust your fees.

As you think about fees, you may also want to ask consumers who have used similar services what they have paid and what they would be willing to pay. Remember, you should *not* be asking colleagues what they charge because this can be viewed as price fixing.[4,5]

There are other ways to determine if your fees are within reason. One way is to look at Medicare's reimbursement rates, which are public information. Private insurance reimbursement rates are proprietary, meaning that they are not public information and should not be shared. But Medicare's rates can provide an idea of what insurance providers are paying. You can contact your affiliate reimbursement representative or go to the Academy of Nutrition and Dietetics website (www.eatright .org) for information on how to obtain the current Medicare fee schedule.

Another way to establish a sense of how to set fees is with the Academy of Nutrition and Dietetics compensation survey. This survey includes salary information for private practice RDNs.[6]

A simple way to judge whether the market will bear your price is to try to gauge patients' reactions when you state your price. If most prospective patients do not balk and schedule an appointment, you know you are on target. If you receive a large number of excuses or people saying they will call back, your fees may be too high.

Consider your *perceived* value. If your rates are consistently lower than those of others providing the same service, you may lose clients because they may think you are not the best. On the other hand, professionals demanding the highest rates tend to have the reputation, experience, and higher levels of specialty that enable them to do so.

Although it is a questionable practice to routinely charge self-pay patients less than insured patients (that is, offer a cash discount), you may occasionally want to provide a discount for a needy or indigent patient. You need to be careful about this from a legal standpoint. Develop a written policy on offering a discount in certain situations and ensure that it is enforced consistently. You may also consider charging differently for home visits or offering a discount for couples. If you do not deal with reimbursement, you may want to offer different fee schedules for day versus night visits. Weekend hours could bring premium rates. You may also want to offer a family rate. Consider having a package deal for patients who schedule several visits. There are different circumstances where your fees may vary. These fees must be in accordance with your policies and applied consistently across the board.

In general, you will have at least two levels of service: an initial visit and a follow-up. Initial visits may take twice as long as follow-ups, so set your fees accordingly. Also, you will have greater administrative expenses from seeing two patients in one hour for follow-up than seeing one patient in one hour. It may be appropriate to set your half-hour fees to account for these increased costs.

When setting fees, do not start too low. It becomes difficult to catch up. You can only raise your rates incrementally at any given time. For example, raising your follow-up rate from $50 to $100 is a 100% increase. That increase would not be palatable to your existing patients. Take your time and carefully consider all the aforementioned variables—and the tips in chapter 3—when setting fees.

If you are thinking that you don't need a fee structure because you plan on accepting insurance, you are wrong. You will need to set a fee structure to bill the insurance provider and for the patient who will pay you out of pocket.

All About Third-Party Payers

RDNs choose to accept third-party payments to quickly build their practices. When enrolling as a third-party provider, your name and contact information will be listed on the insurance company's list of participating providers. The third-party payer is marketing your practice to their beneficiaries and to other health care providers. Clients will be more apt to seek the services of an RDN when they incur no or minimal expense by using their insurance.

Whether you decide to become credentialed and contract with a third-party provider or not, it is important to understand the basic principles and terminology of the health insurance industry, including the types of insurance carriers also referred to as third-party payers. Who are the different parties? The first party is the patient. The second party is you, the provider. The third party is the payer paying on behalf of the patient—hence, this is the third-party payer. There is a whole new language you will learn in reimbursement. The glossary of terms shown on the next page defines many terms important to understand the reimbursement process.[6,7]

Glossary of Terms[7,8]

Accept assignment: A health care provider who participates with an insurance plan. The health care provider agrees to accept the fees specified by the insurance carrier(s) and cannot collect additional fees for the service beyond the copayment and/or deductible.

Accountable care organization: A group of health care providers where reimbursement and patient care are based on meeting quality goals and outcomes to result in cost savings.

Advanced Beneficiary Notice (ABN): A Medicare provider provides the ABN form to be signed by a Medicare beneficiary for those services or items not covered by Medicare. These expenses will be the financial responsibility of the beneficiary.

Beneficiary: Any person who receives insurance benefits from a third-party payer.

Claim: A claim is a request for payment for rendered services.

Complementary and alternative (CAM) network or complementary network (CN): A network of practitioners that includes services of different practitioners—such as massage therapists, nutritionists/RDNs, and acupuncturists—who are considered nontraditional. Firms sell both benefit and access services to insurance companies and employer groups to supplement existing services included in these groups' health benefit plans. Services are provided at a discounted rate of usual fees and are paid directly to the provider by the client.

Copayment/copay: The amount a patient pays for each medical service. A copayment is a set amount specified by the policy that the patient pays for a service.

Current Procedural Terminology (CPT): Procedural codes developed by the American Medical Association for physicians and other health care professionals to describe the provided service. Third-party payers will specify the procedural codes that RDNs can use.

Deductible: The amount a person needs to pay out of pocket for medical costs before the insurance covers costs.

Explanation of Benefits (EOB): A statement from a third-party payer describing coverage for services rendered.

Fee-for-service: A health care provider renders service to a person and is paid for the individual visit. Payment can come from the patient or the insurance provider.]

Form CMS-1500: The form health care providers use to submit Medicare and other insurance claims.

Health maintenance organization (HMO): A type of health insurance plan that delivers previously determined comprehensive services to its policy-holders for a prepaid sum and contracts with health care providers, including RDNs, to deliver service.

In-network provider: A provider under contract with a third-party payer, also known as a participating provider, to render services to its beneficiaries.

International Classification of Diseases, Clinical Modifications (ICD-10-CM): Codes determined by the treating or primary care physician to classify all diagnostic and surgical procedures.

Medicaid: A program jointly funded by federal and state governments but managed by each state to pay for medical assistance for certain individuals and families with low incomes and people with disabilities.

Medicare: The federal health insurance program for people 65 years of age or older, certain younger people with disabilities, and people with end-stage renal disease (those with permanent kidney failure who need regular dialysis or a kidney transplant).

National Provider Identifier (NPI): A unique 10-digit number required for all health care providers. This number is used to identify an individual health care provider for all health transactions. Even if you choose not to accept reimbursement from third-party payers, you should obtain an NPI.

Out-of-network provider: A provider who does not participate with an insurance plan. A patient can pay the provider directly and be reimbursed by his or her insurance company, or the provider can be paid by the insurance company.

Patient-Centered Medical Home (PCMH): A health care delivery model in which the primary care physician's focus is the patient and in which the primary care physician coordinates all the patient's care and treatment through a team of health care providers.

Point-of-service (POS) plan: A health plan that offers its members the option of receiving services from participating or nonparticipating providers.

Preferred provider organization (PPO): A health plan that contracts with medical providers to provide services to its members. Members incur low costs using contracted providers but have the option to receive medical services not in the PPO at a higher cost.

Superbill: A form or invoice that itemizes and describes all services and fees rendered to the patient. The patient can submit the superbill directly to the health care insurer for payment to the insured.

Third-party payer: An organization or company that disburses payment on behalf of an insured party (the patient [the first party]) for medical services to a provider (the second party).

Different Third-Party Payer Options

You have choices when you accept third-party reimbursement. Do you want to only accept Medicare, only accept private health insurance, or accept both?

COMMERCIAL OR PRIVATE HEALTH INSURANCE COMPANIES

Private or commercial health insurance companies provide insurance plans that are not funded by federal or state governments, but they must still comply with federal and state laws concerning insurance. Most individuals insured by commercial or private health insurance obtain insurance coverage through their employer or other affiliations that offer group insurance plans, or if federal and state health insurance plans are offered. There are so many of these commercial plans that it is difficult to list them all here. Some insurance carriers are located nationwide, such as Aetna, Blue Cross Blue Shield (BCBS), Cigna, and United Healthcare, whereas others are regional or very local. Coverage can vary from state to state. Even within the same insurance company, the benefits differ from plan to plan. Although in one state BCBS may provide unlimited visits for MNT, in another state BCBS may only allow three visits annually.

An exception to the aforementioned plans is self-funded or self-insured health insurance plans. With these health plans, a company contracts with a commercial insurance company to administer its health plan. The company decides which services are covered and assumes the financial responsibility for paying the claims. Self-funded plans do not have to comply with all federal and state laws. They may look and sound like a "true" commercial plan, but they may not be. Coverage for MNT can vary.

Managed care organizations' plans are the most popular plans offered in the United States. These include health maintenance organization (HMO) plans, preferred provider organization (PPO) plans, and point-of-service (POS) organization plans.

To be reimbursed by these plans, an RDN must be enrolled as an in-network provider of MNT or other nutrition services. Patients can have a financial responsibility to you as well. They may have to pay you if they have not met their deductible or if there is a copayment. Plans may require some form of preauthorization, such as a referral for coverage. They may limit the number of visits or the diagnoses they cover. The more plans you join, the greater potential for reimbursement.

GOVERNMENT INSURANCE COVERAGE

The Centers for Medicare & Medicaid Services (CMS) is the government agency that establishes guidelines and regulations for federal government insurance plans. These include Medicare, Medicaid, and the Children's Health Insurance Program.

Medicare RDNs are eligible to provide MNT to original Medicare Part B beneficiaries (see the box below for an explanation of the different parts of Medicare coverage). Patients with diabetes or nondialysis kidney disease and those three years post–kidney transplant can receive the Medicare MNT benefit. Beneficiaries are required to receive a written physician referral annually. Medicare beneficiaries can receive three hours of coverage in the first calendar year (from January 1 to December 31) they use their MNT benefit and two hours in subsequent calendar years. With another written physician referral, additional hours of MNT can be provided in a calendar year based on a change in the patient's medical condition, diagnosis, and treatment.

Becoming a Medicare provider requires having the necessary credentials in place to apply and, once you become a provider, staying up-to-date with regulations. Be aware that Medicare's rules and regulations change. For instance, there is an effort for the Medicare MNT benefit to expand beyond coverage for diabetes and kidney disease to include other diet-related diseases. Another example is Medicare's transition of payment from "volume to value" to improve the quality of care while lowering cost.[9,10] The future of insurance reimbursement will be discussed in further detail in later sections of this chapter.

Some potential pitfalls of a Medicare-based practice include the possibilities that the reimbursement rate may not meet your salary expectations, the reimbursement rate may not adequately cover your busi-

The Different Parts of Medicare Coverage

Medicare has different coverage. Parts A and B are original Medicare. RDNs can participate in Parts B and C.

- Part A: Hospital Insurance
- Part B: Medical Insurance
- Part C: Medicare Advantage
- Part D: Prescription Drug Coverage

Medicare beneficiaries with original Medicare Parts A and B can choose Medicare Advantage plans that are administered by private health insurance companies. These plans must comply with Medicare guidelines as the minimum but may provide additional insurance coverage. RDNs must be in-network providers of the private third-party payer to accept Medicare Advantage plans. Stay posted—in the future, Medicare will require providers to be Medicare providers to participate in Medicare Advantage plans.

ness expenses, and the reimbursement process may increase your administrative workload. Your client base will be limited to the diseases and conditions Medicare covers—diabetes and renal disease—until coverage expands to include other diseases.

RDNs who want to become Medicare providers must meet specific criteria. The following are the options with Medicare for RDNs[11]:

- Enroll: Practitioners who meet the provider qualifications can enroll at any time to become Medicare providers.

- Do not enroll: RDNs who choose not to enroll are not able to provide MNT services to qualifying Medicare beneficiaries unless they formally opt out of Medicare Part B. Merely *saying* you are not accepting Medicare reimbursement without opting out while treating and accepting payment from Medicare beneficiaries is a violation of the law. Practitioners who have not enrolled or opted out of Medicare *cannot* provide and bill MNT to beneficiaries with diabetes or nondialysis kidney disease or those post–kidney transplant. Instead, these RDNs should inform patients that they do not participate in Medicare and direct those patients to another RDN who is an enrolled Medicare provider.

- Opt out: In this instance, the RDN formally opts out of Medicare through an affidavit. The RDN can then enter into a private contract with each qualifying Medicare beneficiary in order to provide MNT services. The private contract created for each beneficiary requires very specific requirements as defined by the CMS. Neither the RDN nor the patient can submit a claim to Medicare for payment. Opt-out affidavits signed after June 16, 2015, automatically renew. Before this date, the opt-out period had to be renewed every two years.[11,12]

Refer to the Medicare website (www.cms.gov) for more detailed information about the Medicare program.

Medicaid Medicaid is a federally regulated insurance program administered on a state-by-state basis for low-income individuals and families and disabled individuals. Medicaid coverage for MNT varies by each state. Some states do not cover MNT for Medicaid beneficiaries, whereas other states may contract with private insurance companies to provide Medicaid benefits. Medicaid reimbursement rates vary widely from state to state.

Medicaid programs may also restrict where RDNs can practice because services may have to be billed by a hospital's outpatient department or a physician's office. Further information on specific state regulations can be found at the CMS website specific to Medicaid (www .medicaid.gov).[13] Your state Academy of Nutrition and Dietetics reimbursement representative may also be able to provide assistance or resources on your state's Medicaid program.

Children's Health Insurance Program The Children's Health Insurance Program, better known as CHIP, is a federal program administered by each state to provide insurance to uninsured children up to the age of 19 whose families are ineligible for Medicaid.[14] Like Medicaid eligibility, coverage varies from state to state, as do benefits. Contact your state Academy of Nutrition and Dietetics affiliate reimbursement representative to learn more about your state's CHIP.

Complementary and Alternative Medicine Networks and Discount Programs

Another payment option is for RDNs to join networks. These are often referred to as complementary and alternative medicine (CAM) programs or complementary networks (CNs). Being a member of a CAM network differs from being a provider.

Upon joining the network, RDNs agree to provide their services at a discounted rate to members of that particular plan. In this type of arrangement offered through the CN, the member pays the RDN directly for the service. CNs may also offer benefit CAM services in which the employer or insurer pays for the service.[15]

CAM networks pursue RDNs to join them. Before you join, it is important to determine whether the reimbursement arrangements are a viable option for your practice. Although joining this type of network can potentially increase your referral base, consider the downside. As a member of these networks, you may need to provide deeply discounted fees to members. Some networks offer set fees that do not differ by geographic region. If you practice in a city where the cost of doing business is high, it may not be worth your time to join. Also, joining these networks may associate you with other practitioners such as acupuncturists and massage therapists who have different levels of training and credentialing than RDNs.

How to Become a Provider

To become a provider for a third-party payer, there is professional and practice information you need to have in place before you submit an application. Having this data readily available will make the process easier. The Making Your Business box on the next page provides a checklist of what you may need to complete an application to become a provider.

Making Your Business:
Checklist for Applying to Third-Party Payers

☐ Location where medical nutrition therapy services will be rendered, office phone number, fax number, and business email account

☐ Copy of your malpractice insurance cover sheet. Different third-party payers may specify the amount of malpractice coverage.

☐ Your federal tax identification number, also known as your Tax Identification Number (TIN) or Employer Identification Number (EIN)

☐ Your National Provider Identifier (NPI) number

☐ Copy of your college diploma(s)

☐ Copy of your state certification or license

☐ Copy of any other certifications

☐ Copy of your Commission on Dietetic Registration (CDR) card

☐ Updated resume or curriculum vitae

☐ List of professional and personal references, including their mailing addresses, email addresses, and phone numbers, if requested on the application

Reprinted with permission from Ann Silver.

Obtaining Necessary Identifiers

Third-party payers use two identifiers to identify you: your Tax Identification Number (TIN) and your National Provider Identifier (NPI). In addition to using these identifiers on your application, you will be asked to provide this information when you communicate with a third-party payer.

TAX IDENTIFICATION NUMBER

When you apply to become a participating provider with third-party payers, you must indicate your TIN. You can use your Social Security number if you are a sole proprietor. Once you become a participating provider, the insurer will request your TIN on all communications, even phone calls. Your TIN, if it is your Social Security number, will appear on every Explanation of Benefits (EOB), the claim determination document the patient receives. This means that your Social Security number is publically available; this is why it is advisable to obtain an Employer Identification Number (EIN), as discussed in chapter 2. You will want to use an EIN in place of your Social Security number to protect against identity theft. It is also easier to apply to third-party payers with your EIN than to change it midway through.

NATIONAL PROVIDER IDENTIFIER

A National Provider Identifier (NPI) is required to apply to become a provider with any third-party payer, process a claim, and even when you provide a patient with a superbill to submit to his or her insurer. If you think you do not need an NPI, you are wrong. You do! Every health care provider must have an NPI number. The NPI number is specific to you as the provider. It is your universal identifier for all third-party payers. You will most likely not be assigned a provider identification number from each third-party payer. They will use your NPI. If you are in a group practice, the group will have an NPI, and so will each individual provider. For information about receiving an NPI number, visit the National Plan and Provider Enumeration System (NPPES) website (https://nppes.cms .hhs.gov). You can apply online or by paper application. Call 800/465-3203 for questions and additional information about NPIs.

Applying to Private Insurance Companies

A question you may ask is *For which private insurance companies should I become a provider?* You will want to become an in-network provider for the insurance companies that insure beneficiaries in the vicinity of your office. You may also want to participate in the insurance companies of potential referring health care providers. This way when these providers refer a patient you are already an in-network provider. The box below can assist you with identifying private insurance companies to consider. You will need the name of the insurance company; its mailing

Suggestions for Compiling a List of Potential Insurance Companies

Ask your district and state Academy of Nutrition and Dietetics reimbursement representatives for insurance companies in the state and within your locale.

Ask local colleagues who are already providers of private insurance.

Ask health care providers in your community who they participate with.

Ask your office and home neighbors which insurance they have.

Ask your own physicians which insurance companies they contract with.

Contact local employers to learn which insurance companies insure their employees.

address, website URL, email address, and phone number; and, if possible, the name of the provider representative.

Another deciding factor you should consider in becoming a participating provider is the reimbursement rate. Try to find out the rate prior to applying. If you are dissatisfied with the reimbursement rate, you can try to negotiate with the insurance company. Base your request on facts and not emotions.

To request an application to become a provider, go to the insurance company's website for enrollment information. You can also email or call the insurance company to inquire about becoming a provider. Keep in mind that each insurance company may have a different process, different application, and different timeline for becoming an in-network provider.

COUNCIL FOR AFFORDABLE QUALITY HEALTHCARE

The Council for Affordable Quality Healthcare (CAQH) offers a free and voluntary online database called CAQH ProView for RDNs and other health care providers to store and share their professional and demographic data with third-party payers. With your permission, your information will be provided to private insurance companies for enrollment, credentialing, and any status changes. Not all private insurance companies participate with CAQH—they have to pay to use CAQH's services.

CAQH ProView streamlines the process and stores your information in one place. It makes the application process easier to become credentialed as an in-network provider and to update your information once you are a provider. To learn more about CAQH ProView, visit the CAQH ProView website (www.caqh.org/solutions/caqh-proview).

Applying to Medicare

Medicare's application process for providers is different from that of private insurance. Applications are available at the CMS website (www.cms .gov). You complete and submit the most recent CMS Form 855I, "Application for Individual Health Care Practitioners"; other enrollment forms may also be required.[16,17] The applications can be downloaded from the CMS website or completed online through Medicare's online provider enrollment system, which is called the Provider Enrollment, Chain, and Ownership System (PECOS).[18] The easiest and most efficient way to submit your enrollment application is through PECOS.

Local or geographical Medicare carriers, also known as Medicare administrative contractors (MACs), administer Medicare.[19] The completed application for Medicare will be submitted to your MAC. Some MACs may require you to include additional forms. RDNs should contact their state's Part B MAC with any questions or concerns about enrolling in Medicare or any other issues they may have, including issues regarding claims, reimbursement, and customer services. You can look on the Academy of Nutrition and Dietetics or CMS website for your MAC or contact your state Academy of Nutrition and Dietetics reimbursement representative for assistance.[20] Always check the CMS or your MAC website for the most updated information on Medicare enrollment.

Applying to Medicaid and Children's Health Insurance Program

Because coverage for MNT by Medicaid and CHIP is determined by each state, so too are the applications for credentialing. Check the CMS website (www.cms.gov) or contact your state Academy of Nutrition and Dietetics reimbursement representative about whether your state will recognize RDNs as providers and for help with obtaining a provider enrollment application.

Tips for Completing the Third-Party Payer Application

Read all instructions before completing any applications. Complete all parts of third-party payers' applications. Provide all the requested information or the application will either be sent back or denied. Sign the application.

Keep copies of all submitted applications. Take screenshots on your computer if the process is online. If you are mailing the application, send it certified through the United States Postal Service to confirm receipt of your application. You may need to follow up with the insurer by phone or email to determine the status of the application. You can check on your enrollment with Medicare through PECOS.[18]

Keep in mind that it can take many months to become a provider with third-party payers. If your application is denied, find out why. Be persistent in trying to become a provider. Don't give up!

Now You Are a Provider: What's Next?

As a new participating provider, there is much to learn about the claims process, from first seeing a patient until you are actually paid. With each claim submission, you will gain more experience and knowledge about the process with third-party payers. It will get easier! Don't be afraid to ask questions and research answers. You can post your questions on DPG EMLs, but keep in mind that the replies you receive may not be specific to your region or to the health plan. Reach out to your state or local reimbursement representatives. Research the policies of the third-party payers on their websites. The best source for answers is the insurance company. It can provide guidance; however, the company cannot tell you how to code a claim.

Obtaining Referrals and Preauthorizations

When you accept third-party payments, you need to understand and attend to certain administrative tasks before a patient's first visit.

Although patients should know if they need a referral to see a specialist, such as an RDN, with their health insurance, many may not. You will need to know or find out. Plans within one insurance company can vary if a referral is required. Private insurance companies will not pay you when a referral is required and there is not one provided. In this circumstance, you will not be able to bill the patient. Ultimately, you will not be getting paid for the services you have rendered when a referral is not obtained. The box here includes important questions to ask about referrals.

Medicare Part B requires a written referral on file from the treating physician specifying MNT services and the patient's diagnosis, including the International Classification of Diseases, Clinical Modifications, 10th Revision (ICD-10-CM) code(s).[21]

Regardless of the insurance, if a referral is required, make sure that it will be in place by the time of the appointment. Trying to obtain a referral after you have rendered services puts you at risk of not getting paid.

Questions to Ask Third-Party Payers About Referrals

Are referrals required?

How long are referrals good for?

How will the referrals be sent?

What diagnoses will they cover for medical nutrition therapy?

Is there a limitation to the number of units or visits?

Verifying Medical Nutrition Therapy Coverage

Patients need to understand that health insurance does not guarantee that the insurer will pay all fees for your services. Not all diagnoses are covered, and coverage varies. Even if a referral is in place, this does not guarantee that the visit will be covered. Determine coverage before the first visit. You can call or check online to verify coverage for MNT. However, this can be time consuming. You can place the onus on the patients by requesting that they contact their insurer to confirm coverage. Tell the patients exactly what to ask. Give them conversation points as listed in the box below. With time, you will become familiar with what is and is not covered by different third-party payers.

When MNT is not covered or is questionable, inform the patient that he or she will be responsible for payment. This must be included in your office policies and signed by the patient. Read chapter 3 for more about office policies. Inform the patient what the fee will be—no one likes surprise bills.

If you are rendering services to a Medicare-insured beneficiary for a diagnosis not covered by Medicare, you must inform patients before their visit that they are responsible for payment. Ask clients whether they have additional insurance that might cover the MNT visit. In either case, complete an Advance Beneficiary Notice of Noncoverage, as shown in the figure on the next page. This form verifies that Medicare-insured beneficiaries understand that they are responsible for payment of services not covered by Medicare.[22]

Conversation Points for Patients to Verify Their Insurance Coverage

I am seeing [name of registered dietitian nutritionist (RDN)] for [diagnosis name and International Classification of Diseases, 10th Revision, Clinical Modification (ICD-10) code from your physician] for medical nutrition therapy (MNT).

The dietitian will use Current Procedural Terminology (CPT) codes 98702 and 97803.

Do I have coverage for MNT or nutrition services or preventive services?

How many visits do I have annually or in a calendar year?

Do I need a referral? How do I get it? How is it sent to [name of RDN]?

Do I have a copayment or a deductible? What is it?

Are there any other limitations or information I should know on my policy to see [name of RDN]?

Tips for This Conversation

- Record the name of the representative and request a reference code for the conversation.

- If the insurer states that it does not cover MNT for the given diagnosis, ask the insurance company if it would consider a single case agreement. This can be time consuming, as you need to provide an estimate of needed visits and an assessment and treatment plan.

Making Your Business:
Medicare Advance Beneficiary Notice of Noncoverage (Form CMS-R-131) (03/11)

A. Notifier:

B. Patient Name:

C. Identification Number:

Advance Beneficiary Notice of Noncoverage (ABN)

NOTE: If Medicare doesn't pay for **D.**_____ below, you may have to pay.
Medicare does not pay for everything, even some care that you or your health care provider have
good reason to think you need. We expect Medicare may not pay for the **D.**_____ below.

D.	E. Reason Medicare May Not Pay:	F. Estimated Cost

WHAT YOU NEED TO DO NOW:
- Read this notice, so you can make an informed decision about your care.
- Ask us any questions that you may have after you finish reading.
- Choose an option below about whether to receive the **D.**_____ listed above.
  Note: If you choose Option 1 or 2, we may help you to use any other insurance
  that you might have, but Medicare cannot require us to do this.

G. OPTIONS: Check only one box. We cannot choose a box for you.

☐ **OPTION 1.** I want the **D.**_____ listed above. You may ask to be paid now, but I
also want Medicare billed for an official decision on payment, which is sent to me on a Medicare
Summary Notice (MSN). I understand that if Medicare doesn't pay, I am responsible for
payment, but **I can appeal to Medicare** by following the directions on the MSN. If Medicare
does pay, you will refund any payments I made to you, less co-pays or deductibles.

☐ **OPTION 2.** I want the **D.**_____ listed above, but do not bill Medicare. You may
ask to be paid now as I am responsible for payment. **I cannot appeal if Medicare is not billed**.

☐ **OPTION 3.** I don't want the **D.**_____ listed above. I understand with this choice I
am **not** responsible for payment, and **I cannot appeal to see if Medicare would pay**.

H. Additional Information:

This notice gives our opinion, not an official Medicare decision. If you have other questions on
this notice or Medicare billing, call **1-800-MEDICARE** (1-800-633-4227/**TTY:** 1-877-486-2048).
Signing below means that you have received and understand this notice. You also receive a copy.

I. Signature:	J. Date:

**CMS does not discriminate in its programs and activities. To request this publication in an
alternative format, please call: 1-800-MEDICARE or email: AltFormatRequest@cms.hhs.gov.**

Form CMS-R-131 (Exp. 03/2020)   Form Approved OMB No. 0938-0566

If patients are not covered by insurance, you may need to discuss the advantages and health cost savings they will benefit from by receiving nutrition services. Even without insurance, some patients may decide to see you if they think the services you provide are beneficial.

With time, you will learn all that is required by each third-party payer so the process is not as daunting. You will begin to get a feel for the insurance carriers in your area that reimburse for nutrition services. You will have their websites bookmarked on your computer or their numbers on speed dial to streamline your process.

Other Third-Party Payer Requirements

The plans with which RDNs contract to provide MNT may have other requirements that affect your practice. For example, Medicare and many private insurance plans require the use of protocols. The regulation for the Medicare MNT benefit states that "dietitians and nutritionists would use nationally recognized protocols, such as those developed by the [Academy of Nutrition and Dietetics]."[23] Protocols are available on the Academy of Nutrition and Dietetics online store (www.eatrightSTORE.org) for different diseases and conditions (search for evidence-based guidelines).

Tools for Billing

Once you have determined that an insurance carrier will reimburse you for your services and you have rendered MNT, a claim must be filed. This requires the CMS 1500 Health Insurance Claim form developed by the National Uniform Claim Committee. Commonly referred to as the Form CMS-1500 or the 1500 form, it is used by all third-party payers.

You will need to provide a superbill to patients who self-pay and who seek to be reimbursed by their insurance company. Even if you decide not to accept insurance, you should provide your patients with the necessary forms so they may file a claim for reimbursement.

Diagnosis and Procedure Codes

Both the Form CMS-1500 and superbills use specific alphanumeric identifiers (ICD-10-CM or diagnosis codes) to indicate the diagnosis. These forms also require the Current Procedural Terminology (CPT) code. The CPT code identifies the procedure provided by the RDN. Whether you are directly submitting a claim to a third-party payer or your patient is submitting paperwork to his or her insurance company, this information needs to be specified for you to be reimbursed.

INTERNATIONAL CLASSIFICATION OF DISEASES, CLINICAL MODIFICATIONS, 10TH REVISION

International Classification of Diseases, Clinical Modifications, is the manual that contains a listing of the diagnoses and their assigned alphanumeric codes.

The ICD-10-CM codes, usually referred to as the ICD-10 codes, are used when submitting claims to a third-party payer. The correct diagnosis code(s) must be obtained from the patient's physician, physician assistant, or nurse practitioner. RDNs cannot determine the medical diagnosis; this is not in an RDN's scope of practice. There are many ICD-10 codes to describe a diagnosis. It is the patient's physician or other health care provider who determines the code that most accurately represents the patient's diagnosis or condition. Selecting a medical diagnosis based solely on a client's statement can expose you to claims of insurance fraud.

Always be sure you are using the most recent codes. You can purchase an International Classification of Diseases manual from the American Medical Association (www.ama-assn.org), an online bookstore, or a local bookstore. There are also resources on the internet where you can obtain the ICD-10 codes for free. The Centers for Medicare and Medicaid Services, also referred to as CMS, has a free and easy-to-use ICD-10 Medicare Coverage Database (www.cms.gov/medicare-coverage-database/staticpages/icd-10-code-lookup.aspx). You can conduct your search using either the ICD-10 code or a keyword. The box below lists the ICD-10 codes with the diagnosis commonly seen by RDNs.

International Classification of Diseases, Clinical Modifications, 10th Revision, Codes Commonly Used by Registered Dietitian Nutritionists[a,24]

Diagnosis	ICD-10-CM code[b]
Abnormal weight gain	R63.5
Abnormal weight loss	R63.4
Abnormal glucose (prediabetes)	R73.09
Anemia, unspecified	D64.9
Anorexia nervosa, unspecified	F50.0
Arteriosclerotic heart disorder (ASHD)	I25.10
Asthma, unspecified	J45.909
Bowel, irritable bowel syndrome without diarrhea	K58.9
Bulimia nervosa	F50.2
Celiac disease	K90.0
Cholecystitis, unspecified	K81.9

Diagnosis	ICD-10-CM code[b]
Chronic kidney disease, unspecified	N18.9
Cleft palate with unilateral cleft lip, unspecified	Q37.9
Congestive heart failure, unspecified	I50.9
Constipation, unspecified	K59.00
Crohn's disease, unspecified	K50.90
Cystic fibrosis with pulmonary manifestations	E84.0
Degenerative disc disease, unspecified	M51.9
Degenerative joint disease	M19.90
Diabetes, gestational, unspecified control	O24.419
Diabetes, type 1	E10.9
Diabetes, type 2	E11.9
Diabetes with pregnancy	O24.319
Diabetic nephropathy	E11.21
Diarrhea	R19.7
Diverticulitis	K57.80
Diverticulosis	K57.30
Dysphagia	R13.10
Eating disorder, unspecified	F50.9
Excess weight gain, pregnancy, unspecified trimester	O26.00
Failure to thrive, child	R62.51
Food allergy, dermatitis	L27.2
Gastritis	K29.60
Gastroenteritis	K52.89
Gastroesophageal reflux	K21.9
Gout	M10.9
Human immunodeficiency virus (HIV) disease	B20
Hyperlipidemia	E78.2
Hypertension, essential	I10
Hyperthyroidism	E05.90

(Continued on next page)

International Classification of Diseases, Clinical Modifications, 10th Revision, Codes Commonly Used by Registered Dietitian Nutritionists[a,24]
(continued)

Diagnosis	ICD-10-CM code[b]
Hypoglycemia	E16.2
Hypothyroidism	E03.9
Impaired fasting glucose	R73.01
Irritable bowel syndrome	K58.9
Lactose intolerance	E73.9
Low weight gain, pregnancy	O26.11
Malnutrition	E46
Menopausal disorder	N95.9
Myocardial infarction, old	I25.2
Obesity	E66.9
Obesity, morbid	E66.01
Osteopenia	M85.80
Osteoporosis	M81.8
Overweight	E66.3
Parkinson's disease	G20
Peptic ulcer disease, chronic site unspecified	K27.7
Phenylketonuria (PKU)	E70.0
Postgastric surgery syndrome	K91.1
Pregnant state, incidental	Z33.1
Renal disease	N28.9
Sleep apnea, unspecified	G47.30
Ulcerative colitis	K51.90
Underweight	R63.6
Vitamin deficiency, unspecified	E56.9

[a] Always consult the most up-to-date International Classification of Diseases to confirm the accuracy of all codes. ICD-10 codes can be very specific.

[b] ICD-10 = International Classification of Diseases, Clinical Modifications, 10th Revision

CURRENT PROCEDURAL TERMINOLOGY CODES

CPT codes are the codes used to describe medical services and procedures. The 2017 CPT manual contains specific codes for MNT counseling by RDNs. The box below specifies the CPT codes used by RDNs.[25,26] These codes are used by both Medicare and private insurance companies. The MNT codes are time based. Codes for individual MNT are based on 15-minute increments, and group codes are based on 30-minute increments. They can be billed in multiple units. Keep track of the amount of the face-to-face time you are with the patient to bill accurately. For example, if the initial MNT visit lasts 60 minutes, four units are billed.

In addition to the codes listed in the box below, private insurance companies may accept other CPT codes. Ask if the insurance companies you participate with permit RDNs to use CPT codes in addition to MNT codes. If they do, learn the criteria for the codes and the reimbursement rates to assess the appropriateness for your practice.

Medical Nutrition Therapy Current Procedural Terminology Codes[a,25,26]

- **97802:** Medical Nutrition Therapy (MNT), initial assessment and intervention, individual, face-to-face with the patient, each 15 minutes

- **97803:** Reassessment and intervention, individual, face-to-face with the patient, each 15 minutes

- **97804:** Group (two or more individuals), each 30 minutes

The Centers for Medicare and Medicaid Services requires the use of two MNT codes for billing additional hours of MNT. A Medicare beneficiary can receive MNT beyond the three hours of initial episode of care in the first calendar year and beyond the two hours of follow-up episode of care in each subsequent calendar year when the physician determines that there is a change in diagnosis or medical condition that makes a change in diet necessary. This requires a new referral from the physician.

- **G0270:** MNT reassessment and subsequent intervention(s) following second referral in same year for change in diagnosis, medical condition, or treatment regimen (including additional hours needed for renal disease), individual, face-to-face with the patient, each 15 minutes

- **G0271:** MNT reassessment and subsequent intervention(s) following second referral in same year for change in diagnosis, medical condition, or treatment regimen (including additional hours needed for renal disease) group (2 or more individuals), each 30 minutes.

[a] Current Procedural Terminology codes, descriptions, and material only are copyright ©2017 of the American Medical Association.

Centers for Medicare and Medicaid Services Form CMS-1500

Most insurance carriers only accept a Form CMS-1500 (see the figure below), especially from in-network providers.

Making Your Business: **Blank Centers for Medicare and Medicaid Services Form CMS-1500**

HEALTH INSURANCE CLAIM FORM

APPROVED BY NATIONAL UNIFORM CLAIM COMMITTEE (NUCC) 02/12

PICA | | | PICA

1. MEDICARE MEDICAID TRICARE CHAMPVA GROUP HEALTH PLAN FECA BLK LUNG OTHER   1a. INSURED'S I.D. NUMBER (For Program in Item 1)
  (Medicare#) (Medicaid#) (ID#/DoD#) (Member ID#) (ID#) (ID#)

2. PATIENT'S NAME (Last Name, First Name, Middle Initial)   3. PATIENT'S BIRTH DATE MM DD YY SEX M F   4. INSURED'S NAME (Last Name, First Name, Middle Initial)

5. PATIENT'S ADDRESS (No., Street)   6. PATIENT RELATIONSHIP TO INSURED Self Spouse Child Other   7. INSURED'S ADDRESS (No., Street)

CITY STATE   8. RESERVED FOR NUCC USE   CITY STATE

ZIP CODE TELEPHONE (Include Area Code) ( )   ZIP CODE TELEPHONE (Include Area Code) ( )

9. OTHER INSURED'S NAME (Last Name, First Name, Middle Initial)   10. IS PATIENT'S CONDITION RELATED TO: 11. INSURED'S POLICY GROUP OR FECA NUMBER

a. OTHER INSURED'S POLICY OR GROUP NUMBER   a. EMPLOYMENT? (Current or Previous) YES NO   a. INSURED'S DATE OF BIRTH MM DD YY SEX M F

b. RESERVED FOR NUCC USE   b. AUTO ACCIDENT? YES NO PLACE (State)   b. OTHER CLAIM ID (Designated by NUCC)

c. RESERVED FOR NUCC USE   c. OTHER ACCIDENT? YES NO   c. INSURANCE PLAN NAME OR PROGRAM NAME

d. INSURANCE PLAN NAME OR PROGRAM NAME   10d. CLAIM CODES (Designated by NUCC)   d. IS THERE ANOTHER HEALTH BENEFIT PLAN? YES NO If yes, complete items 9, 9a, and 9d.

READ BACK OF FORM BEFORE COMPLETING & SIGNING THIS FORM.
12. PATIENT'S OR AUTHORIZED PERSON'S SIGNATURE I authorize the release of any medical or other information necessary to process this claim. I also request payment of government benefits either to myself or to the party who accepts assignment below.

SIGNED DATE

13. INSURED'S OR AUTHORIZED PERSON'S SIGNATURE I authorize payment of medical benefits to the undersigned physician or supplier for services described below.

SIGNED

14. DATE OF CURRENT ILLNESS, INJURY, or PREGNANCY (LMP) MM DD YY QUAL.   15. OTHER DATE QUAL. MM DD YY   16. DATES PATIENT UNABLE TO WORK IN CURRENT OCCUPATION FROM MM DD YY TO MM DD YY

17. NAME OF REFERRING PROVIDER OR OTHER SOURCE   17a. 17b. NPI   18. HOSPITALIZATION DATES RELATED TO CURRENT SERVICES FROM MM DD YY TO MM DD YY

19. ADDITIONAL CLAIM INFORMATION (Designated by NUCC)   20. OUTSIDE LAB? YES NO $ CHARGES

21. DIAGNOSIS OR NATURE OF ILLNESS OR INJURY Relate A-L to service line below (24E) ICD Ind.   22. RESUBMISSION CODE ORIGINAL REF. NO.

A. | B. | C. | D. |
E. | F. | G. | H. |
I. | J. | K. | L. |

23. PRIOR AUTHORIZATION NUMBER

24. A. DATE(S) OF SERVICE From To MM DD YY MM DD YY | B. PLACE OF SERVICE | C. EMG | D. PROCEDURES, SERVICES, OR SUPPLIES (Explain Unusual Circumstances) CPT/HCPCS MODIFIER | E. DIAGNOSIS POINTER | F. $ CHARGES | G. DAYS OR UNITS | H. EPSDT Family Plan | I. ID. QUAL. | J. RENDERING PROVIDER ID. #
1 | | | | | | | | | NPI
2 | | | | | | | | | NPI
3 | | | | | | | | | NPI
4 | | | | | | | | | NPI
5 | | | | | | | | | NPI
6 | | | | | | | | | NPI

25. FEDERAL TAX I.D. NUMBER SSN EIN   26. PATIENT'S ACCOUNT NO.   27. ACCEPT ASSIGNMENT? (For govt. claims, see back) YES NO   28. TOTAL CHARGE $ 29. AMOUNT PAID $ 30. Rsvd for NUCC Use

31. SIGNATURE OF PHYSICIAN OR SUPPLIER INCLUDING DEGREES OR CREDENTIALS (I certify that the statements on the reverse apply to this bill and are made a part thereof.)

SIGNED DATE

32. SERVICE FACILITY LOCATION INFORMATION   a. NPI b.

33. BILLING PROVIDER INFO & PH # ( )   a. NPI b.

NUCC Instruction Manual available at: www.nucc.org   PLEASE PRINT OR TYPE   APPROVED OMB-0938-1197 FORM 1500 (02-12)

CARRIER

PATIENT AND INSURED INFORMATION

PHYSICIAN OR SUPPLIER INFORMATION

FORM CMS-1500 ELECTRONIC SUBMISSION

Filing claims electronically is the state of the art. It is the preferred format for claim submission and is the only method of transmission accepted by most third-party payers. There are numerous advantages to submitting forms electronically. It eliminates paper, claim submission is easier, and payment is faster than with paper claims.

There are three options to submit claims electronically:

- Use a billing website or software to submit to all third-party payers.

- Submit forms using individual third-party payers' websites.

- Contract with a billing service or biller to submit the claims on your behalf.

When you submit a claim electronically, it is important to be aware of and abide by Health Insurance Portability and Accountability Act (HIPAA) privacy and security rules. We will discuss each of these three options—along with HIPAA regulations—in more detail in the following sections.

Billing Websites and Software Many RDNs use billing websites to submit claims. They may use a billing website exclusively for billing purposes or as part of their electronic health record (EHR). Some billing websites offer claim submission for free; however, they will most likely charge a separate fee for the EHR to do charting.

The RDN or administrative staff enters all the necessary information for a patient into the software to complete the Form CMS-1500 and submit the claim for processing. Once you have all the patient information entered in the software to complete the Form CMS-1500, it is then easier and less time consuming for patients' subsequent visits. You merely update the date of service and billing information for the date of service and press *Send* to submit the claim. Some websites provide immediate feedback as you complete the form or once it goes to a clearinghouse prior to being sent to the third-party payer. This allows you to learn quickly whether you incorrectly completed the form and need to edit the errors.

With a billing website or software, you may be able to track the status of the claim and post payments. This can enable you to easily print an invoice for any outstanding patient financial responsibility.

Third-Party Payer Websites Individual third party payers, including MACs (for Medicare billing), maintain their own websites for claims submission. This can be the best option if you are an in-network provider with only one or two insurers. Otherwise if you are a provider of multiple insurance carriers, you will spend a lot of time going to each website to submit and track claims.

Billing Services RDNs who prefer not to do their own electronic claims submission can contract with a billing service or biller. Based on an informal survey of RDNs using billers conducted by the authors, the fees can range from a flat fee of $6.00 per claim up to 10% of the collected reimbursement, and some billers may charge a setup fee or monthly fees. For an RDN who plans to handle a multitude of insurance claims, using one of these companies to handle insurance billing can free up time to perform other functions within his or her practice. You will have to weigh the money you would spend for a biller versus the valuable time spent doing it yourself. Keep in mind that you still have to invest time to communicate all the patient's information to the biller to complete the Form CMS-1500, as shown in the box below.

If you are interested in using a billing service, post your inquiry on DPG EMLs for recommendations of billers. They do not have to be in your town or state. You can search the internet or contact local billing service or other health care professionals in your area for billers. You will want references for the billers. Use a biller familiar with MNT codes. The Academy of Nutrition and Dietetics website (www.eatrightPRO.org) has valuable information to consider when selecting a biller.[27,28]

Information to Share When Using a Biller

Patient's name, date of birth, address, and phone number

Copy of the front and back of the insurance card

Date of service, ICD-10[a] code(s), and CPT[b] code(s) with the number of units

Referral information

Patient payments for copayment or deductible

Payments received from the third-party payer

[a] ICD-10 = International Classification of Diseases, Clinical Modifications, 10th Revision
[b] CPT = current procedural terminology

Health Insurance Portability and Accountability Act Information

According to HIPAA, if you are a health care provider who transmits protected health information (PHI) electronically, you are a covered entity. The question you have to ask yourself is *Will I send PHI electronically?* When you submit a claim, it is being processed electronically somewhere along the way, so the answer is YES.[29]

As a covered entity, you must abide by the privacy and security rules of HIPAA. You are required to provide a notice of your privacy practices to all patients and make a good-faith effort to obtain written acknowledgment from patients of their receipt of the notice.[29] Basically, you are informing patients about how you will protect their health information.

The federal government has outlined specific policies and procedures to which covered entities must adhere, such as posting privacy notices and computer access procedures, to comply with HIPAA.[30] Most hospitals or large clinic facilities have a privacy notice that covers all practitioner services provided at that location. However, RDNs in private practice will need to create a personalized privacy notice and patient acknowledgment form to meet the HIPAA requirement. A sample HIPAA privacy notice is shown in the form below and a sample patient written acknowledgment confirming receipt of the privacy notice is shown in the Making Your Business box on the next page.

Making Your Business:
Health Insurance Portability and Accountability Act Sample Notice of Privacy Practices

Notice of Privacy Practices
Effective Date: _____

THIS NOTICE DESCRIBES HOW HEALTH INFORMATION ABOUT YOU MAY BE USED AND DISCLOSED AND HOW YOU CAN GET ACCESS TO THIS INFORMATION. PLEASE REVIEW IT CAREFULLY.
If you have any questions about this notice, please contact:
Provider name
Title
Street address
Town, State, Zip code
Phone number
Email address

OUR LEGAL DUTY:
We are required by applicable federal and state law to maintain the privacy of your health information. We reserve the right to change our privacy. Before we make a significant change in our privacy practices, we will change this Notice and make the new Notice available. You may request a copy of our Notice at any time. For more information about our privacy practices or for additional copies of this Notice, please contact us using the information at the top of this page.
USE AND DISCLOSURE OF HEALTH INFORMATION
Treatment: We may use or disclose your health information to a physician or other healthcare provider providing treatment to you.
Payment for Services: We may use or disclose your health information to obtain payment for services we provide to you.
Healthcare Operations: We may use or disclose your health information in connection with our healthcare operations. Healthcare operations include quality assessment and improvement activities, case management, review the competence or qualification of healthcare professionals, evaluating practitioner and provider performance, conducting training programs, accreditation, certification, licensing and other activities.
Required By Law: We will disclose your health information about you when required to do so by federal, state or local law.
Abuse or Neglect: We may disclose your health information to appropriate authorities if we reasonably believe you are a victim of abuse, neglect or domestic violence or the possible victim of other crimes. We may disclose this type of information to the extent necessary to avert a serious threat to your health or safety or the health or safety of others.
Business Associate: We may disclose information to business associates who perform services on our behalf (such as billing companies;) however, we require them to appropriately safeguard your information.
Appointment Reminders: We may use or disclose your health information to contact you as a reminder (such as voicemail messages, email, postcards, or letters) that you have an appointment for treatment or medical care with [insert provider name].
PATIENT/CLIENT RIGHTS
Access: You have the right to inspect and copy your health information, with limited exceptions. Submit your request in writing to [insert provider name]. A fee will be charged for the costs associated with your request. There are certain situations in which we are not required to comply with your request. In these circumstances, we will respond to you in writing, stating why we will not grant your request and describe any rights you may have to request a review of our denial.
Disclosures Accounting: You have the right to receive a list of instances in which we or our business associates disclosed your health information for purposes, other than treatment, payment, healthcare operations and certain activities, for the last 6 years, but not before [insert date]. If you request an accounting more than once in a 12-month period, you will be charged a reasonable cost-based fee for responding to these requests.
Amendment: You have the right to request that we amend your health information. (Your request must be in writing and it must explain why the information should be amended.) We may deny your request under certain circumstances.
Restrictions: You have the right to request we place additional restrictions on our use of your health information. We are not required to agree to additional restrictions, but if we do, we sill abide by our agreement (except in an emergency).
Alternative Communications: You have the right to request that we communicate with you about medical matters in a certain way or at a certain location. For example, you can ask that we only contact you at work or by mail. To request alternative communications, you must make your request in writing. We will accommodate all reasonable requests.
Right to a Paper Copy of This Notice. You have the right to a paper copy of this Notice at any time by contacting [insert provider name].
QUESTIONS AND COMPLAINTS
If you want more information about our privacy practices or have questions or concerns, please contact us at:
If you are concerned that we may have violated your privacy rights or you disagree with a decision we made about access to your health information or in response to a request you made to amend or restrict the use of disclosure of your health information or to have us communicate with you by alternative means or at alternative locations, you may record your complaint to us by using the contact information at the beginning of this Notice. You also may submit a written complaint to the Secretary of the Department of Health and Human Services. We support your right to the privacy of your health information. If you file a complaint, we will not take any action against you or change our treatment of you in any way. We support your right to the privacy of your health information.

Making Your Business:
Patient Written Acknowledgment Confirming Receipt of Privacy Practices Notice

Receipt of Privacy Practices Notice

Please read the copy of [RDN's name] Notice of Privacy Practices (on the next page).

Your signature with date acknowledges that you have received and read [RDN's name] Notice of Privacy Practices.

Signature: _____

Relationship to patient:_____

Print name: _____

Date: _____

In addition to federal HIPAA guidelines, your state may have laws that protect PHI. Even if you only treat self-pay patients and you are not a covered entity, your state laws for privacy may apply. Generally, the stricter laws for the protection of PHI apply. Additional information on HIPAA is accessible from the members-only section of the Academy of Nutrition and Dietetics website (www.eatrightPRO.org).[31]

CENTER FOR MEDICARE AND MEDICAID SERVICES 1500 PAPER CLAIMS

Paper CMS 1500 claims forms are being phased out. Some third-party payers still use this archaic way to submit claims. Paper Form CMS-1500s can be purchased from some office supply stores or medical office supply catalogs. Third-party payers do not accept scanned or downloaded CMS 1500 paper forms; to be submitted as a paper claim, the form must be an original. The original form is red and will be read electronically. These paper forms can be quite time consuming. Each time you see a patient, you will have to complete the form by hand. This means that for repeat visits, you are rewriting all the information about the patient, you, and the visit. Form CMS-1500s must be properly completed to the specifications of the insurance carrier. Forms that are filled out incorrectly or incompletely will be returned to the provider for completion and resubmission. It may be beneficial to purchase a computer software program that can complete the form and take care of this administrative task. You can search online for this software and post inquiries for recommendations to colleagues on DPG EMLs.

HOW TO COMPLETE A CENTER FOR MEDICARE AND MEDICAID SERVICES 1500 FORM

Using software to complete a Form CMS-1500 can make it easy. The figure below shows an example of a form completed on a billing website for a commercial third-party payer. Use this sample form as a basis for completing the form.

Making Your Business:
Sample Completed Center for Medicare and Medicaid Services 1500 Form

When submitting forms to Medicare, you may have to enter quality measures. Check on the CMS website (www.cms.gov) and the Academy of Nutrition and Dietetics website (www.eatrightPRO.org) for the most up-to-date information on reporting quality measures.

If you will be submitting a paper claim and entering the information by hand, use black ink. The CMS provides detailed information on completing the form.[32] There is a learning curve with manually completing a Form CMS-1500 correctly. When information is incorrect or incomplete, the claim will be denied. You will need to figure out what you did wrong, fix the error, and resubmit.

Be mindful of the time frame for claims submission. Most insurance companies require claims to be submitted within 90 days from the date of service. The time frame for Medicare is 12 months. Check with each third-party payer to be aware of deadlines. It is a good habit to submit claims soon after rendering services to a patient.

Superbills

A superbill is a different type of claim form. This bill can be provided as a receipt when a patient has paid you out of pocket for your services or if the patient plans to seek reimbursement from the insurance company. The RDN completes the form at the end of each visit. The RDN provides the patient with the superbill with the understanding that the insurance company may or may not pay for counseling. This puts the responsibility of collecting reimbursement on the patient. The patient submits the superbill to his or her insurer. Reimbursement for the service will depend on the insurance company and whether the patient has out-of-network benefits. If you are an in-network provider, you cannot submit a superbill.

A superbill must have certain components, as shown in the sample in the figure on the next page. Collect samples of superbills from other health care providers and colleagues. You can pattern yours after these samples. You can create your own superbill using your computer or purchase camera-ready superbills.

Accounting and Reimbursement Issues

Be sure to set up a system to record your accounts receivable. Whether or not you accept third-party payments, you need to track payments and outstanding balances. You should get into the habit of having patients pay you at the end of their visits. This minimizes the amount of billing and paperwork you need to complete for self-pay patients and for co-payments or deductibles with insured patients.

Making Your Business:
Sample Superbill[33]

Medical Nutrition Therapy (MNT) Superbill

Date of Service:		Provider name:
Patient name:		Tax ID#:
Address:		NPI:
Phone:		License #:
DOB:		
Referring Provider Name:		Referring provider NPI:

Diagnoses

✓	ICD-10	ICD-10 Description	✓	ICD-10	ICD-10 Description

Office Procedure

✓	CPT Code/Description	Units	Fee

Total Charge	
Amount Paid	
Balance Due	

RDN Name:_____

RDN Signature: _____

Information to Include to Track Payments

Date of service

Patient name (as it appears on the insurance card)

Patient date of birth

Third-party payer or self-pay

Patient identification number for third-party payer

Referral number, if required

CPT[a] code and number of units

ICD-10[b] codes

Fee for services rendered

Copayment or other payments made, including the date

Date(s) billed to patient and/or third-party payer

Communications from third-party payers

[a] ICD-10 = International Classification of Diseases, Clinical Modifications, 10th Revision
[b] CPT = current procedural terminology

Tracking Claims and Payments

Tracking claims you submit to third-party payers is more involved. You will have more paperwork. Using a billing website or software will streamline the process. Most EHRs have a billing feature that, in addition to submitting claims, can track payments and generate invoices. Whatever you choose, develop a system or routine that makes the task easier. The box here provides criteria to include when setting up a form to track monies owed to you by both self-pay patients and insurance providers. You can create a form in a spreadsheet or table using the standard software programs on your computer.

The figure below shows an example of a spreadsheet to track payments monthly. You can also monitor payments by date of service, by third-party payers, or by whatever will work best for you.

Making Your Business: Sample Spreadsheet for Tracking Payments

Date of Birth	Payee	ID #	Referral #	CPT/units	ICD-10	Billed	Insurance Paid	Ins. Date paid	Copay/ Pt Paid	Date	Communication from 3rd Party payer	Comments
8/1/1967	BCBS	ABC12345		97803/4	E11.9	$XXX.00	$YZK.BY	2/3/16				
6/1/1938	Medicare	123456789A		97803/4	E11.65	$XXX.00	$YKZ.FJ	1/26/16				
10/10/1978	UHC	9876543	123487	97803/4	E11.9	$XXX.00	$YQN.YK	2/18/16				
3/21/1944	Medicare	987654321A		97803/4	N18.9	$XXX.00	$YZK.BY	2/25/16				
7/6/1983	BCBS	DEF23456		97802/5	E10.9	$AAA.00	$YXZ.JK	2/4/16				
12/15/1967	Aetna	W123456		97802/5	F50.0	$AAA.00	$RT.BH	1/29/16	$CC.00	2/16/16		
5/26/1952	Medicare	876543219A		97802/4	K90.0	$XXX.00						ABN signed. Patient owes $XXX.00
2/17/1999	Self-pay			97803/4	F50.9	$XXX.00			1/6/16	$XXX.00		
4/15/1959	BCBS	GHI34567		97803/4	E11.65	$XXX.00	$YYY.YY	2/3/16				
TOTALS	-						$TYZX.RZ		$XRR.00	$TYYZ.RZ		

Reprinted with permission from Ann Silver.

How Will You Get Paid?

Getting paid is an important part of your private practice. You can receive payments from a third-party payer, from a patient, or from both depending on the practice model you choose. It is easiest when the payment process goes smoothly, but if you have trouble getting paid, you want to be prepared for the next step.

THIRD-PARTY PAYMENTS

After completing and submitting the Form CMS-1500, follow up on every claim you submit. You will receive an EOB from private insurers and an Explanation of Medicare Benefits (EOMB) from Medicare in response to your claim. This can be a paper statement but will most likely be communicated electronically. If you do not receive a response to your claim submission within 45 days, resubmit the claim. Keep in mind that there is a shorter time limit on claims submission with private insurance companies than with Medicare.

Review the EOB or EOMB. Determine whether the claim was paid and how much. If the claim was paid, GREAT! You are making money. Your payment may be deposited directly into your checking account by electronic funds transfer (EFT). EFT can be arranged once you are approved as an in-network provider. Otherwise, you will receive a check in the mail.

Denied Claims Denied claims can produce a lot of angst. It goes with the territory. If the claim was denied, you need to find out why. The EOB will specify the reason for the denial.

Most likely, there was an error or omission of information. Once you make the correction, resubmit the claim.

The EOB description for the denial can be vague or use unfamiliar terminology, and you might not understand why the claim was denied. You will have to pursue it. Contact the third-party payer for assistance. Ask colleagues, such as your state reimbursement representatives with more third-party payment experience, for help. Do not accept *no* as the answer if you believe that the claim should have been paid. You can also enlist the assistance of the patient to help get the claim paid. Teach patients to advocate for themselves.

PATIENT PAYMENTS

It is important to establish the routine of collecting payment for each patient visit. This way, you will not have to bill the patient and limit your accounts receivable.

There are different ways you can receive payment from a patient, as discussed in chapter 3. You can receive payment from cash, checks, credit cards, or debit cards. Sometimes the patient may play a role in deciding how he or she will pay you, but in the long run, you just need to ensure that you are getting paid.

Accepting credit cards and debit cards makes it easier to get paid. In addition to debit cards issued by a bank, there are debit cards for health savings accounts (HSAs) and flexible spending accounts (FSAs). HSA and FSA debit cards are processed like other debit cards. These accounts are funded by pretax monies set aside for an individual to use for specific medical expenses, including copayments, deductibles, and even paying an RDN for MNT.[34] Refer to chapter 3 for additional information on credit and debit cards.

Changing Your Payment Model

Do not think that the payment option you start your practice with is the one you must have forever. As your practice evolves, who pays you may change. There may be different reasons why you may want to only accept self-pay patients into your practice or why you may want to begin accepting third-party payments. The Words of Wisdom box below shares the story of an RDN who transitioned from accepting third-party payments to accepting self-pay patients only.

Words of Wisdom

One Registered Dietitian Nutritionist Discusses Changing Her Payment Model

Bonnie R. Giller, MS, RD, CDN, CDE
of BRG Dietetics & Nutrition, P.C., www.brghealth.com

It was November 2011. I woke up and realized I dreaded going to work that morning. I had been in private practice for 25 years at that point, and while I loved my work during most of that time, the last two years were taking their toll on me.

I was a provider for 10 insurance companies. I learned the policies and procedures of each company, I knew the ins and outs of the coding system, and I was helping other dietitians work through the insurance challenges they were having. And, while each insurance company did have a different fee schedule, I still made a very nice income.

Then, health care took a turn and the fee schedules changed. I found myself working longer hours and seeing more patients to earn the same income. What I also noticed was [that] the quality of my patients changed. With zero copay under preventive medicine benefits, they had less motivation to commit to the work we were doing together. I was no longer enjoying my work.

I decided to slowly discontinue my participation with each insurance company, one at a time. I contacted provider relations to discontinue my participation. There was a waiting period until it took effect. I did not drop all insurance companies at one time. I did this over the course of one-and-a-half years. I sent a letter to all patients informing them of my status change and offered to continue seeing them at my out-of-pocket rate.

My next step was to hire a business coach to help me increase the number of self-pay clients and patients that I had. I created programs that I started offering to potential clients so that I could move away from the "pay-per-hour model."

The Future of Insurance Reimbursement

What is on the horizon for RDNs who accept third-party reimbursement? Change. What is the change? The change is a new paradigm for reimbursement and improvement of the quality of care delivered. Having a basic understanding of these paradigms will guide you in your future.

Third-party reimbursement, as discussed earlier in this chapter, has traditionally been paid on a fee-for-service (FFS) basis. FFS is a payment model in which the patient receives a service, such as an office visit, a blood test, or a procedure, and payment is made for the individual service. This system can encourage providers to render more patient visits and treatments because payment is based solely on the quantity of care. FFS is contributing to the soaring health care costs in the United States and does not address or guarantee quality of care. In 2007, to target this inequality, the Institute for Health Improvement developed the Triple Aim. The three goals of the Triple Aim are to[35]:

- improve the patient care experience,

- improve the health of a population, and

- reduce per-capita health care costs.

Health care organizations such as third-party payers, hospitals, and medical practices are restructuring to comply with the Triple Aim goals.

Following the theme of the Triple Aim to improve quality of care while reducing the cost of health care in the United States was the passage of the Patient Protection and Affordable Care Act (PPACA) in 2010.[36] As a result of the Triple Aim and the PPACA, new health care delivery and payment systems have emerged and continue to appear from the CMS and the private sector. Patient-Centered Medical Homes (PCMHs) and accountable care organizations (ACOs) are two examples of new health care delivery systems with similar goals.[36,37]

PCMHs are not new. The concept of a "medical home" was first developed in 1967, with the pediatrician and his or her practice responsible for providing coordinated and comprehensive care to children with special needs.[38] In recent years, the philosophy has been adopted and has evolved into the PCMH health care delivery model recognized by third-party payers and professional health organizations. Using the primary care setting as ground zero, the goal of PCMHs is for primary care physicians and their teams, which can include RDNs, to provide comprehensive and coordinated care for each patient to improve the quality of care while decreasing costs.

ACOs, as defined by Medicare, are groups of health care providers such as RDNs coming together to jointly provide coordinated high-quality care to their patients, especially those with a long-term illness, to reduce costs.[39] The groups can be doctors, primary care practices that are PCMHs, hospitals, other health care providers, insurance companies, and nonprofit organizations.[37]

Reimbursement for PCMHs and ACOs is based on alternative payment models that account for quality of care, patient outcomes, patient satisfaction, and reduction of costs. These alternative payment models can include FFS but with other financial incentives to improve value.

The CMS has also been transitioning Medicare's payment from one based on FFS to one based on quality. Medicare RDNs have been reporting quality measures using the Physician Quality Reporting System (PQRS).[40]

As Medicare continues to reform payment to their providers, the Medicare Access and Chip Reauthorization Act of 2015 has implemented a new quality payment program. One of the programs that will most likely apply to RDNs is the Merit-based Incentive Payment System (MIPS).[41] The MIPS combines Medicare's numerous existing quality programs, including PQRS, into one. The new quality program is based on four components:

- quality;
- resource use;
- clinical practice improvement activities; and
- advancing care information.

These four weighted components become the basis for a provider's composite score on a scale of 0 to 100. Based on the MIPS score, providers will receive an increase or decrease or no adjustment in their annual payment. RDNs are forecasted to join the ranks of MIPS-eligible clinicians by about 2019.

What Can Registered Dietitian Nutritionists Do to Prepare for the Future?

First, you may be wondering if this will affect you in the future. It will, especially if you accept reimbursement. With the spotlight of this new paradigm being patient centered, RDNs can play a pivotal role. RDNs prevent and treat diseases and conditions through MNT. MNT has a health benefit and is a cost-saving measure.[42] This is consistent with the focus of the new health care and payment models. RDNs who can demonstrate that they can improve health while saving money will be integral and valued members of health care teams.

While these new programs are in the planning stages, RDNs need to "pull a chair up to the table" and express how they are essential to improving health care and decreasing health care dollars. What should you do? Become knowledgeable about these evolving and new programs. Read articles from the Academy of Nutrition and Dietetics, attend meetings, and listen to webinars about the changes in reimbursement. Get involved. The box below offers a look at some things RDNs can expect for the future.

Words of Wisdom

The Future of Reimbursement

Marsha Schofield, MS, RD, LD, FAND, Senior Director of Governance and Nutrition Services Coverage at the Academy of Nutrition and Dietetics

How will the changes in the future of reimbursement affect private-practice registered dietitian nutritionists (RDNs) who accept third-party payers?

Private practice RDNs will still be able to contract as in-network providers with third-party payers. Reimbursement will move toward value-based

(Continued on next page)

Words of Wisdom (continued)

payments that are built on a fee-for-service architecture. RDNs may be held more accountable for patient outcomes with payment based on quality and cost. [There will be a] continuing shift to community-based care so that third-party payers may cover services where people work, live, eat, and pray. The idea being: Go to where the patient is to make it convenient. This can include third-party payers expanding coverage for telehealth services.

Will these RDNs become employees of accountable care organizations (ACOs), Patient-Centered Medical Homes (PCMHs), or other new similar programs, or can they remain in private practice?

[Although] some ACOs, PCMHs, and similar-type programs will want to employ RDNs, others will be happy to use contractors, such as RDNs in private practice. Team-based care can be "virtual," meaning everyone does not need to work within the same four walls and be receiving a paycheck. Opportunities will be there for RDNs to be their own business owners, and what that looks like is only limited by one's creativity and vision. RDNs will need to be open to new business models, especially with primary care providers. And they will need to be able to talk the "value proposition" in language the stakeholders will understand.

RDNs have a great skill set that is underutilized in health care because RDNs themselves, as well as others, put them in a box, meaning we are seen as only doing medical nutrition therapy. RDNs need to and can do much more than that, and others have to recognize that fact. RDNs [should] step up their game and be willing to do things like nutrition-focused physical exams, case/care management, quality improvement/outcomes tracking/data management, and other higher-level functions—maybe even get a practice doctorate. And RDNs may need to restructure their sessions with clients to be able to see more patients in a day. Shorter, more focused, person-centered counseling sessions may be the new norm.

Billing Options: A Summary

Before you start a private practice, you have many business decisions to make. If making all these decisions seems overwhelming, consider seeking the advice of professionals, such as accountants, business advisers, or other RDNs. Some private-practice RDNs and RDN career coaches are available to mentor entrepreneurs on a consulting basis. Remember, they too must be paid for their professional services. Budget accordingly, and seek professional advice when necessary (see chapter 2 for more on selecting advisers). Additionally, keep the following points in mind:

- Deciding to accept third-party payments or only self-pay patients is a decision you will have to make. You can always change your payment model as your practice evolves.

- Some RDNs are strictly paid by their patients and do not accept third-party payments. They inform patients that payment is due at the time of their visit. Other RDNs are reimbursed for MNT by private insurance plans, Medicare, Medicaid, and CHIP.

- RDNs should use a superbill when receiving payment from self-pay patients. If an RDN is filing insurance claims, a Form CMS-1500 must be used. Up-to-date ICD and CPT codes are required for successful claims processing.

- Keep current with changes in reimbursement as new programs develop.

References

1. Leonard K. Doctors, hospitals say 'no' to Obamacare plans. US News website. November 14, 2015. www.usnews.com/news/articles/2015/11/04/doctors -hospitals-wont-accept-obamacare-marketplace-plans. Accessed May 10, 2017.

2. MNT: cost effectiveness, cost-benefit or economic savings of MNT (2009). Evidence Analysis Library website. www.andeal.org/topic.cfm?cat=4085 &evidence_summary_id=250816&highlight=mnt%27&home=1. Accessed May 10, 2017.

3. MNT Medicare Provider. Chicago, IL: Academy of Nutrition and Dietetics; 2004.

4. Price fixing. Federal Trade Commission website. www.ftc.gov/tips-advice /competition-guidance/guide-antitrust-laws/dealings-competitors/price -fixing. Accessed May 10, 2017.

5. Setting Fees. Smart Business Practice and Management. eatrightPRO website. www.eatrightPRO.org/resources/practice/getting-paid/smart-business -practice-and-management. Accessed May 22, 2017.

6. Academy of Nutrition and Dietetics. Compensation & Benefits Survey of the Dietetics Profession 2015 (Downloadable). www.eatrightSTORE.org/product /B2112E17-FF41-418C-8208-27539D3E5C0F. Published 2016. Accessed June 6, 2016.

7. Glossary. Centers for Medicare & Medicaid Services website. www.healthcare .gov/glossary/. Accessed June 17, 2016.

8. Academy of Nutrition and Dietetics. Coding and billing handbook: a guide for program directors and preceptors. www.eatrightSTORE.org/product/72D93968 -26F0-44BB-AE78-C9D2AD2C8ABD. Published 2015. Accessed April 15, 2017.

9. Conway P. Continuing the shift from volume to results in American healthcare. The CMS Blog website. https://blog.cms.gov/continuing-the-shift -from-volume-to-results-in-american-healthcare/. Accessed May 10, 2017.

10. Academy of Nutrition and Dietetics. The two Ps of healthcare: provision and payment. *MNT Provider*. 2015;14(5):1,4. www.eatrightPRO.org/~/media/eatright PRO%20files/news%20center/in%20practice/mntprovider/mntprovider -october2015.ashx Accessed April 15, 2017.

11. RDN considerations for participating in the Medicare program. eatrightPRO website. www.eatrightPRO.org/resource/practice/getting-paid/smart -business-practice-and-management/rdn-considerations-for-participating. Accessed May 10, 2017.

12. Opt out affidavits. Centers for Medicare & Medicaid Services website. www.cms.gov/Medicare/Provider-Enrollment-and-Certification/Medicare ProviderSupEnroll/OptOutAffidavits.html. Accessed May 10, 2017.

13. Centers for Medicare & Medicaid Services website. www.medicaid.gov. Accessed May 10, 2017.

14. Children's Health Insurance Program (CHIP). Centers for Medicare & Medicaid Services. www.medicaid.gov/chip/chip-program-information.html. Accessed May 10, 2017.

15. CAM and discount programs for nutrition services. eatrightPRO website. www.eatrightPRO.org/resource/practice/getting-paid/who-pays-for -nutrition-services/cam-and-discount-programs-for-nutrition-services Accessed April 15, 2017.

16. Medicare enrollment application: physicians and non-physician practitioners (CMS-855I). Centers for Medicare & Medicaid Services website. www.cms.gov /Medicare/CMS-Forms/CMS-Forms/Downloads/cms855i.pdf. Accessed May 10, 2017.

17. Quick reference new Medicare provider. Centers for Medicare & Medicaid Services website. www.cms.gov/Outreach-and-Education/Medicare-Learning-Network -MLN/MLNProducts/downloads/Quick_Reference_New_Provider.pdf. Accessed May 10, 2017.

18. Medicare Provider Enrollment, Chain, and Ownership System (PECOS). Centers for Medicare & Medicaid Services website. https://pecos.cms.hhs.gov. Accessed May 10, 2017.

19. What is a MAC? Centers for Medicare & Medicaid Services website. www.cms .gov/Medicare/Medicare-Contracting/Medicare-Administrative-Contractors /What-is-a-MAC.html. Accessed May 10, 2017.

20. Who are the MACs? Centers for Medicare & Medicaid Services website. www.cms.gov/Medicare/Medicare-Contracting/Medicare-Administrative -Contractors/Who-are-the-MACs.html. Accessed May 10, 2017.

21. Additional clarification for medical nutrition therapy (MNT) services. Centers for Medicare & Medicaid Services website. www.cms.gov/Regulations-and -Guidance/Guidance/Transmittals/downloads/AB02059.pdf. Accessed May 10, 2017.

22. Advanced Beneficiary Notice of noncoverage tutorial. Centers for Medicare & Medicaid Services website. www.cms.gov/Outreach-and-Education/Medicare -Learning-Network-MLN/MLNProducts/ABN-Tutorial/formCMSR131tutorial 111915f.html. Accessed May 10, 2017.

23. Decision memo for medical nutrition therapy benefit for diabetes & ESRD. Centers for Medicare & Medicaid Services website. www.cms.gov/medicare -coverage-database/details/nca-decision-memo.aspx?NCAId=53&ver=8&view AMA=Y&bc=AAAAAAAAIAAA&. Accessed May 10, 2017.

24. Medicare Coverage database. Center for Medicare & Medicaid Services website. www.cms.gov/medicare-coverage-database/staticpages/icd-10-code-lookup .aspx. Accessed July 1, 2016.

25. Medical nutrition therapy services for beneficiaries with diabetes or renal disease. Centers for Medicare & Medicaid Services website. www.cms.gov /Regulations-and-Guidance/Guidance/Transmittals/downloads/B0148.pdf. Accessed May 10, 2017.

26. Clarification regarding non-physician practitioners billing on behalf of a diabetes outpatient self-management training services (DSMT) program and the common working file edits for DSMT & medical nutrition therapy (MNT). Centers for Medicare & Medicaid Services website. www.cms.gov/Regulations -and-Guidance/Guidance/Transmittals/downloads/AB02151.pdf. Accessed May 10, 2017.

27. Factors to consider when selecting a professional billing service. eatrightPRO website. www.eatrightPRO.org/resource/practice/getting-paid/nuts-and -bolts-of-getting-paid/selecting-a-professional-billing-service. Accessed May 10, 2017.

28. Billing: vendors and services. eatrightPRO website. www.eatrightPRO.org /resource/practice/getting-paid/nuts-and-bolts-of-getting-paid/billing -resources#Vendors. Accessed May 10, 2017.

29. Covered entities and business associates. US Department of Health and Human Services website. www.hhs.gov/hipaa/for-professionals/covered -entities/index.html. Accessed May 10, 2017.

30. HIPAA basics for providers: privacy, security, and breach notification rules. Centers for Medicare & Medicaid Services website. www.cms.gov/Outreach -and-Education/Medicare-Learning-Network-MLN/MLNProducts/Downloads /HIPAAPrivacyandSecurity.pdf. Accessed June 24, 2016.

31. HIPAA and Registered Dietitian Nutritionists. eatrightPRO website. www.eatrightPRO.org/resource/practice/getting-paid/smart-business -practice-and-management/hipaa-requirements. Accessed April 15, 2017.

32. Medicare claims processing manual: chapter 26—completing and processing form CMS-1500 data set. Rev. 10-28-16. Centers for Medicare & Medicaid Services website. www.cms.gov/Regulations-and-Guidance/Guidance /Manuals/downloads/clm104c26.pdf. Accessed May 10, 2017.

33. Superbill for MNT services. eatrightPRO website. www.eatrightSTORE.org/ product /6511E8CF-B27A-44C0-9E60-FA6D45C268AC. Accessed December 4, 2016.

34. Norris L. What is the difference between a medical FSA and an HSA? January 16, 2017. www.healthinsurance.org/faqs/what-is-the-difference-between-a -medical-fsa-and-an-hsa/. Accessed May 10, 2017.

35. Case J. A primer on defining the Triple Aim. October 17, 2014. Institute for Healthcare Improvement website. www.ihi.org/communities/blogs/_layouts /ihi/community/blog/itemview.aspx?List=81ca4a47-4ccd-4e9e-89d9-14d88ec 59e8d&ID=63. Accessed May 10, 2017.

36. Boyce B. Emerging paradigms in dietetics practice and health care: patient-centered medical homes and accountable care organizations. *J Acad Nutr Diet*. 2015;115(11):1765-1770.

37. Jortberg BT, Fleming MO. Registered dietitian nutritionists bring value to emerging health care delivery models. *J Acad Nutr Diet*. 2014;114(12):2017-2022.

38. Lipscomb R. Understanding the patient-centered medical home. *J Am Diet Assoc*. 2009;109(9):1507-1508.

39. Accountable care organizations (ACO). Centers for Medicare & Medicaid Services website. www.cms.gov/Medicare/Medicare-Fee-for-Service -Payment/ACO/index.html?redirect=/Aco/. Accessed May 10, 2017.

40. Medicare Physician Quality Reporting System (PQRS). Evidence Analysis Library website. www.eatrightPRO.org/resource/practice/getting-paid/nuts -and-bolts-of-getting-paid/medicare-physician-quality-reporting-system. Accessed May 10, 2017.

41. MACRA: Delivery system reform, Medicare payment reform. Centers for Medicare & Medicaid Services website. www.cms.gov/Medicare/Quality -Initiatives-Patient-Assessment-Instruments/Value-Based-Programs/MACRA -MIPS-and-APMs/MACRA-MIPS-and-APMs.html. Accessed May 10, 2017.

42. What is the evidence to support the cost-effectiveness, cost benefit or economic savings of outpatient MNT services provided by an RDN? Academy of Nutrition and Dietetics Evidence Analysis Library. www.andeal.org/topic .cfm?cat=4085&evidence_summary_id=250816&highlight=mnt&home=1. Accessed May 10, 2017.

8 | Marketing: Getting the Word Out

You've decided on your office location (whether home, private office, or virtual), your website is live, you know how you're going to bill patients, and you obtained a new phone number. So what's the next step? You need to begin working on your marketing plan. Your marketing plan is the way you will bring new clients or patients into your office. A solid plan will help build your practice and grow your brand.[1] You want people to remember you and what you do. Be creative and unique. As your practice develops and grows, you must regularly review the effectiveness of your plan and adjust it as needed. From time to time, you will need to revise and modify it to ensure that it is bringing in new clients.

There are numerous ways to market your practice. Your plan will be specific to you. Use a combination of marketing efforts. Don't simply try one method and wait to see if your phone rings. Use different approaches to find clients or patients. Ask new clients how they came to you. Have a Referral Source section listed on your registration form. You can track the information on a spreadsheet to determine what is working and not working for you. Modify or discontinue those marketing efforts that are ineffective. Almost everything you do that is related to your practice should promote your business.

This chapter focuses on specific marketing strategies for building a successful private practice. There are several important components to consider when marketing your practice, including developing your referral sources, determining the right tools to help reach your target market, and using technology to market your services. You are going to create a fabulous private practice—you just have to let everybody out there know!

Initial Office Contact

A phone call to your office is often someone's first contact with your practice, so if her or she has not seen you before, it is often your first chance to promote yourself. What is the caller's experience when calling your office? Will he or she speak with a person or hear a voice mail message? Is the voice representing your office business-like and harried, or is it friendly and professional? Ask friends or family members for feedback about their experiences when calling your office or designated work phone number. You may obtain valuable suggestions.

Prospective patients and referral sources call your office because they are interested in your services. You want to capture that interest. Make the telephone exchange as pleasant and welcoming as possible. This can be your first (and possibly only) chance to make the "sale." When you are unavailable and a caller leaves a voice mail message, call back by the end of the day or within 24 hours. Also leave the URL for your website on your voice mail, and let prospective clients know they can find more information about your practice there. You can also link up with a service, such as Zocdoc or Healthie, that allows patients to book appointments on your website.

You may receive emails inquiring about your practice or to schedule an appointment. Check your email frequently throughout the day. Reply to email messages in a timely fashion. The amount of time it takes you to respond to phone calls or emails may make or break someone's decision to use your services. Delays can be lost business.

Other examples of promoting you and your practice include your business cards, your website, and advertisements. Always carry your business cards with you; you may find opportunities to distribute them at social events, at the gym, and even while out shopping. Store your business cards in a variety of places so you are always prepared. You will be pleasantly surprised how often people will request your card once they learn what you do.

Whenever you can, direct people to your website. Your website is quite often the first introduction clients have to you, your philosophy, and your services. Your website describes you and the services you provide. Make sure that it aligns with how you want to portray yourself to prospective clients. To get clients to visit your site, display your website address (URL) wherever you can. Make sure that it's on your business card, email signature, social media profiles, letterhead, and anywhere else you can list it. Have your URL on your voice mail so prospective clients can find out more about you and your services. You should also add it to your social media accounts.

Make sure your practice is listed on the internet. Do a Google and Yahoo search and see where—or if—you show up. If you are low on the list of dietitians and nutritionists, consider investing in search engine optimization (SEO), which can help bring you higher up on the list when a prospective patient is searching for your services online. Quite often you can obtain this service through your website developer or hosting company. Many people look online to find nutrition services. You can advertise in local newspapers. However, make sure your ads will be worth the money you spend. These can be costly and not worth the rate of return. Consider placing a display ad or even an image of your business card in newsletters, directories for schools and places of worship, or any other publication in which you can promote your practice. But remember that you need to advertise regularly, as a one-time ad will rarely get you clients.

Getting Referrals: Who Are Your Sources?

A steady flow of referrals from a variety of sources can keep your practice busy. Ask for referrals from people you already know, and invest time and resources in building new contacts. As you begin your search for potential referral sources, start with those who know you and the quality of your work. For example, reach out to physicians, physician assistants, nurse practitioners, mental health specialists, and other health care professionals from prior work settings. These potential referrals are easy to tap. Let them know that you are in private practice and ready to help their clients and patients. They may even refer your services to their colleagues. Think of this as "word of mouth" among professionals.

Referrals from Local Health Care Providers

Do an online search to develop a list of health care professionals near you who could provide referrals. As they will not be familiar with you or the quality of your counseling, it may take some time for them to feel comfortable referring clients to you. They may need to hear about you from a variety of sources. This may include satisfied clients.

There are no absolutes about how to market your services to health care professionals. You can begin by sending a letter of introduction, including a brief description of your practice and how your services will benefit their patients. You may want to include your curriculum vitae or resume. In the letter, offer to meet the health care professional or his or her office manager. Include some business cards. Keep the letter brief and to the point. Follow up with a phone call. If you can contact an office manager for a health care practice, requesting a time when you can speak to the entire staff can be very beneficial. If it is a small practice (eg, a few physicians and a nurse), offering to cater a light lunch can bring huge rewards. Pharmaceutical reps do this all the time. It can be a business deduction and a worthwhile investment for your practice.

Referrals from Insurance Providers

If you accept insurance, insurance providers can be another source of referrals. Your practice information will be listed as an in-network provider on their website. They will also give out your name when a member calls who is seeking the help of a registered dietitian nutritionist (RDN) in your locale. To limit out-of-pocket expenses, people with health insurance will most likely seek the services of an RDN who accepts their insurance. Be aware that some people may have out-of-network benefits and may still be able to see you even if you aren't an insurance provider.

Referrals from Other Registered Dietitian Nutritionists

Network with colleagues in your area. Remember, fellow RDNs in private practice are your colleagues and friends, not your foes. These RDNs, even those in the same town, can be assets if you handle the situation appropriately. Their target market might be a different population, or you may refer patients to each other when one practice accepts a type of third-party payment and the other does not. When you are on vacation, they can cover for you and vice versa. Build bridges; don't burn them. Working together can bring many rewards.

Referrals for Telehealth

Working in telehealth is a great way for RDNs to help people stay well and prevent disease without patients having to come to your office. And instead of having patients come to you for one-on-one counseling, you can host webinars, cooking classes, and nutrition classes in a virtual group format. You can build up your practice by attracting clients to your services. How do you get clients in a virtual world? You need to know who your ideal client is. What types of people do you want to work with? Do you want to work with millennials, busy professionals, pregnant women, senior citizens?

You need to know who you want to help, and you have to give them what they are looking for. It helps to have a strong presence on social media. Are you on Facebook, Twitter, and Instagram? If you want to work with busy professionals, are you on LinkedIn? Be active on the platforms where your ideal clients are. Let your followers know that you offer virtual services. When you create new programs, advertise them on your social media platforms. Do you have a blog? Blogs are very important for growing your virtual practice. When a prospective client is checking a search engine to find help with an issue, your blog may appear. Make sure you tag and categorize your blog posts appropriately so they show up on search engines. Let your blog readers know that you can help them virtually. Video is also very important. Become active on YouTube so people can find you. Email marketing is another important tactic. Draw people to your website and ask them to sign up for your mailing list for your weekly newsletter or blog. Include your new programs in your website, blog, email signature, and videos. Make your online presence known so you will be at the top of people's minds when they decide they want to work with an RDN.

See the Words of Wisdom box below for more tips on getting referrals from two RDNs.

Words of Wisdom

Tips for Getting More Referrals

Felicia Stoler, DCN, MS, RDN, FACSM, FAND

Promote yourself online and in local papers and collaborate with local businesses.

Make referral pads—just like other specialists. This is an easy way for other health care professionals to "refer" a patient to you—it seems official (and it is). Make sure all your contact information is on the referral sheet.

Take a few hours a month to network with other health care professionals—whether you drop off cards, brochures, or referral pads, go meet other professionals (or their office staff). This makes a HUGE difference!

Be the best, most caring professional you can be because the best referrals come from word of mouth!

Maria Bella, MS, RD, CDN

Aim for top-of-mind marketing: Referrals come to those who first come to mind. It helps to send consult notes immediately after appointments and include a few business cards with each letter. You can also mail out holiday cards and provide a regular newsletter.

Provide quality care. It sounds simple, but you never want to have patients go back to physicians and complain about subpar care. Physicians also want to receive a consult note explaining what happened during the appointment—is the patient motivated to make lifestyle changes? What are your recommendations?

Find your niche. If you are the only pediatric gastrointestinal dietitian in your area, getting all of the referrals to come to you will not be a problem.

Maintaining Referral Sources

Once you have established a referral source, you want to keep and maintain it. To expedite the process for busy medical offices, provide them with a preprinted pad with tear-off pages to complete when referring patients.

Acknowledge your gratitude for the referral. To a referring physician, a follow-up letter regarding the patient is an excellent form of ongoing marketing (see an example in the Making Your Business box below). In this letter, explain the nutrition services provided to the referring physician's patients and include business cards. (Note: You must have your patients sign a release to allow you to send a follow-up letter. You can ask them to do this during their first visit. Refer to chapter 6 for a sample patient release form.)

Another way to promote your practice and thank those who refer patients to you is to send a holiday gift or other gift during the year (think March for RDN Month!). A subscription for a health or cooking magazine is a gift that lasts all year and is an ongoing reminder of you. Health-related books and cookbooks also make great gifts for other health professionals.

Making Your Business:
Sample Physician Follow-Up Letter

[Date]

[Physician's name and address]

Re: [Patient Name]

Date of birth: [Patient date of birth]

Dear [Physician Name]:

Thank you for referring [Patient Name] for medical nutrition therapy for [diagnosis]. [Patient name] came to see me on [appointment date] for an initial consultation.

[Patient Name] is [height in feet and inches] tall and weighs [weight in pounds]. [His or her] body mass index (BMI) is [number].

A complete nutrition assessment indicated that [description of findings].

I reviewed my findings with [name of colleague], and together we established strategies to achieve [his or her] goals for [Patient Name].

A follow-up appointment has been scheduled for [date].

Thank you again for referring [Patient Name]. Your referrals are always appreciated.

Regards,

[Your name], RDN

Marketing Directly to Patients and Clients

In addition to physician referrals, you will want to market directly to potential patients and clients. Start by thinking about who your clients or patients will be. Do they belong to a particular age group or do they have a specific diagnosis, such as diabetes? Once you have identified the population you want to concentrate on (read more about determining your target market in chapter 4), learn everything you can about these potential patients or clients. Understanding all aspects of the population you wish to target will assist you in marketing to them. What are the demographics of this group? What are their socioeconomic backgrounds? Where do they go for medical services? For example, if you want to specialize in pediatrics, your marketing plan will be more directed to parents but will appeal to children, pediatricians, and family practitioners.

What will you call the people who receive your services: clients or patients? These terms can affect your marketing and signal to individuals whether you are the right nutrition professional for them. You may choose to use clients if your practice is wellness based or specializes in eating disorders. *Patients* is the preferable term for RDNs who provide medical nutrition therapy (MNT).

People need to hear your name repeatedly from a variety of sources to believe that you are reputable and that they can trust you.[1,2] Remember that before a prospective patient finally calls you for an appointment, he or she may find your listing in a Google search, review your website, listen to your presentation at the local library, or hear about you from a physician or from a neighbor.

Clients and patients may go to online patient referral directories, such as HealthProfs and Zocdoc, to find a nutrition professional. Listing your practice with these directories can be helpful. Perform an internet search to find these directories. Some are free; others charge a fee annually or monthly for a listing. Before paying a fee to include your practice in a directory, make sure it is worth your investment. Talk to colleagues or post on a dietetic practice group (DPG) electronic mailing list (EML) to learn about the directories you are considering.

There is no limit to the amount of money you can spend to market your practice, especially to patients and clients. Be careful that you don't end up wasting valuable marketing dollars. To make your marketing budget worthwhile, determine whether you are spending your money wisely on marketing. Figure out how many people you would have to treat to pay for the cost of advertising. Ask yourself whether the amount is realistic. For example, if you don't have a virtual assistant to answer the phone and book appointments for you, using a referral service, which schedules online appointments for you, may be a good business decision.

When you promote your practice, you may attract inappropriate clientele or unrealistic requests. Be prepared. Don't be surprised if you receive a phone call from someone who asks you to mail them a diet plan so they can lose weight. You may receive a random email with a food record inquiring whether it is healthy or which supplements to purchase. Although you want business, you do not want to give your professional services away for free! Use these situations to market your practice. Your conversation can be something like this: "It's difficult for me to determine what would be best for you to do nutritionally without knowing anything about you. If you'd like, let's make an appointment for me to review your medical and nutrition history and other information and for us to develop a plan specifically for you." Of course, at times you may want to give back to the community and provide your services at a reduced fee or for free. However, you do not want to give away your professional services to everyone who asks. Be sure that *you* make the decision about when you want to provide community service. And if money is an issue, limit the amount of times you provide free services in a given year.

There are circumstances—such as when a physician refers individuals to you or they find you through their insurance provider—when you may think that promoting your practice directly to patients and clients may be unnecessary. Not so. You always need to promote yourself. The doctor and insurance company may present patients with choices of RDNs. The patients may then check these names online. If they find nothing about you but find information about the other recommended RDNs, this will affect their decision about which RDN to see. Remember that the patient needs to learn about you from a variety of sources. This is why your marketing needs to be multifaceted.

There is no better publicity than a satisfied client or patient. Your patients are your best marketing tools. How you speak to and treat your clients will influence their willingness to say, "I have this great RDN who I highly recommend." Ask your patients for testimonials that you can post on your website. Positive testimonials only add to your credibility.

Creating a Marketing Plan

You may be on the cutting edge of prenatal nutrition, have written a bestseller, or have the highest success rate with helping triathletes, but if no one knows about you, your practice can fail. Success in business is all about marketing. Marketing separates you from your competition and lets your clients know you are out there. Good marketing translates into a successful business.

A marketing plan is different from a business plan. A business plan is the blueprint that guides you as you get your business up and running. Your marketing plan is a strategic plan to get your name out to customers to make money. Many small businesses may develop a business plan

Marketing Tips

Evaluate your marketing knowledge and get professional help in areas where you feel inadequate.

Successful marketing requires a "hook." Think about all the things that are unique about you and your business.

Networking is essential to your success. Find out where your networks exist and learn how and when to network effectively.

but stumble through the marketing process. Some cite insufficient cash, lack of knowledge, and having other priorities as reasons for not having a marketing plan. However, marketing is vital. To successfully market your services, your marketing plan needs to define the following:

- your target market (refer to chapter 4);

- the services you are selling (which is your expertise); and

- the tools you will use to ensure that your services reach the market.

It is as basic as that. When you are marketing your private practice, you need to develop a plan that will be revised, refined, and reformulated as your business develops. The box above includes several helpful marketing tips.

Focus Groups

If you're uncertain about whether a specific idea or service is worth marketing, one way to conduct research before beginning to market it is by forming a focus group. Traditional focus groups are conducted with a group of neutral individuals who are not going to benefit directly from your service. When manufacturers are introducing a new product, they always conduct focus groups to get feedback. You can operate your business the same way. Focus groups are an inexpensive way to conduct market research. Another way to query your intended market is to develop an online survey that you can email to potential clients or referral sources. SurveyMonkey offers a free membership that allows you to create simple surveys that can gather much-needed information for you to use when developing new programs for your patients.

Suppose you have an idea to offer a nutrition lecture series for new parents. To determine whether this is a good idea, consider asking a pediatrician's staff to serve as your focus group or, better yet, request that they give your contact info to new parents who express interest in nutrition. Ask if you can learn their opinions of your idea. Because members of focus groups expect to receive something in return for their time, offer to provide the first class to them as a thank-you. Also, ask if you can leave info on your nutrition lecture series in the waiting room.

Perhaps you want to develop educational materials for the athletes you counsel. After you conduct an internet search to determine what has already been published on this topic, take your idea directly to the athletes. Call your local running group. Offer to give a lecture, and in return ask the participants to evaluate your handout ideas.

Volunteer to give a free lecture to a group of senior citizens residing in a retirement community. In return, gather feedback on an idea to provide Cooking for One classes. Those attending your seminar have just served as your focus group. The only cost to you is the time you spend preparing and presenting a lecture, plus the cost of the food.

Tools and Methods for Reaching Your Target Market

Potential clients will learn about your business through your marketing efforts. The goal of marketing is simple: Get your name out there and keep it out there in a cost-effective way. There are many marketing tools available. When selecting marketing tools and strategies, you will need to consider your market. The tools you use may be different if you are marketing to a health club, a physicians' practice, a corporation, or a consumer group in the community. Focus on what seems appropriate for the market. Ultimately, you want to know who your customer may be so you can begin to think like your customer and identify the most effective way to market to him or her.

There are five general categories for promoting your services: self-promotion, networking, advertising, publicity, and word of mouth. Finding the right mix of promotional activities to get your name out and keep it out there, in an affordable way, should be your goal.[1,2,3]

Self-Promotion

In private practice, you are the practice! You are the product you are selling. When you market your practice, you are ultimately marketing yourself. Thus, you need to be on 24/7. The way you dress, the way you speak, and the image you project in your professional and personal lives send a message about you and your practice.[3,4] Even when you shop for food or dine out, you are promoting yourself. People who know that you are an RDN will watch your food selections just a little more closely. If you advocate physical activity in your counseling, you should set an example by exercising. Those interested in seeing you professionally will want to know whether you practice what you preach. Keep in mind that your lifestyle is a form of marketing your practice.

Networking

Networking is defined as "the deliberate process of exchanging information, resources, support, and access in such [a] way as to create mutually beneficial relationships for personal and professional success."[5] New entrepreneurs are sometimes uncomfortable with the concept of networking. Some view it as using others. True networking is building relationships that work two ways. It is about giving *and* receiving. Don't just take.

Networking is not simply going to an event, handing out your business card, and collecting other people's business cards. Networking requires you to have a plan to connect with others, share information, and receive something in return to further your professional or personal goals.[5,6]

FINDING YOUR NETWORKS

Any situation where you can meet people, share your vision, gather information from the group, and hopefully offer them something in return is a network. You can start by creating a list of your existing networks. This list should include your personal and professional acquaintances. Your personal networks include your friends, your relatives, and your children's school, as well as your place of worship, your exercise class, and your community association.

Your professional networks include your colleagues at work (if you are still employed), dietetics organizations and DPGs, other health professionals such as doctors and therapists, organizations such as college alumni groups, and civic organizations.

In addition to joining the Academy of Nutrition and Dietetics, you will want to join and become an active member in other professional organizations where you can meet a targeted audience. Explore membership in business networking groups outside the world of dietetics in the vicinity of your practice, such as the Chamber of Commerce. Simply becoming a member of an organization is not networking. Being an active and participative member means that you give and receive. DPGs, health organizations such as the American Diabetes Association, and professional organizations such as the National Speakers Bureau will provide opportunities to share and learn from others with similar interests and goals.

Online social networks, such as Facebook and Twitter, can be other forums for networking with colleagues, patients, friends, and family.[7,8] Be aware that these are social platforms, and you need to consider the image you portray as you mix your personal and professional lives. For instance, if you post a controversial political point of view, it may affect a potential client's willingness to contact you. Some RDNs have separate personal and professional social media accounts in order to avoid these issues. Social media is discussed in greater detail later in this chapter.

Remember to network with competitors. One of the best existing networks is other RDNs. RDNs new to self-employment fear that RDNs with established practices will perceive them as competition or a threat. However, other RDNs can be an excellent referral source. Get to know their practices so that when you get a referral you cannot handle, you can reciprocate. Providing referrals for others is an important aspect of doing business.[9]

NETWORKING STRATEGIES

Learning how to network is an art. Attend professional meetings, social gatherings, and even family events with a networking frame of mind. Don't wait for people to seek you out. You must make the effort to get to know your networks. Think about who your networks are and put yourself in a position to be active within those networks. If you are focusing your practice on diabetes management, become active in the local American Diabetes Association chapter. If you are specializing in geriatrics, look at networking opportunities offered through the AARP.

Take advantage of your membership in organizations and the networking opportunities that are available. Professional organizations, including the Academy of Nutrition and Dietetics, offer formal networking events. Toastmasters International clubs (www.toastmasters.org) as well as business and civic groups also provide formal networking classes.

Every time you attend a meeting, a social gathering, or even a family dinner, you can network. Set a networking goal for yourself for each event you attend. Networking goals can include meeting a new person, providing a referral or resource, or following up with a new contact within five days of the networking event.

Make your address book or contact list meaningful by keeping names memorable. When you meet people, use the back of their business card to jot down something about your meeting to help you remember them. It could be a shared birthday, their recent promotion, or their love of baseball. Rely on this when you reconnect. People will be impressed that you've taken an interest in them, and then they will be more likely to refer you to others.

Invite conversation by practicing a welcoming introduction. When first introducing yourself, have an elevator speech prepared (see chapter 4). This is a creative, memorable speech about yourself that is no longer than the time spent in an elevator ride.

Think of ways to encourage people to tell you about themselves. This is relationship building. It may take many introductions and meetings before people remember who you are. Come up with 10 items you can share with someone. Use key words to make it easier for people to remember you.

Words of Wisdom

Networking Strategies from Successful Registered Dietitian Nutritionists

Felicia Stoler, DCN, MS, RDN, FACSM, FAND

ALWAYS have business cards on you—you NEVER know who you will meet. Even if there is not an immediate need, over time, an introduction can become a lucrative work opportunity.

Step outside of the box—get involved with other organizations (like the American College of Sports Medicine [ACSM]) or on state or local boards, networking groups, and so on. The best way to get work is from other professionals—not necessarily dietitians!

Yvette Quantz, RDN, CSSD, LDN

Step out of your comfort zone. All too often at networking events, we get comfortable meeting and mingling with the people we already have built a relationship with (and this is very important), but we must not forget to reach out and meet new people.

Be interested instead of interesting—listen more and be interested in what other people are doing in their careers and lives. Ask questions, stay engaged, and remember details they share with you. Avoid making the conversation all about you and instead focus on the person you are talking to.

Collect and follow up. Collect contact information and be sure to follow up. Send a personal email or note directly after you meet and then send consistent follow-ups with your e-newsletter.

Refer to the Words of Wisdom box for networking strategies from some of your successful RDN colleagues.

Networking is about exposure and having fun. Plan to network at least once a week in a variety of settings. Networking can include lunch with a colleague or a power walk with a friend. Always follow up a formal or informal networking function with a note, email, or phone call thanking the person for his or her efforts in helping you build your network.

Anyone you meet is a potential resource for you. Learning how and when to nurture those connections is important. Practice a subtle but direct approach. Asking someone *What can you do for me?* is a turn-off. Craft your questions carefully. For example, ask *Who else should I speak with?*

Networking is an ongoing activity. As long as you are in private practice, you will need to keep your networks alive. Always be "on." You never know who that person in line at the grocery store may be.

Advertising

Good advertising means getting the word out often. For advertising to be effective, the message must be repeated several times. There are plenty of low-cost advertising tools. Regardless of which tools you use, you should employ two basic advertising concepts: (1) Your advertising must be catchy, and (2) your audience must see it repeatedly.[1,2] In *The Small Business Bible*, Steven Strauss explains that you may see the same advertisement repeatedly and never notice it until the day you need what it advertises.[1] Great ads solve problems—does yours?

When you are first starting out, choose the most appropriate media and upgrade as you can afford it. The most appropriate media might be different for different RDNs, depending on what your niche is. However, whichever form of media you choose, advertising allows you to control your message. Take the time to plan out a well-designed advertisement. If you can't afford to have it professionally designed, have it evaluated by friends and colleagues. Take their input seriously, and revise your advertising until the message is presented in a clear, concise, and catchy way.

NEWSPAPERS

Newspapers can be good advertising tools, although ads in some newspapers can be very costly. If you live in a large metropolitan area, advertise in a small community-based newspaper. It will be more affordable and will reach a more targeted audience.

Think carefully about ad placement. If your paper has a health edition or a food edition, placing an ad in that section will reach an already-interested audience. If you are focusing on sports nutrition, have your ad placed on the sports page. Some newspapers offer a type of bulletin board that advertises classes, community events, or lectures. This is free advertising. If you can, be sure to take advantage of this opportunity.

When planning your newspaper ad, remember to budget for several releases. Good advertising needs to appear several times. A one-time newspaper ad will likely not generate the attention you want. Consider smaller ads that appear more often rather than larger ads that appear less frequently. When buying bulk advertising—that is, running the same advertisement multiple times—you will be offered a discount. Also, do not forget to design your ad so that it is punchy and informative.

NONPRINT MEDIA: TELEVISION AND RADIO

Airtime, regardless of your locale, is usually cost-prohibitive. A paid commercial is probably beyond the budget for most RDNs just starting out. Cable and satellite TV are less expensive than network TV but may not be a wise use of your marketing money. If you are trying to advertise an event as opposed to your own business, networks and radio stations may offer the opportunity for a public service announcement. Exposure and name recognition are important, so do not pass up this opportunity if it exists.

DIRECT MAIL

Direct mail includes any promotional piece that connects directly with the consumer. There are many options available to you, each with a unique selling power. Direct mail includes emails, postcards, brochures, announcements, and newsletters. Even a follow-up letter to a referring physician is a form of direct mail.

Targeted mailing lists can be purchased from several different organizations. If you are advertising to other RDNs to promote a class or a product, you can purchase mailing lists from the Academy of Nutrition and Dietetics that are specific to certain geographic regions or specialty areas. Other professional organizations sell lists, too. Your local medical society may be a good source if you are mailing to physicians or other health professionals.

To access an existing mailing list, think about the target group you identified and what other services they may use. If you are offering a class for new parents, think about the products all new parents will be purchasing and contact a product source, such as a local baby clothing store, to see if a list is available. You can also generate your own mailing list for free from your email address book and other personal contact lists.

FOLLOW-UP LETTERS, THANK-YOU NOTES, CARDS, AND GIFTS

An overlooked piece of direct mail is the follow-up letter you mail to a physician or a thank-you note you send to a referral source. With so much reliance on email, receiving a letter or note the old-fashioned way can provide a personal touch to make you stand out, which customers may really appreciate. Follow-up letters are direct mail pieces with very targeted and receptive audiences. You might also include an article on a relevant nutrition topic. The name of the game in advertising is to keep your name out there. Always include business cards and a brochure or other promotional material, if possible.

Sending holiday cards to your referral sources and client base is direct mail advertising. It is another way of keeping your name out there. Purchase or design cards that reflect you and your practice. Add a personal note. Also consider sending holiday gifts to referral sources. A fruit basket, a nice cookbook or nutrition book, or a subscription to a health newsletter or magazine are all appreciated gifts. National Nutrition Month and Registered Dietitian Day provide opportunities for marketing your services by sending a gift, article, or card. Be creative in finding ways to develop referrals for your business. Once you establish a relationship with a referral source, sustain it by sharing your appreciation.

NEWSLETTERS

Although a newsletter is a great way to advertise, it should not be the first tool you use to promote your business. It might be wise to wait until you have been in practice for at least a year so you have a database of patients to send it to. You can also advertise it on your website and in your email signature and let people sign up from either of those platforms. Creating a newsletter can be time consuming, but there are several companies that provide enewsletter templates that you can customize and send through email. You can customize the newsletter to fit your philosophy and specialty area of nutrition. It can be added to your bag of tricks when you are looking to grow and diversify your business, but consider your target population and what they will read.[10] For example, if you are marketing your services to seniors, consider that they will more likely read paper newsletters sent through snail mail than enewsletters.

DIRECTORIES

Many organizations publish the names of all members in their directories, and some directories include paid advertisements. Look for opportunities to be listed or advertise in multiple directories. For example, your DPG or the local chapter of the American Heart Association or Women in Business may have directories that will reach different populations. Medical societies often publish directories for physicians and other health care professionals. If your medical community publishes a directory but does not include RDNs, suggest that it add the section. This will make the directory more complete.

Search the internet for directories that include nutrition businesses or services. Create a profile or listing for your business on these directories. When prospective clients search your name on the internet, they will be guided to your listing. On some of these sites, visitors can post reviews of your business. Review what others are reading and writing about your services.

Remember to think of all your networks: your child's school, your garden club, or your place of worship. Do they publish a directory? Does it reach your target audience? If so, advertise in it.

Directories can be a very inexpensive form of advertising. Sometimes a reprint of your business card can take the place of a formal ad.

Publicity

Publicity is basically free advertising. It includes anything that gets your name out to your target population. It can be a quote you've given to a newspaper, an article you've written, or publicity flyers distributed for a talk you are giving. Your target market will view good publicity as more credible than paid advertising. Readers often think that you must be credible if an article features you or relies on you as an expert or if you've been asked to speak to a group. Publicity tends to have greater longevity than paid advertising. Readers will likely remember it better than advertising. The key is learning how to become noteworthy enough to attract good publicity.

As you seek publicity, remember that you cannot fully control what is said about you. For example, when you are interviewed, the interviewer can use your comments in any way he or she wishes to fit a story. Although reporters are not out to make you look bad, they do determine what they write about the interview. You can request to review an article for accuracy prior to publication, but this doesn't give you control of the message.

PRESS RELEASES AND PRESS KITS

The first step in attracting publicity is to develop a press release. Send a press release to anyone who believe might have any interest. Perhaps you have a new software program to analyze recipes, a new piece of equipment to measure percentage of body fat, or you are starting a cooking program for senior citizens. These could all seem newsworthy to the right media source. A press release can lead to free publicity. You should create a press kit if you plan to promote yourself or an event to the media or to organizations interested in hiring you to speak.

WRITING FOR PUBLICITY

Having a byline and getting published are great publicity. Although many RDNs are paid for writing, others write to gain name recognition or as a stepping stone to larger projects. If you are writing for free, negotiate for free advertising space in return for writing an article.

Writing takes time, talent, and drive. You do not need to start with a large daily newspaper to be published. Think about what your target market reads. Perhaps you are working with a pediatric population. Writing for a locally produced parenting magazine or newspaper or even contributing an article for the local Parent Teacher Association (PTA) newsletter would provide you with exposure to your target population. If your interest is in sports nutrition, find a local fitness center with a monthly newsletter and volunteer to write an article. Perhaps you are interested in conducting supermarket tours. If so, check if your local supermarket chain might be interested in having you write a column for their newsletter.

PUBLICIZING YOURSELF WITH REPRINTED ARTICLES WRITTEN BY OTHERS

If you do not have the time or are not interested in writing an article, find a relevant article written by someone else and distribute copies to raise awareness of a topic related to your business. Let readers know that you are a local expert on that topic. Before you distribute any published material, be sure to request permission to have it reprinted and ask how the author and publisher should be cited. Costs for reprint permissions vary significantly. Some articles may be free of charge; others can be quite expensive to use.

GETTING QUOTED AS AN EXPERT

To become a local expert, you will need to develop relationships with the local media. Learning how to work with the media is an art that is not mastered overnight. Present yourself as an expert by sending the local media a press release about a program you are presenting in the community, by providing a press kit that includes information about your practice, or by simply calling them to respond to a story they ran. The media will appreciate your availability as a credible source rather than as an RDN who is trying to get her name in print.

Reporters appreciate hearing about story ideas. However, not all ideas are considered. For serious consideration, a story idea should be unique, topical, or present a new angle on a previously covered topic. If one reporter is not interested in the topic, ask if he or she is aware of someone who might be interested. Be persistent, but do not be a pest.

Generally, reporters always need information yesterday. If a reporter calls you, be sure to respond in a timely fashion. Oftentimes, the reporter will talk to the first person who returns his or her call. If you know the time and topic of the interview, be prepared. If you are not prepared with an answer when a reporter calls, ask if you can return the call in 15 minutes. In that time, collect your thoughts. Have a few important sound bites of information. Limit your answers to the questions asked. The more you talk to reporters, the more comfortable you will become asking them to repeat what you've said to minimize the risks of being misquoted. Follow up promptly if a reporter requests supporting information. If you aren't familiar with the topic, the best thing you can do is provide the reporter with the name of someone who is.

This process can be frustrating. You might provide 45 minutes of your time and in return receive a two-second sound bite or a one-sentence quote. Sometimes you might receive no mention at all. Follow up by contacting the writer after the article has appeared. Give him or her feedback. Thank the reporter for including your information or for consulting you, even if you were not mentioned.

Pay attention to when other RDNs are quoted in the press, then contact them and ask how they became a resource to the media. If an RDN has a relationship with the media, relay your expertise to him or her. Professionals should recognize their limitations and, if they are aware of your expertise, may refer the media to you.

SPEAKING ENGAGEMENTS AND PRESENTATIONS

Name recognition and keeping your name visible are the cornerstones of marketing. One easy way to become well known is by making yourself available for speaking engagements. To find opportunities, join speakers' bureaus, such as the National Speakers Bureau (www.nationalspeakers.com) or the speakers' bureaus of professional organizations. You will learn how to become a better speaker and, with some marketing, can be called upon as a speaker.

Nutrition is a topic of interest to almost everyone, including your colleagues. It's important to learn how to speak publically to different audiences. Research your audience before giving a talk. Do not focus on selling your services to the audience. If you do a good job, the audience members may request a business card. Be sure to have handouts available when you speak, or make them available as a PDF on your website. Tell attendees they can download them from your site. Always include contact information. If you are giving a PowerPoint presentation, make sure to have your contact information on the first and last slides.

As you look for speaking and presentation opportunities, concentrate on your target market. If you want to target physicians, you may offer to provide a lunchtime presentation on a relevant topic at their office. If pediatrics is your focus, present at a PTA meeting. Your goal is for referring sources to see you as an expert.

HEALTH FAIRS

Many organizations conduct health fairs, and these events can be opportunities to market your services, network, assess interest in topics, showcase new products, or get feedback on educational materials you sell or use. If the health fair reaches your target audience, it can be a good way to get your name out and earn credibility. Although a health fair that doesn't reach your target population is unlikely to bring you business, it may be a good opportunity to practice speaking with an audience that you probably will not address again. Be wary of health fairs that charge a fee. Consider whether it is worth your time to spend your marketing dollars on hosting a booth.

Word of Mouth

A satisfied customer is your best marketing tool. You can't control this free advertising, but it is definitely the best. Being competent and caring for your client base will lead to satisfied clients. Satisfied clients will promote you to their physicians as well as their friends and relatives. Satisfied clients are what will ultimately promote your services and build your practice. Having happy clients is truly the best way to grow your private practice.

Summary

Refer to the box on the next page for a summary of tips to help promote your practice.

Tips to Promote Your Practice

Advertising, although costly, needs to be repeated to be meaningful. One-shot ads are generally not worth the investment.

There are many different forms of media—including newspapers, radio and television, websites, direct mail, email, brochures, announcements, flyers, follow-up letters, holiday cards, newsletters, and online directories—that are available to you for advertising. Evaluate the cost, image, and effectiveness of each for your particular practice.

Publicity is free advertising. You have little control over what is said about you, but it tends to give credibility to your services. To position yourself for publicity, create a press release or press kit, write an article, or offer your expertise to the media. Free publicity also comes from giving talks, volunteering at health fairs, and being involved in your community.

A satisfied client is the best form of advertising.

You are your practice. Promoting yourself will be promoting your practice.

Prospective clients need to hear your name repeatedly from a variety of sources. Reach out to patients in multiple ways.

Your best advertising is through word of mouth.

Using Technology to Market Your Practice

Technology is changing so fast that it can be difficult to keep up. To compete in today's market, however, you must change with the times. Although you do not need to run out and purchase the latest and greatest gadget the minute it appears on the market, you do need to be aware of new technology and assess its usefulness to you. For example, in today's market, you cannot effectively have a practice without using the internet. This section will explore ways to use technology to enhance your business.

Website

A website is an essential tool in doing business. No matter the size of your practice or where you conduct your business, your website is where many prospective clients will find you. Regularly check Google and other search engines to make sure that their information about you is current. If you move to a different office space, check Google Maps to make sure that your new location is listed. If your information is incorrect, clients could come to the wrong location! See chapter 5 for more in-depth information on setting up your website.

Email Marketing

Email has greatly increased productivity. In most cases, email has replaced the telephone and snail mail. RDNs use email with patients in a variety of ways, including providing nutrition consultations, communicating with patients, and sending out meal plans and other nutrition information. They also communicate by email with other health care professionals regarding particular patients (provided that they comply with Health Insurance Portability and Accountability Act [HIPAA] regulations).

Email is an effective marketing tool. For example, you can collect email addresses from your patients or clients and email them the recipe of the month or the nutrition tip of the month. Make sure that you have permission from recipients to email them, however. You do not want to be the source of unwanted email.

The most basic use of email as a marketing tool is sending every email with your signature, which provides complete contact information about your business. This is free advertising every time you send an email. Take advantage of this and make sure that your signature reflects your brand. Another way to use email as a marketing tool is to use an email marketing website. These websites can assist you with developing professional, polished-looking emails for a nominal fee and can provide other services as well.[2]

There is a downside to email. Checking email can be time consuming, and you may become sidetracked by certain emails. Some RDNs find it helpful to set up separate email addresses for business and personal use so they can focus on one at a time. Others schedule specific times of the day to focus solely on email to increase productivity and decrease distractions.

Electronic Mailing Lists

EMLs are wonderful free tools for RDNs. An EML is a forum for discussion via email. You can subscribe to EMLs that pertain to your area of interest. Be mindful that when you send an email message to an EML, everyone who is subscribed receives the email. RDNs can use EMLs to obtain clinical and business advice from colleagues, announce consulting positions, and locate referrals for patients who are moving.

The Academy of Nutrition and Dietetics has a general EML open to all members. Most of the Academy of Nutrition and Dietetics DPGs also have EMLs, which are more specialized by area of practice. Even within DPGs, EMLs exist among subgroups. For example, the Nutrition Entrepreneurs DPG has a general EML for its members as well as specific EMLs for RDNs who specialize in private practice, writing, speaking, internet and business technology, corporate health, and coaching. Participating in the DPG EMLs requires DPG membership.

If you choose to subscribe to multiple EMLs, the volume of mail can become excessive. Consider the option of receiving the information in the digest version. This will provide you with a daily summary rather than multiple emails coming in throughout the day. Another option is to set up a separate email address for EML subscriptions. Then you can check these messages periodically.

Conducting Research on the Internet

Staying current is essential in the field of nutrition. Your patients or clients will want your opinion of the latest diet or today's news about food safety. To stay current, you can read online editions of major newspapers, such as the *New York Times*, *Wall Street Journal*, or *Washington Post*. You can also subscribe to the Weekly News email published by the Academy of Nutrition and Dietetics Knowledge Center. It provides a daily summary of nutrition and health articles from major media outlets. Another great Academy of Nutrition and Dietetics feature is the New in Review section of the *Journal of the Academy of Nutrition and Dietetics*. Each month, New in Review compiles articles from scientific and professional periodicals of interest to food and nutrition professionals as well as reviews of nutrition-related books and websites. This members-only benefit is available on the journal's website (www.andjrnl .org). Another great benefit from the Academy of Nutrition and Dietetics is the colorful *Food & Nutrition Magazine*. This publication is loaded with great articles covering such areas as food and diet trends, nutrition research, resources for both public health issues and policy initiatives, and product reviews. It addresses the diverse needs of the nutrition profession by providing superb content for a large variety of readers. It is an excellent resource for a private practice RDN.

You can access educational materials online, but be aware of legal rules regarding the distribution of such documents to patients or clients. Materials published by the US government are generally part of the public domain and usually can be distributed without needing permission to do so. Other material on the internet is copyrighted. Many websites allow you to reprint copyrighted documents for free if you are using them for educational purposes.[4] However, you should always verify that reprints are permitted before you distribute materials. You may need a signed release form from the copyright holder. Some copyright holders will charge a fee for use. Another option is to direct your patients or clients to some of the sites you deem appropriate and accurate.

Internet Marketing

One way you can use the internet as a marketing tool is to subscribe to online referral listings. The Academy of Nutrition and Dietetics Nationwide Nutrition Network provides a referral listing at no charge to Academy of Nutrition and Dietetics members. Be sure to check other associations, such as the American Diabetes Association or the National Speakers Association, for opportunities to list your practice or services. If you accept insurance, most insurance providers will include you in their online listing for RDNs. Thus, accepting insurance as payment is another way to help you obtain patients.

It is common to include your practice email address, website URL, and business telephone number in referral listings (see chapter 5 for more information on how to create your website). Make sure that prospective patients can email you directly from your website. Once you do, be prepared to receive inquiries about your services via email.

Social Media

If you aren't using social media yet, you should consider jumping on the bandwagon to promote your practice. When you use online platforms (such as Twitter, Facebook, LinkedIn, and YouTube) and blogs, you are building a social network that can help your practice grow. With social media, you can reach many people quickly and easily. Social media can boost your profile, build your brand, and help maximize your credibility.[9,10] You also have the potential to be more influential and to increase the value of your opinions, thoughts, and expertise. This is excellent exposure for an entrepreneur. And you don't need a budget unless you hire someone to handle your social media accounts.

The main expense associated with participating in social media is your time. Find out which platforms your target market is using and work on integrating those platforms into your practice. Sign up for a few accounts, such as Instagram and Twitter, to help you network and build your private practice. If you have a Facebook account and want to use it for both personal and business activities, be careful what you post. Do you want your clients to know what is going in your personal life? Do you want them to know where you were last Saturday night? Think before you post. Otherwise, set up a Facebook page for your business and connect with your clients there. Be aware that some target markets, such as senior citizens, may not use social media. You may need to find other ways to reach them, such as by advertising in local newspapers. However, staying active on social media may help you reach people who could refer others to your practice.

It's smart to limit yourself to two online platforms at first, especially if you don't have someone to help you, such as a social media intern. If you think that an intern could help you market your practice, seek out a nutrition student who is knowledgeable about social media. Quite often you can find a nutrition student who is looking to gain more experience in the field. If you start off using too many platforms and do not have help, you could be spending valuable time on social media that you should be using to build relationships with your patients and referral base. To stay visible on social media, you need to be consistent—limit your platforms so you can be fully engaged with your followers.[9]

TWITTER

If you're new to social media, Twitter is easy to use and a great place to start (www.twitter.com). Twitter asks you one question: *What's happening?* With a 140-character limit, you can answer that question and share it with your followers. Twitter can be a very powerful marketing and networking tool. Use it to market yourself as an expert and connect with your network. You can post the latest food and nutrition information as well as get involved in conversations with other nutrition and food leaders in your Twitterverse. A Twitter account is easier to set up than a blog and takes much less time to manage. Over time, you should find that you can make amazing connections on Twitter to help grow your practice; you just have to put yourself out there. Try it out for yourself and find ways to make it work for you.

Adding a graphic to your tweet increases the odds that it will be read and retweeted. Having others retweet your tweets is a great way to share your wisdom to an even larger community.

When you create an account with Twitter, you set up a profile and look for people to follow. Make sure to compose a profile that tells people who you are and what you do. Adding some widely used hashtags to your profile is a great way to come up in a Twitter search, so be sure to include a few. And don't forget to add your picture or logo to your profile. People need to be able to identify you. If you don't have a picture, they will be less inclined to follow you. To find people to follow, you can look for people who are influencers in your area of expertise. You can also find people to follow by searching in a topic area such as *health* or *food*. Alternatively, you can enter your email address and Twitter will find the people in your address book who also have accounts. When you follow people, their tweets show up on your home page. One good tip to get more followers is to follow people back who are following you. This is a great way to build your Twitter network. You can always unfollow people if you feel they tweet misinformation or if you feel they don't add any-thing of relevance to your network. You can also unfollow people if you find that you are following so many people that it becomes overwhelm-ing to stay informed by those you truly want to follow.

Twitter is an easy way to stay informed about what people in your network are blogging about, reading in the news, or doing in their work that may be of interest to you. You can skim your Twitter stream to get quick bits of information, discover news, and retweet content to your followers. You can ask people in your network questions such as *Anyone have healthy, gluten-free snack ideas?* You can share links to your recent blog posts, videos, newsworthy nutrition studies, or special practice pro-motions you may be offering to get the word out quickly.

Twitter has features to manage your contacts. You can create lists that allow you to group people you follow into categories (for example, RDNs or Chefs). You can also use Twitter's trending tools, which allow you to follow current conversations by clicking a button.

Several social media platforms have created applications to help you manage your online presence. For example, TweetDeck (www.tweet deck.com) and Hootsuite (www.hootsuite.com) allow you to post tweets from multiple Twitter accounts all on one screen. You can also schedule posts in advance if you are going on vacation or have a media campaign to schedule. You can post updates on Hootsuite to connect with several of your social media pages. This saves you time (and money!) and keeps you in the loop.[10]

FACEBOOK

Facebook (www.facebook.com) is a powerful social networking platform that can help promote your brand and grow your business.[8] If you have been using Facebook to solely connect with family and friends, it is now time to use Facebook to grow your practice.

One of the useful Facebook features for business owners is the Pages feature for branded entities. Businesses, individual products, nonprofits, public figures, music groups, sports teams, and TV shows are all exam-ples of branded entities. If you have a presence on Facebook, you can create a public page for your business and invite your contacts to be-come fans. Anyone with a Facebook account can join your page, which allows all of your fans to communicate with you and with each other. This enables you to establish your own online business community. You can provide special offers such as classes and webinars, provide incen-tives to your fans, ask them for feedback, or share news and information.

If you want to set up a Facebook page, all you need to do is create an account on the website. Facebook has customizable privacy permis-sions that allow you to select what profile information is public and what is for friends only. Some entrepreneurs are not comfortable with mixing business and pleasure and don't know whether they should "friend" clients, business colleagues, and family. This is a personal decision. Based on your area of practice, you may need to be careful about what your clients and professional contacts see. As social media can affect your reputation, it is a good idea to be careful what you post. If you want to keep patients away from your profile, you can decline their friend invitations and send them a request to join your business page instead.

You can place an ad on Facebook to promote your business to your target market. The advantage of advertising on Facebook is that you can target their billions of daily users by many demographic and psychographic filters, and it's relatively easy to set up your own advertising based on your budget. If your audience is on Facebook and you have some advertising money, consider the value of using Facebook's powerful targeting tools to stretch your dollar. As a first step, expand your network on Facebook through people you already know. Consider paid placement when you have funds available for advertising. If you decide to move forward with an ad, consider offering a discount to people who mention the ad so you can measure your return on investment.[11]

YOUTUBE

YouTube (www.youtube.com) is one of the oldest social media sites. It is a great place to share videos to help build your practice. Create a compelling profile so people will be more likely to watch your videos. Although people can comment on videos, YouTube does not have the power of Facebook or Twitter as a social networking website. However, it integrates well with these and other sites. You may decide to record video blogs, which you can do easily using a smartphone. You can post the videos to YouTube; embed them in your blog; and upload them to other social media sites, such as Twitter, Facebook, and Pinterest. If you are interested in speaking, spokesperson, or media opportunities, you can start by recording your own videos. Think of this as a cheap way to practice and improve your speaking skills as well as a way to build up examples of your work.

YouTube also allows you to record a video to sell yourself. Highlight your unique qualities, background, and anything else that makes you stand out. YouTube limits video file size, so most videos need to be less than 10 minutes in length. Most people prefer to watch short videos (one to three minutes), so the time limitation should not be a problem.

PINTEREST

Pinterest is a terrific platform to share your interests through a series of beautiful photos. The images you share don't have to be your own. You can use your own images or find other images on the internet to pin. If you would like to set up a Pinterest account to help grow your brand, take the time to create a profile that will help followers learn more about you and what you do. As with other social media platforms, include your picture and an interesting bio so people can identify you. You can then create boards that reflect your interests and personal brand. For instance, if you have expertise in pediatric nutrition, consider creating boards devoted to your passion, such as healthy snacks for kids and quick and healthy brown-bag lunches for adults.

Choose your own images to pin or find other images to help fill up your board. When you share an image on Pinterest, each picture is called a pin. When you share someone else's pin on Pinterest, it's called a repin. You can group images or pins together by categories on the boards in your profile. You can use images you find online, or you can directly upload your own images. There is a Pin It button available on your Pinterest page. Use the Pin It button to share images directly in your browser from any webpage.[11] You can also share your pins on Twitter and Facebook. You can search categories unique to your brand to find images to repin. Sign up for a Pinterest account and get pinning!

INSTAGRAM

Instagram is a great visual marketing tool for building your business. To increase your network of followers, post interesting pictures related to your brand. People who like your photos will follow you, and you can follow them back. Download the app on your phone and start taking photos of intriguing subjects. Or feel free to use photos that are already stored on your phone. Choose a high-quality photo that resonates with your brand. If you want your picture to stand out, make sure that it is a great photo.

If you are new to Instagram, here's some advice: When you create your account, choose a username that reflects your brand. Your name or the name of your practice are two good choices. This will make your profile easily identifiable as you add followers on Instagram. For your profile, use either your picture or your business logo to align your brand with the images you post. Make your account public so that all Instagram users can view your profile and interact with your business. Provide a creative overview of your business. And don't forget to add the URL of your website in your bio so users can easily connect with you to find out more about you and to access your services.

To help your photo gain more attention, include a caption with your photo and a hashtag that portrays your photo's description. Viewers use hashtags to search for content that is of interest to them. Don't use a simple hashtag such as #fruit, which is too vague. If you post a photo of tangerines, use #tangerines or #citrus so the image shows up in a more specific search. Try to limit the number of hashtags to three so your post doesn't look messy.[12] Many major brands post to Instagram only once per day, so don't feel the need to take a lot of time out of your day to have an impact on Instagram. Once a day is optimal.

BLOGS

If you haven't started writing a blog, you may want to tap into this medium. Having a blog is a great way to showcase your brand. A blog is a great forum for engaging in conversations on trends and topics that matter to you and that are also in line with your business.[13] Blogging is a great way to position yourself as a credible nutrition expert and build your private practice. It also helps increase your website's search ranking or SEO, which allows your target customers to find you more easily without the cost of paid advertising.[12]

Blog authors (also known as bloggers) have a chance to let their style and personality shine through their topic choices, writing ability, and dialogue with readers. Your blog may include text, photos, video, and audio. Blogs display the most recent content first, and prior entries follow down the page in descending order. Bloggers write posts in a conversational style to encourage dialogue, which leads to interaction with your readers in the form of questions or comments.

Blogs are easy to set up and maintain. If you are interested in starting a blog, come up with a theme that supports your brand and professional interests. Successful blogs tend to be centered on a specific theme and deal with current issues that are relevant to their target audience. Some RDNs love to cook, so they use their blogs as a way to share photos, test recipes, and get feedback from others. Others may only blog about their practice specialty, such as polycystic ovarian syndrome, diabetes, or celiac disease. As you blog, you will discover which types of information you like to share and what works best for you.[13]

Plan to spend 30 to 60 minutes on most blog posts and maybe even more time when you are first getting started. But don't get overwhelmed. If time is an issue, you can hire a nutrition intern to help you blog. But make sure to carefully edit the intern's work, as your blog is an extension of your brand. You want to make sure that what is posted on your blog reflects your image. Your content should be well written, easy to read, enjoyable, and credible. People don't like to read long posts online—they prefer to skim. Aim to keep your blog posts between 300 and 500 words. Write compelling headings that will pull your readers in and make them want to read your blog. Use bullet points and include visual media, such as photos or videos. These strategies will improve the readability of your blog posts. If you have a hard time sticking to the word count, consider splitting the blog into several posts.

Blogging can have a downside as well. You have to learn how to use the software and publish posts on a regular basis. Keeping a blog current can be a serious time commitment. You have to write often (at least one post a week), respond to reader comments, and build an audience. Usually, obtaining more followers involves reading and commenting on other blogs or linking to them in one of your own posts.

It is possible to obtain a free or inexpensive blog. Blogging platforms such as WordPress (www.wordpress.com) provide free or inexpensive blogging applications. If you want to have your own unique domain for your blog, you will most likely have to pay an annual fee.

Most blog communities allow you to sync your blog within their platform using really simple syndication (RSS) or start your own blog within the community. The power of blog communities is the power of numbers. Dietitians on the Blog is a great example of a blog community supported by RDNs.

SOCIAL MEDIA STRATEGIES TO GROW YOUR BUSINESS

Be strategic as you explore how you can use social media to promote your business. Your marketing plan is a great place to start. Review your goals and ask yourself *How can social media help?* If you're considering a blog, be sure to ask yourself *Why do I need to blog?* If you are starting to build your private practice, maybe you want to establish yourself as an expert. This will help justify the time investment you'll put into building your presence on social media. Think about the people you need to connect with, whether they are people you know or those you need to learn from. Explore the leading social media websites, such as Facebook, Twitter, Instagram, and Pinterest. If you decide you want to participate, you'll need to create accounts on the various websites. Keep in mind that you can't just set up a profile and abandon your social media presence. Make sure you upload a picture of yourself and a short bio. Make it interesting and fun so people will follow you. Include some hashtags that are relevant to your brand in your profile, which will help you come up in online searches. Plan to maintain your blog on a long-term basis. Success may not come overnight, but the only way you will really know if social media works for you is to give it a try.[13]

After you have a social media presence, you need to integrate it. Maximize your reach and minimize your time investment by making sure your Facebook fans know how they can follow you on Twitter. Think of your website as home base, and make sure you have social media icons on your website that link to your entire social media presence. Include social media icons on your website, on your blog, and in your email signature. To find free icons, search online for social media icons.

Although the thought of entering into uncharted territory may be overwhelming, using social media as a marketing and communications tool is necessary for your business to thrive and prosper. If you are a little hesitant to jump in, take advantage of the many free resources available on the internet. Take small steps when you are first getting started to gain confidence, and before you know it you will be a social media guru.

If you find yourself searching for ideas for how to use social media in your private practice, the box on the next page should help get those entrepreneurial juices flowing.

8

Ten Social Media Tips to Market Your Business

1. Read blogs in your specialty area to stay on top of what other registered dietitian nutritionists and health professionals are writing about.

2. If you have an enewsletter, include your recent blog posts and recipes for your clients.

3. Find blogs you like to read and offer to provide a one-time guest post. You gain more credibility when viewers see you as a guest expert.

4. Start a blog in your nutrition specialty area. Post thoughts, tips, and timely news related to your brand.

5. Create a LinkedIn account and find contacts who may help you achieve a business goal.

6. Tape short videos of yourself giving nutrition tips or preparing a recipe and upload them to social networking sites that support video, such as YouTube, Twitter, and Facebook.

7. Tweet story ideas to members of the media to get a story spot or quotation.

8. Find health experts important to your area of expertise to follow on Twitter and read their blogs. Communicate with them to develop a referral network.

9. To help gain more followers, include your social media links in your email signature, blog, and enewsletter.

10. Tell your clients to sign up for your blog or follow you on Twitter for the credible nutrition information you provide.

Multimedia Tools to Market Your Business

Once you are using the internet to streamline your work and you have developed your website for marketing, you may want to take technology to the next level. Many multimedia tools, including video clips, podcasts, webinars, teleconferences, and telehealth can be added to your technology toolbox to grow your business or enhance your products and services. See chapter 5 for more information on telehealth.

Video Clips

One of the simplest ways to enhance a website is to add video clips. For example, many RDNs post videos of themselves giving television interviews, teaching classes, or conducting cooking demonstrations. This is a great way to showcase your talent and expertise.

Podcasts

A podcast is an audio file available on the internet that you can listen to on computers and handheld devices. Podcasts include video in addition to audio. (Some people include videos under the term podcast.) Some podcasts are offered for free, whereas others require payment to download them. For example, some medical journals offer free podcasts of their articles, sometimes with added content.[7]

There are many ways for RDNs to enhance their businesses by offering podcasts. Consider providing free podcasts on various nutrition topics through your website. This could be an excellent way of regularly updating your site and encouraging repeat visitors. For example, you could post a weekly or monthly podcast that provides sports nutrition tips and recipes. Alternatively, you could charge a nominal fee for downloading podcasts, particularly if you have an interesting area of expertise and produce podcasts that people are willing to buy. Some RDNs turn the classes they teach into podcasts for purchase.

Making a podcast is fairly easy. There are numerous How To articles available on the internet to walk you through all the steps. You can even find podcasts on how to make a podcast. You need specific equipment to make a podcast, but it is fairly inexpensive and not complicated. If you decide to offer podcasts, make sure that they are recorded in a professional manner, using quality sound recording equipment. Do the taping in a quiet place where you won't have the interference of outside sound. Prepare a detailed outline or script for your podcast to help you stay on track and refrain from using "um" when you get stuck in a thought. If you are interviewing someone for you podcast, make sure the person has all the questions you will be asking beforehand so he or she can have answers well-prepared.

Webinars and Teleconferences

You can obtain continuing education, conduct business meetings, and even counsel clients from the comfort of your own home if you have the right equipment.

A webinar (short for web-based seminar) is a presentation, lecture, workshop, or seminar that is transmitted over the internet. Webinars are interactive. Generally, participants call in or listen through audio on the computer, and a guided slide presentation or video is provided for participants to watch while an expert talks. Participants can type questions or ask them over the phone. Many RDNs receive continuing education through webinars. Webinars can also be used to provide nutrition education programs to the public. Perhaps you have developed a great presentation for executives about healthy eating on the run. Consider filming your presentation, turning it into a webinar, and marketing it to area law firms.

Teleconferences are telephone meetings among two or more people. Traditionally, teleconferences were audio only, but with added equipment, it is now possible to include video images. Teleconferences tend to be used more and more to hold meetings or disseminate information. For example, you could hold weekly weight management support teleconferences for your patients who may be interested in this type of format. You could also use teleconferencing if you are working with families virtually to help with meal planning. There are many ways to incorporate teleconferencing into your practice.

Marketing: A Summary

You will need to market your business to have a successful private practice. This will be an ongoing process. As your practice grows, you will need to continually update and tweak your marketing approach. You will need to spend money to make money, but in today's world, you don't have to spend a lot. Here are some tips to keep in mind from this chapter:

- Social media is free and is a great way to get people to recognize your business and seek you out.

- You need to determine how much you can spend on marketing to get the biggest bang for your buck. Be realistic. This does not mean that you should forgo marketing; it simply means that you need to do your research and invest your money where you will reap the biggest rewards. There are less expensive ways to market—seek out these opportunities. Be creative.

- You will need to constantly monitor the effectiveness of your marketing.

- Advertising allows you to control the message but is more costly. Publicity and word of mouth, although free, do not allow you to control the message, only influence it. Marketing is a dynamic and ongoing process. You do not create a marketing plan, try it out, and go into practice. From the inception of your business until you retire, you need to be marketing and reevaluating and revising your marketing methods as needed. Marketing should be fun and allow you and your practice to shine.

References

1. Strauss S. *The Small Business Bible: Everything You Need to Know to Succeed in Your Small Business*. 3rd ed. Hoboken, NJ: John Wiley & Sons, Inc; 2012.

2. Johnson KD. *The Entrepreneur Mind: 100 Essential Beliefs, Characteristics, and Habits of Elite Entrepreneurs*. Atlanta, GA: Johnson Media Inc; 2013.

3. Levinson JC, Levinson J. *The Best of Guerrilla Marketing: Guerrilla Marketing Remix*. Irvine, CA: Entrepreneur Press; 2011.

4. Longer B. *Networking: 42 Keys to Career Growth—Communication Skills, Building Relationships, Influence. 2nd edition*. Brett Longer Publishing; 2015.

5. Koszyk S. Marketing: Are You on Top of Your Game? NEDPG website. https://nedpg.org/sites/default/files/Members/Toolkit/2012%20Marketing/AreYouOnTopOfYourGame.pdf. Published 2012. Accessed June 12, 2017.

6. Tyson E, Schell J. *Small Business for Dummies*. 4th ed. Hoboken, NJ: John Wiley & Sons Inc; 2012.

7. Cobun D. *Networking Is Not Working: Stop Collecting Business Cards and Start Making Meaningful Connections*. Washington, DC: IdeaPress Publishing; 2014.

8. Hollenberg J. *Love at First Site: How to Build the Website of Your Dreams*. Australia: Five by Five Online Marketing Pty Ltd; 2014.

9. Social media & self-promotion: what works and what doesn't. *Ventures Newsletter*. https://issuu.com/mitchellgraphics/docs/ventures_2016_summer_issue?e=8652869/37315727. Published Summer 2016. Accessed June 12, 2017.

10. MacCarthy A. *500 Social Media Marketing Tips*. Andrew MacCarthy; 2016.

11. Kawasaki G, Fitzpatrick P. *The Art of Social Media*. New York, NY: Penguin Group; 2014.

12. Gunelius S. *Blogging All-in-One for Dummies*. 2nd ed. Hoboken, NJ: John Wiley & Sons, Inc; 2012.

13. Williams J. *Social Media: Marketing Strategies for Rapid Growth Using Facebook, Twitter, Instagram, LinkedIn, Pinterest, and YouTube*. John Williams Publishing; 2016.

9 | From Scheduling Your First Patient to Running a Successful Practice

All is in place for the inauguration of your nutrition practice. You are ready to open for business and see your first patient. How exciting! Finally, you will see all your hard work and planning coming together. You might be a little nervous. That's normal. This is a new venture.

Over time, your practice will grow, especially as you become more comfortable in what you are doing. You may find that attracting patients is fairly easy but that keeping their business is more difficult. To generate follow-up sessions, which in business terms translate into repeat business, you may need to reconceive your professional purpose and transition your approach. This chapter explores the process of scheduling your first patient appointment to sustaining a successful nutrition practice.

Things to Consider for Setting Up Appointments

Initially, you may feel overwhelmed. With time, you will develop a routine and it will become automatic and natural for you. Let's work through what you'll need to know to successfully set up those very first appointments.

Scheduling the First Appointment

There is a great deal of information you will share and obtain when scheduling an appointment with a patient. Even seasoned registered dietitian nutritionists (RDNs) and their staff may forget to obtain important information. Developing a checklist for scheduling a new patient, as shown in the box on the next page, can prove to be invaluable.

When a patient contacts your office, whether by phone or electronically, to make his or her initial appointment, establish the reason for the visit and how you will be paid. If you accept insurance, inquire first about the patient's insurance prior to getting into any discussion about the visit. You want to make sure that you participate with the insurance company and that you can avoid wasting time. Briefly screen the patient to determine that your services are appropriate for him or her and, if not, refer the person to another colleague who will be a better fit. When speaking with a prospective patient on the phone, aim to limit your time. Get the information you need. Once the patient has you on the phone, some patients want to share his or her life story or get quick nutrition information from you. Politely inform the patient that you will discuss all this when you meet.

If the patient's insurance company requires a referral, inform him or her of this prior to the appointment. You will want the referral to be in place by the first appointment. Some private insurance identification cards will indicate if a referral is needed. If you are unsure if a referral is required, contact the patient's insurance company. You will need the patient's full name as it appears on the insurance card, the patient's date of birth, and the insurance identification number. You can also enlist the help of the patient to find out this information. It is good for patients to know about their own insurance. With most private insurance, the referral is generated from the primary care provider's office through the insurance company. In the case of Medicare, it is not generated through Medicare but is a written referral from the patient's physician making the referral including the International Classification of Diseases, Clinical Modifications, 10th Revision (ICD-10-CM) code. The referrals you receive from private insurance companies may not specify the ICD-10-CM code. The physician determines the ICD-10-CM code. Either you or the patient can obtain the patient's diagnoses with the ICD-10-CM code from the physician. Chapter 7 includes information about referrals and the ICD-10-CM codes.

Inform the patient of the information you will need for the first appointment. This can include your new patient forms; a food journal; a medications list, including over-the-counter medication and supplements; a copy of his or her recent laboratory test results; an insurance card and payment for the copay or the office visit; and anything else you may need for the appointment. Samples of many of these forms can be found in chapter 6.

Making Your Business:
Checklist for Scheduling a New Patient

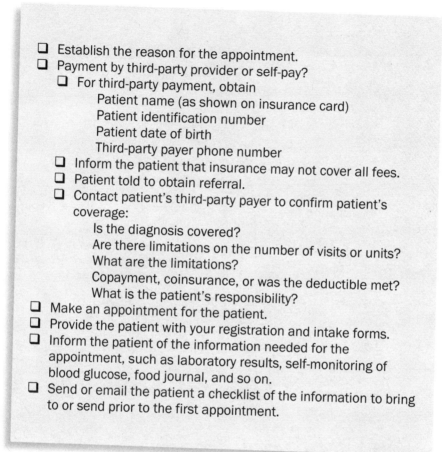

❑ Establish the reason for the appointment.
❑ Payment by third-party provider or self-pay?
   ❑ For third-party payment, obtain
      Patient name (as shown on insurance card)
      Patient identification number
      Patient date of birth
      Third-party payer phone number
❑ Inform the patient that insurance may not cover all fees.
❑ Patient told to obtain referral.
❑ Contact patient's third-party payer to confirm patient's coverage:
      Is the diagnosis covered?
      Are there limitations on the number of visits or units?
      What are the limitations?
      Copayment, coinsurance, or was the deductible met?
      What is the patient's responsibility?
❑ Make an appointment for the patient.
❑ Provide the patient with your registration and intake forms.
❑ Inform the patient of the information needed for the appointment, such as laboratory results, self-monitoring of blood glucose, food journal, and so on.
❑ Send or email the patient a checklist of the information to bring to or send prior to the first appointment.

Providing your patient with access to your new patient forms prior to the appointment can save time. Some dietitians prefer to complete parts of their patient intake forms with the patient as part of the initial visit. They feel that they learn more about the patient by asking for the information and also ensure that they do not miss any details. This is an individual choice. Regardless of your choice, share with new patients what they need to bring for this first appointment. The Making Your Business box on the next page shows an example of an email to send to new patients as a reminder of what to bring to the appointment.

You have your first appointment scheduled with a patient. Congratulations!

Making Your Business:
Sample Email for Patient's First Visit

Dear [patient name],

I am excited that you have scheduled an appointment for [date, time, and location]. I need to receive the following information from you prior to our appointment. Prior to the appointment, you can email the information to [RDN's email address] or fax it to [fax number]. If you prefer, you can bring the information with you to the appointment.

1. Your completed New Patient Questionnaire.

    The questionnaire can be found at this link [provide link] or attached to this email.

2. A food diary maintained for three days prior to your appointment as instructed at this link [provide link] or attached to this e-mail.

3. A copy of your latest blood (lab) report.

4. Blood glucose logs (if you maintain one) or your glucose meter.

5. Your insurance card, copay, or payment for the appointment.

6. Your physician's referral, including the ICD-10-CM diagnosis code.

I look forward to meeting you.

Healthy regards,

[Your name]

[Contact information]

Adapted with permission from Ann Silver.

The First Appointment

When you first meet your patient, introduce yourself. Ask for his or her name to be sure you have the correct person. Ask how he or she prefers to be identified. Some patients may have a nickname; older patients may want to be referred to in a more formal manner. However the patient wants to be addressed, be welcoming and cordial while being respectful. There may be times you are not working directly with the patient but with the patient's guardian or designated representative. Be sure to confirm his or her name and relationship to the patient and document his or her presence in your chart notes.

To start the conversation with a patient, engage in some friendly banter about the weather, a news event, or something that will relax both you and your patient. Avoid discussing controversial topics like politics. Keep it light and short, but don't instantly jump into *Why are you here?*

Get the administrative chores out of the way at the beginning of the session, unless you have an assistant who will be performing these tasks. If you accept insurance, make a copy of the front and back of their insurance card. Make sure that you participate with their insurance company and that the patient has a referral if needed. Read through the completed new patient forms. Ask questions to clarify or gather additional information. Confirm that the patient has signed your office and Health Insurance Portability and Accountability Act (HIPAA) policies. You must have a signature on file to bill the patient's insurance. Obtain a signed release of information from the patient giving you permission to communicate with the patient's health care provider and other persons the patient designates. Chapter 6 provides samples of these forms. The Making Your Business Box below provides a checklist of information you will want to obtain from the patient.

Now you are ready to get down to work. You may ask the patient again why he or she comes to see you and how you can help. Sometimes what is indicated on the new patient forms is not the reason for the visit. Explore what the patient wants to achieve from meeting with you on this first visit and future appointments. Review and document all the information you need to complete the patient's nutrition care plan and documentation of the visit.

Ultimately, you strive to develop a collaborative, long-term relationship with your patient that includes trust, honesty, and respect. You want

Making Your Business:
Checklist for First Appointment

☐ Completed patient registration forms

☐ Signed acknowledgment of Health Insurance Portability and Accountability Act (HIPAA) and all office policies

☐ Authorization for release of information to other health care providers, other designees, and third-party payers

☐ Copy of front and back of patient's insurance card(s)

☐ Referral or preauthorization from referring physician for third-party payer

☐ Physician's diagnosis with ICD-10-CM code

☐ Payment for copay or office visit

☐ Superbill and/or receipt

☐ Next appointment scheduled.

Adapted with permission from Ann Silver.

the patient to look up to you as a nutrition expert. As the provider, you want the patient to feel that you sincerely care about him or her. Focus on the patient. Do not take phone calls during the appointment or respond to text messages. Of course, there may be extenuating circumstances when this can occur, but make it rare. Excuse yourself and apologize to the patient for taking time from the appointment.[1] Remember: This is ALL about your patient.

Do not discipline a patient for not bringing a food record or other information. There is likely a reason why he or she did not do the homework, and this can provide insight for you about the patient making changes.

At an appointment, avoid giving a patient so much nutrition information that he or she departs in information overload. Try not to be the nutrition dictator or food police of eat this and not that. Your goal is to foster a patient-centered relationship. The questions you should be answering are:

- What does the patient want?

- What is the patient willing to do?

Building Your Practice as You Transition from Educator to Counselor

As you treat more and more clients and begin seeing them for follow-up visits, your new status as a business owner in your own practice can be very different from your previous employment setting. Finding your modus operandi and approach with patients will develop over time.

RDNs employed in traditional settings, such as hospitals or outpatient clinics, may have a difficult time envisioning how to counsel patients in a private-practice setting. Many RDNs wonder: *How do you structure the session? What do you do in follow-up sessions? How do you encourage patients to return?*

One reason RDNs in traditional settings ask these questions is that they may have been using a medical model of patient care. This model, as explained in the box on the next page, is appropriate in hospital and clinical settings where RDNs have historically practiced.[1]

This traditional medical model relies on short-term nutrition intervention. The RDN generates goals for the patient, focusing on what the patient needs to learn. Typically, the RDN needs to develop only a superficial relationship with the patient. In this model, nutrition counseling

9

Medical Model vs Nutrition Therapy Model[1]

	Medical Model	Nutrition Therapy Model
Scope of intervention	Short-term intervention	Long-term care
Patient-provider relationship	Minimal relationship	Significant relationship
Type of treatment plan	Primarily educational	Highly individualized
	Often standardized plan of action	Evolves over time

includes assessing the patient's status, planning necessary diet changes, and providing information. Counseling, in this sense, is really educating.[1,2]

Generally, inpatient consultations are brief. A diet consultation may be requested when the patient is about to be discharged from the hospital, and the patient is usually preoccupied with other issues at this time. The consultation may take place in a setting that is not private, so it is unlikely that the patient can be completely candid. In an outpatient setting, you might have more time with the patient, but you may still seize the opportunity to teach the patient instead of engaging in actual counseling, as you may never see the patient again. It can be difficult for an RDN practicing in an inpatient hospital setting or an outpatient department to truly serve the patient as a nutrition therapist; rather, the RDN serves a useful but quite different function as a nutrition educator.

Thus, traditional nutrition counseling, by necessity, is very different from the nutrition therapy process that is used in a private practice setting. Nutrition therapy is a dynamic relationship between the RDN and the patient and often between the RDN and other health care providers. Although clinical nutrition principles are incorporated into the nutrition therapy process, the techniques used to impart the information and the pace at which information is shared differ. In 2002, Julie O'Sullivan Maillet, former President of the Academy of Nutrition and Dietetics, predicted that "in 2017, much [will have] changed...the role of the clinical dietitian [will] become that of a nutrition therapist."[3] Julie was on target! The future is now. Nutrition therapy is the state of the art.

Nutrition therapy is a client-centered approach that focuses on beliefs, emotions, and behaviors, particularly as they relate to food and eating. It results in the formation of a long-term relationship with your patients. Treatment plans are highly individualized and evolve over time.[4]

Nutrition therapy is a widely accepted approach in the eating disorders arena, where RDNs have learned that simply educating a client about dietary changes does not mean that the client will be able to

Words of Wisdom

Developing Skills

Rebecca Bitzer, MS, RD/LD, CEDRD

Just as you develop your technical skills and stay up-to-date on the latest nutrition research, you also need to develop your counseling and people skills. Remember that clients want more than just facts from you; they are also seeking compassion, connection, and care. Therefore, seek out training in such things as communication and people skills. This will help ensure that you develop long-term clients rather than one-time appointments.

Reprinted with permission from Empowered Enterprises.[5]

implement the changes. To see real change in individuals with eating disorders, you need to incorporate nutrition therapy and nutrition education skills. In fact, the nutrition therapy approach can be useful, even necessary, to your development as a skilled counselor working with *any* patient population.[2] For example, this approach can be very useful in helping patients with diabetes make the necessary dietary changes to achieve blood glucose control.

The Words of Wisdom above provides some insight on developing crucial counseling skills.

Although some of your patients' goals will be accomplished merely by providing them with factual information, it is unlikely that you will be able to build a practice based on one-time nutrition education sessions. If you try this approach, as your patients fail to make lifelong changes, you will get frustrated and look for ways to help your patients become more successful. A nutrition therapy approach will enable you to better help your patients. Your success will be measured by your clients' success. You will have more follow-up visits, and your satisfied clients will help you build your practice.

Becoming a Nutrition Therapist

The transition from nutrition educator to nutrition therapist is a process that happens over time and through experience. This process takes training and practice.

TRAINING AND EDUCATION

Making the transition to becoming a nutrition therapist requires learning counseling skills. Typically, RDNs receive basic training in counseling skills; however, it is recommended that those who want to work with patients on an ongoing basis seek additional training.[6,7] You can benefit from reading counseling books, attending formal counseling courses, and receiving supervision from an RDN experienced in private practice. The Academy of Nutrition and Dietetics dietetic practice groups (DPGs)— Behavioral Health Nutrition; Nutrition Entrepreneurs; Weight Management; and Sport, Cardiovascular, and Wellness Nutrition—offer counseling skills workshops, devote columns in their newsletters to this topic, and share information about this topic on their websites. Chapter 11 includes additional resources for you to develop your skills as a nutrition therapist.

INCORPORATING NUTRITION THERAPY SKILLS

There is no protocol for developing nutrition therapy skills when counseling patients. Although formal education is often the first step, some RDNs may intuitively use these skills from the beginning without realizing it. Other RDNs who do not feel confident with the concept of nutrition therapy can gradually introduce these skills into their counseling style.

EFFECTIVE LISTENING SKILLS

Our role as educators often prevents us from listening to our patients. We sometimes feel we don't have the time to listen. However, what clients actually want from the session is sometimes very different from what they need, and you need to listen to hear the difference. Being a good listener will require you to be flexible in your approach. What you think a patient may be ready to address in your session may very well not be what he or she is ready to do or wants to do.[8] Take your cues from the patient. What does the patient want? This does not entail compromising your ethics or practice approach. For example, a patient may be emphatic at the first appointment and say, "I never ate breakfast and I don't plan on eating breakfast." In your professional opinion, not eating breakfast may be setting up the patient for out-of-control eating later in the day. But obviously the patient has made his or her stance. Respect it. Honor the patient without compromising your ethics, practice model, or scope of practice. You can experiment with different approaches to work around the patient's position. Perhaps in future sessions, you can readdress it and the patient will be more receptive. Keep in mind that a satisfied customer is the best form of marketing. The same applies to a satisfied patient!

You may feel uncomfortable if there is silence in the room, but there will be times when your response should be silence. For example, during a nutrition therapy session, a patient may tell you that she has not cooked much since her spouse died. She then becomes tearful. Your role is to sit with her and her sadness, not to jump in and try to fix it. You may also be surprised by what you learn from your patient when you allow silence to fill the room. As awkward as it may seem initially, silence will provide your patient time to divulge more information. This process may be very valuable to the patient's overall success.

A good listener should be able to paraphrase what a patient says. Referred to as mirroring or reflective listening, this allows the patient to have an opportunity to review the topics discussed in the session so he or she can clarify any misunderstandings and feel more valued.[9,10]

EMPATHY AND SUPPORT

When your patients respond to questions, you need to assume a non-judgmental position. They may never have felt secure enough to realize how food is intertwined with the rest of their lives and talk openly about it. When patients realize that you are not there merely to provide the latest food and nutrition information, they may be more willing to share their feelings about the difficulty they face in making important and necessary diet changes. You can validate those feelings and be knowledgeable about how and when they can make changes.

In your practice, as in your life, you will encounter diversity. Your patients may be different from you. They can differ from you in terms of race, culture, language, religion, gender, sexual orientation, socioeconomic status, age, weight, or physical ability. These factors may affect patients' food choices in addition to their willingness to be open and honest with you. Exhibit sensitivity. Be understanding. Ask questions to gain knowledge. Do additional research to learn more about dealing with your patient. Consult a colleague with more expertise and skill if you ever feel that you are unable to treat a patient. Learn more about diversity by reading articles and books and by attending conferences and presentations on the topic.

CARE AND TRUST

Nutrition therapists must be caring and genuinely interested in helping their patients. These are attributes you cannot fake. Your patients must feel safe to talk freely about food and their issues around food. Listen to their concerns and respond in a caring manner.

Acquiring Counseling Techniques

When you are first attempting to make the shift from educator to counselor, you may find it difficult, daunting, and unnatural. There are many strategies you can use to expand your work into the counseling arena, improve outcomes with your patients, and generate repeat visits.

Consider expanding your studies to develop new skills. Take a psychology class that includes information about personality disorders, cognitive behavioral interventions, family systems theory, and different counseling styles. You can also take courses or participate in workshops on counseling techniques.

TYPES OF NUTRITION COUNSELING INTERVENTIONS

The counseling styles used by RDNs have been adopted from other fields, especially psychology. The two most common nutrition counseling interventions practiced by RDNs in private practice are motivational interviewing (MI) and cognitive behavioral therapy (CBT).[4,11] These approaches have been practiced by RDNs primarily for the treatment of patients with eating disorders.[12] The use of these counseling techniques has transitioned to nutrition counseling for other diagnoses to implement and support patient-centered behavior changes.[13-15]

Motivational Interviewing Training in MI can improve your counseling skills and clinical strategies. MI is a patient-centered communication approach that focuses on a patient's ambivalence and facilitates behavior change by "strengthening a person's own motivation and commitment to change."[16] MI is an effective counseling style in which the clinician collaborates with the client to help promote dietary behavioral change.[17-19] With MI, the RDN and the patient work together. The RDN is not coming across as an authoritative nutrition expert but as a facilitator. The Words of Wisdom box below provides information on how MI can be helpful to RDNs.

Words of Wisdom

A Conversation About Motivational Interviewing

Molly Kellogg, LCSW, CEDRD[a]

How can motivational interviewing (MI) help private-practice registered dietitian nutritionists (RDNs)?

As RDNs, we know that much of our advice will be useless unless the client adopts the diet changes we recommend. Behavior change is complex and often difficult. Many change theories can be applied to nutrition counseling. MI is a practical method for engaging clients in effective change conversations. As a collaborative, goal-oriented style of conversation, MI is designed to strengthen a client's motivation for and movement toward a specific goal by eliciting and exploring the person's own reasons for change. It encourages exploration and resolution of ambivalence to change. The counselor guides the client rather than directing.

MI is a good fit with the medical nutrition therapy process because it is both client centered and evidence based. It allows us to embed our advice in the most effective conversational process. We thereby avoid resistance and increase the likelihood of acceptance.

(Continued on next page)

Words of Wisdom (continued)

What's involved in training to become proficient with MI?

MI is both practical and relatively easy to understand. That does not mean it is easy to learn. Research on training has shown that a two-day workshop increases knowledge about MI and self-perceived proficiency. However, careful study of work samples shows only modest gains: "In short, the workshop convinced clinicians that they had acquired MI skillfulness, but their actual practice did not change enough to make any difference to their clients."[20] Further research has shown that months of practice interspersed with several cycles of observation and individual feedback or coaching are necessary to bring MI practice up to a level of proficiency that affects patient outcomes.

[a] Molly Kellogg is a member of the Motivational Interviewing Network of Trainers (www.motivationalinterviewing.org/about_mint). She trains RDNs in MI.

Reprinted with permission from Molly Kelllogg.[22]

By asking broad, open-ended questions and using reflective listening, MI elicits the patient's own thoughts and ideas for motivation and change.[21] Closed-ended questions are answered with a single word or a very short response. You do not learn much about the patient. On the other hand, open-ended questions (see the box below for examples) are answered with a longer response and can provide additional information. Reflective listening, or mirroring, is paraphrasing what the patient says. This clarifies what the patient says and also encourages the patient to provide more information. The box on the next page provides examples of mirroring.

Examples of Open-Ended Questions

Instead of:	Ask:
You are here to lose weight, right?	What are your concerns?
When do you eat breakfast?	When is the first time in the day you eat or drink something?
Do you avoid certain foods?	What foods do you not eat?
Do you think you are gaining weight because you eat too much?	What do you think has contributed to your weight gain?
Do you need help with improving your blood sugar levels?	How can I help you with managing your diabetes?

Examples of Mirroring with Words

"What I hear you saying is..."

"So you feel..."

"Let me see if I heard you correctly. You..."

"It sounds like..."

"You really care about/want..., don't you?"

"Is there more that I've missed...?"

Reprinted with permission from Molly Kelllogg.[22]

Cognitive Behavioral Therapy CBT is a common and effective technique used in nutrition counseling for a variety of conditions.[21] The premise of CBT, as applied to nutrition, is that eating behavior and food choices are generated by feelings and thoughts. These beliefs and misconceptions are challenged to restructure thinking in order to establish new, healthier thought processes and to change behavior.[11]

As in MI, CBT is a collaborative approach between the RDN and the patient. CBT and MI are frequently practiced together.[15,21] In CBT counseling, the RDN first has to learn the patient's thinking and how it is influencing patient behavior. The next step, which can be time consuming, is changing the patient's thought process or beliefs to promote changes in eating.

Take the case of an obese patient who is being treated for weight management. The patient insists that he or she can never, ever again in his or her life eat bread to lose weight. He or she associates eating bread with not losing weight. With CBT, the role of the RDN is to explore with the patient the origin of this information, provide convincing evidence that bread will not impede weight loss, and work with the patient to acquire new thinking to change behavior and eat bread.

Health Coaching Health coaching, also referred to as wellness coaching or just plain coaching, is another patient-led approach that RDNs can consider using in private practice.[23,24] Insurance companies, corporations, and businesses use coaches for prevention and wellness. A collaborative effort, health coaching incorporates tenets of MI and other counseling techniques to initiate behavior change.[23] The change considers the whole person and other aspects of his or her life. The client (not referred to as a patient) determines the focus of each session.

Health coaching is *not* medical nutrition therapy (MNT) or nutritional counseling.[24] There is a difference. The difference between coaching and MNT, as explained in the box on the next page, is that the RDN coach

Comparison of Coaching Model with Traditional Medical Nutrition Therapy Model

Coaching model	Traditional Medical Nutrition Therapy model
Client is the expert. Client prioritizes what gets done, including the order and how it gets done.	Registered dietitian nutritionist (RDN) comes across as the expert. Patient is told what to do and how to do it.
All solutions are 100% tailored to the individual. The client identifies a lot of the solutions.	Solutions can be somewhat less personalized. RDN provides solutions.
Uses intrinsic motivation to stay the course.	Uses extrinsic motivation (told or led by the RDN).
Collaborative relationship to help move along the behavioral change continuum.	Patient needs to facilitate the change.
No handouts needed. Sessions geared toward exploring the clients' vision, setting goals, and goal attainment. Focuses on the HOW.	Usually requires patient education/dietary handouts. RDN mostly gives specific recommendations for a particular illness, disease, or symptoms. Focus tends to be on the WHAT.
Common methods used in a coaching session: positive psychology, mindfulness, appreciative inquiry, curiosity and optimism, transtheoretical model of change, cognitive behavioral therapy (CBT), social cognitive theory, and motivational interviewing (MI).	Some of these psychological theories can be integrated into MNT. MI and CBT are occasionally interwoven into sessions, depending on RDN's expertise.
No referral needed. Can be performed anywhere in the world.	Referral may be needed. State licensure or certification limits practice to within the state.

Adapted with permission from Lesli Bitel.

provides guidance and support to the client in achieving his or her goals by promoting action rather than by telling the client how to eat and what diet or foods to choose. Be careful not to circumvent state licensure laws by calling yourself a coach when you are indeed performing MNT.

If you have nutrition expertise and background as an RDN, coaching can be a natural fit.[24] Anyone can be called a coach; however, training and certification are highly recommended. The International Coach Federation (www.icf.org) is the certification agency for the different coaching training programs. Training programs vary significantly. Coaching has been pretty much unregulated, although the International Consortium for Health & Wellness Coaching (www.ichwc.org) now offers a national certification.

Unlike MNT, which must comply with state licensing laws for RDNs, coaching does not fall under state licensure or certification. RDNs can practice coaching around the globe. Coaching can be conducted in person or through technology such as on the telephone or through video conferencing, making it the most convenient for the client and the RDN.[24] RDNs have become health coaches as a way to expand their practices, increase return visits, and develop long-term relationships. RDNs share their experiences with working as health coaches in the Words of Wisdom box. Additional information on coaching is available on the Nutrition Entrepreneurs DPG website (www.nedpg.org) and in chapter 11.

Words of Wisdom

What Are Registered Dietitian Nutritionists Saying About Health Coaching?

Lesli Bitel, MBA, RD, LDN

The coaching model is rapidly gaining momentum and popularity, in part because there is a large body of research now available to support its efficacy. I've not met anyone who has regretted adding coach training to their credentials. In fact, I believe most registered dietitian nutritionist (RDN) coaches would agree that becoming a certified coach is a life-changing experience, from both a personal and a professional perspective. Most coaches do not work with clients for less than three

(Continued on next page)

Words of Wisdom (continued)

months at a time because they recognize that helping their clients achieve sustainable lifestyle changes can be difficult and requires a minimum of 12 weeks to achieve success. Client referrals are obtained the same way an RDN does. You can get referrals from physicians, other health professionals, friends, family, your website, blogs—ANYONE! The key is to focus on the results and transformation you're helping your clients to achieve versus the process.

Linda Eck Mills, MBA, RDN, LDN, FADA

The coach is not saying *You need to do X*. Instead, the coach is saying *What do you want to do?* Coaching is THE best investment a professional can make to accelerate their success.

Jennifer Neily, MS, RDN, LD, FAND

I find [that] through coaching, when I take off my expert hat and facilitate the conversation, my client comes up with the answers. I also find [that] the client is more inclined to follow through. Prior to my coach training, I always considered myself a coach. I realized going through the training and becoming certified [that] I was really not, in a true coach sense. Coaching totally changed my business model. I offer package programs and don't provide individual sessions anymore. It takes weeks or months to build the behavior changes and lifestyle modifications clients need for long-term success.

Chere Bork, MS, RDN

Client retention is great. I have a package of 12 weekly sessions, which is often renewed more than once. The RDN coach-client relationship is so deep that often I hear what the clients do not say, which is tethered to their values and personal needs, which often surprises them and empowers them to easily make decisions. With coaching, you start to listen (I mean *really* listen), and you decrease what you are saying so your clients speak more. It ignites your passionate curiosity, and magic happens for the client and for you. It is life-changing. Coaching has changed my whole life. I have a deeper relationship with my family, I am happier, and [I] earn lots more money than I ever dreamed of when I [first] became an RDN.

Building Networks

Although you may want to build up your networks to grow your business, as discussed in chapter 8, this can also help with your personal growth as an effective clinician.

NETWORKING

Discuss your interests or any skills in counseling you want to develop with professors, colleagues, friends, and others who can enhance your knowledge in counseling techniques related to your particular area of interest (such as eating disorders, weight management, diabetes, and so on). A mentor can aid you in this process. Many of the Academy of Nutrition and Dietetics DPGs provide mentoring services.

EXPLORING THE BENEFITS OF SUPERVISION

You might want to discuss your own relationship to food, weight, exercise, and body image with a therapist. This work will give you the opportunity to experience what a counselor-client relationship is like and discover what techniques, approaches, and counseling styles you prefer.

As stated in the Academy of Nutrition and Dietetics Code of Ethics, "The dietetics practitioner assumes a life-long responsibility and accountability for personal competence in practice, consistent with accepted professional standards, continually striving to increase professional knowledge and skills and to apply them in practice."[25] To advance as a nutrition therapist, supervision may be necessary and beneficial.

Supervision is a concept that is widely used in the psychotherapy world. As RDNs, we may be unfamiliar with it. In a personal communication, Molly Kellogg, LCSW, CEDRD, defined *supervision* as follows:

> [Supervision is when] one or a group of nutrition therapists contract with an experienced professional to help them advance their counseling skills. It includes such things as discussion of cases, exploration of the therapists' own issues that come up in client sessions, practice of new skills, advice on what to try next with a particular client, support for limit setting, handling burnout, etc. The emphasis is on the *process* of counseling rather than on the content. It is assumed that participants have other sources of information on disease states, diet recommendations, etc.

Consider being supervised by a skilled therapist or counselor who you respect. You can receive supervision from an experienced RDN, a psychotherapist, or a psychiatrist. Look for a professional counselor with whom you connect well and who shares your philosophies. Another option is to form a mixed peer supervision group. Consider including psychotherapists, psychiatrists, and nutrition therapists in the same group. This allows professionals from different disciplines to learn from each other while gaining further insight into how the team approach works.

Supervision is not mentoring. Mentors do not expect reimbursement, but when you engage in a professional supervision relationship with any health professional, you should expect to pay for the service.

Respecting Professional Boundaries

As you move beyond the role of nutrition educator, you must be completely informed of the Academy of Nutrition and Dietetics Code of Ethics and Standards of Professional Practice.[23,25] Behaviors play a role in how, what, why, and when we eat. Our work as RDNs will always be grounded in nutrition, food, and eating. To truly motivate a patient to change, the boundaries of nutrition therapy and psychotherapy will sometimes seem blurred. You should never assume that you are the psychotherapist—you are the nutrition therapist. You need to understand your boundaries within your scope of practice and know when you should refer a patient to a psychotherapist. Generally, the goals in nutrition therapy are related to medical conditions, food behaviors, and possibly the patient's relationship with food and his or her body, as well as motivating the patient toward changing behaviors related to eating, food preparation, and other medical conditions. If you find that your patient is bringing up topics outside your scope of practice, the box below provides statements to help. Psychotherapy focuses more on mood, relationships, treating mental illness, and healing from trauma.[22] If you are in a state that requires licensing, become familiar with your legal limitations. Always be knowledgeable of and respect the Academy of Nutrition and Dietetics Code of Ethics.[23,25]

Managing Discussions out of Your Scope of Practice

Transition the conversation to food with a question:

"How do you think that affected your eating?"

"I'm so glad you had that experience! Tell me—did it make a difference in your eating?"

When a patient wants your input on something unrelated to food:

"That would be a great topic to discuss with your counselor" (if the patient has one).

"I don't feel qualified to discuss this. Let me think of someone who could help you."

"I can see that this is an important area for you to discuss, but I know I'm not the best person to advise you on this issue. Have you ever considered meeting with a counselor?"

Adapted with permission from the Academy of Nutrition and Dietetics.[4]

Due to personal prejudices, a need to be confrontational, or misconceptions about mental health counseling, some RDNs may hesitate to make referrals to mental health professionals. However, the Academy of Nutrition and Dietetics Code of Ethics requires that RDNs know how and when to make appropriate referrals, and this will be necessary in your expanded role as a nutrition therapist.[25]

To make good referrals, you need to know who is in your community. Keep your network up-to-date (see more information on this in chapter 8). Mental health professionals need to know about you, too. They need to know what you do and what to expect when they refer a patient to you. Networking allows you and others to supplement your respective practices.

If your client is under the care of a mental health professional, communication is essential. There will be some overlap, but this can actually be helpful to the client and to you.

Selling Nutrition Therapy

The success of your practice depends on you and how well you can sell yourself. Your referral sources and prospective clients must be aware of your approach as a nutrition therapist. Be prepared to address preconceived ideas of what you do as an RDN. For example, patients and their families may believe that you will focus on nutrition education and expect quick results. In such cases, you may need to help them understand that nutrition counseling is part of a longer therapeutic process (see the case study in the box below).

Case Study: Explaining Nutrition Therapy to Patients and Their Families

DJ, a 14-year-old girl, was referred for nutrition counseling because she was a picky eater. Her parents were frustrated with her limited food choices and thought that a nutrition consultation to tell her what to eat was in order. During the first visit, without DJ present, the nutrition therapist explained to the parents that she would first need to establish a relationship with the daughter, who they described as sassy, to determine why she didn't eat certain foods before instructing her about what she needed to eat.

DJ was extremely thin, had not yet started menstruating, and had always been a picky eater. She informed the nutrition therapist that she knew all about MyPlate, so the session would probably be a waste of time. As DJ's relationship with food was explored, it was clear that

(Continued on next page)

(continued from previous page)

she had been a restrictor since the age of eight because she was afraid of becoming fat. Upon the RDN's input and further medical evaluation, she met the diagnostic criteria for anorexia nervosa. The RDN conveyed her findings to DJ's physician, who was then able to make the diagnosis.

Upon diagnosis, DJ was referred to a family therapist and a pediatrician skilled in working with adolescents, and she had subsequent sessions with the nutrition therapist. With this professional help, she explored the struggles she was having with food. She is now a healthy, recovered, 21-year-old college student who has a normal weight and eats a wide variety of foods. Had the nutrition therapist merely told her what was necessary for her to eat during a single visit, her eating disorder would not have been diagnosed.

Similarly, physicians may refer their patients to you with the expectation that you will teach a prescribed diet. Although you may ultimately do this, nutrition therapy may involve many other steps in between. Therefore, you will need to educate referring physicians about your philosophy, style, and broader therapeutic approach. Communicate this to your referral base. Help them understand that patients may not initially lose weight, reduce their blood pressure, or have greater control over their diabetes. Goals for their patients may not be immediate or measurable in the conventional way. Patients may take small steps toward resolving issues that have kept them from achieving long-term dietary compliance. It may take time for them to reach their ultimate goals. That goal in the end may be different from the physician's original plan. For instance, a healthier lifestyle without dieting may be a more appropriate goal for a long-term dieter who is depressed. If the physician is using weight loss to assess progress, he or she may need to appreciate the much larger goals you have helped the patient achieve (see the case study in the box on the next page).

If your practice will largely be sourced by third-party payers, your financial success may depend on high volume. Some third-party payers provide coverage based on a predetermined number of visits or units (time). You may need to see many patients for shorter visits, and/or your number of visits with patients may be limited. When insurance coverage is limited, it can compromise the patient's outcome. Ideally, you will be able to help those patients *and* assist them in lobbying their insurance plans to allow the necessary number of visits with you to achieve the identified nutrition goals. It may take some effort, but it is possible to work with third-party payers to increase the number of covered visits. When requesting additional visits for patients from third-party

Case Study: Explaining Nutrition Therapy to Physicians

SD was referred by his physician for nutrition counseling for hypertension and obesity. During the initial visit, the nutrition therapist learned that SD had recently lost his job, was forced to move back in with his family, and was overeating in response to the stress. SD wanted to improve his diet, lose weight, and begin exercising. However, the nutrition therapist and SD agreed that his precious health care dollars would be better spent working with a therapist to help him deal with the other stresses in his life.

The nutrition therapist communicated this to the referring physician, who at first was disappointed that his patient would not be tackling his obvious nutrition problems. After the nutrition therapist explained the overall goals to the physician, he had more realistic expectations for SD and agreed to monitor his weight and blood pressure. The referring physician also agreed to provide encouragement to SD to work through his personal problems and then to return for help improving his nutrition.

payers, state the facts and leave out emotions. Speak money. Money is the language of third-party payers. You can explain how you will save the third-party payer money. Compare the cost of appointments with you to one hospitalization in dollars if the patient does not implement dietary changes. Another option—although this must be stated in your office policies and be consistently applied—is to allow the patient to pay you out of pocket at the same rate the insurance was paying to continue working with you. Chapter 8 provides more information about third-party reimbursement.

Getting Patients to Return for Follow-Up Appointments

Many RDNs who are new to private practice have difficulty getting patients to return for follow-up appointments. They are not sure what, in addition to a therapeutic approach that conveys trust and a desire to help patients, the actual mechanics are that bring patients back. In the Words of Wisdom box on the next page, some colleagues share useful techniques you can use to encourage follow-up compliance.

How to Get Patients to Return

Lori Auerbach Sullivan, MS, RD, CDN

Retention of clients has always been of concern to me, first as an outpatient dietitian for a hospital, and now in my own private practice. Fifteen years ago, a challenging middle-aged woman struggling to lose weight complimented me at her third session. The compliment has always resonated. She said:

"You are always positive and can help me see the light at the end of the tunnel. When I said I scarfed down over 10 Oreos, you responded, 'You could have eaten the entire package but chose not to.' You help me see my small steps of progress and that makes me want to stick with this."

[As a result of working with this] memorable client, my hallmark has been making my patients feel good and encouraging small changes.

Andrea Chernus, RDN, CDE, CSSD, CDN

I find that it is important to ascertain the patient's goals. Often, people hope to tackle a number of health concerns all at once. Make clear at the beginning of the session how much time is available and the volume of material that is reasonable to cover. Let them know what may be covered in today's visit and which topics may need to be addressed in future visits. Avoid overwhelming patients with too much information all at once.

One tool that has been helpful in repeat visits is the use of body composition testing. My patients love to return to see their progress in terms of body composition changes. I use a high-end bioelectrical impedance scale that provides a detailed handout that is both helpful and impressive.

Cathy Leman, MA, RD, LD

From the first point of contact with a potential new client, I work to establish rapport. I share that I am a nutrition therapist who works individually with each client. I explain [that] I employ an open-ended therapy model, which simply means that we work together for as many or [as] few sessions that their particular nutrition concerns require. I send a handwritten thank-you card to every new client. It is important to let them know how much I value their business and the trust they have in me as a nutrition professional. My clients appreciate the personal touch!

If you do your own scheduling, you can set the stage from the first inquiry about your practice. Share your philosophy. Let the prospective client know that there is a process involved in making changes and that change takes time. You might share how you structure your sessions. For instance, if you are using the first session to provide a thorough assessment, it is important to inform the patient of this so he or she does not expect that first session to include in-depth counseling.

With some types of patients, a technique referred to as previewing may be helpful. Previewing allows prospective patients to know, or preview, some of the topics you hope to address together. Weight management programs often use previewing by outlining topics that will be covered in subsequent sessions.

If you choose to outline goals with your patients, make sure that you break the goals down into achievable baby steps. It is in an RDN's nature, as a caregiver and a teacher, to provide patients with as much information as time allows (as the RDN did in the story in the Case Study with SD on page 211). As a result, the patient may leave a session suffering from information overload (see the box below for information on how to avoid information overload). This technique backfires because it does not allow patients to break the information down into a usable form. Instead, practice providing information in small manageable messages or sound bites. Patients are much more likely to return if they feel they are making progress. They are also much less likely to feel overwhelmed. There are certain medical conditions where this can be an exception. This is a judgment call on your part as a practitioner as to what will be best for the client.

You might find it useful to enter into a contract with a patient, outlining what you both hope to accomplish. This type of previewing encourages follow-up because the patient has a clear sense of what will be covered in subsequent sessions. When setting up a plan with your patients, be prepared to modify it on the basis of their needs and readiness to use the in-

Words of Wisdom

Avoiding Information Overload

Dana Magee, RD, LD

A common mistake I used to make is giving too much information in my first session. My young age prompted me to overcompensate and provide too many nutrition facts to prove my expertise. I now take the time to really listen to clients and only give them bite-sized pieces of information.

Reprinted with permission from Empowered Enterprises.[5]

formation. A simple technique to assess your patient's readiness to change is to ask during initial intake *How do you feel about making changes to your eating habits?* You may be surprised at the answers you receive.

Learn how and when to end sessions. About 10 minutes before the end of the appointment, inform the patient of the time. You can say something to the effect of *We have 10 minutes left. Is there anything you'd like to discuss before we stop?* Or you can ask if the patient has any questions, what he or she will be working on until the next appointment, or if he or she has any feedback on the session. This provides the patient with a sense of time and closure.

Sometimes a patient will have more to discuss than time allows in a session. If a patient brings up a topic as the session is ending, acknowledge the importance of the topic and let the patient know you will be happy to discuss it at the next appointment. Although the patient may feel unsatisfied, it is important that he or she understand and respect your need to adhere to your schedule. Be sure to explain to the patient your desire and intention to answer the questions, allowing the time they warrant. Patients will appreciate your ability to manage your time, and will establish time boundaries. To encourage a patient to return for a follow-up session, close the session with an open-ended question: *When would you like your next appointment?* or *I'd like to see you in one week; what are your thoughts?* If you know that more work needs to be done, you could say *Let's schedule your next visit* as opposed to *Do you want to come back for follow-up?*[22] Open-ended questions encourage the patient to assume an active role in treatment. Be sure you allow time at the end of a session to schedule a follow-up appointment rather than asking the patient to call you. The chances of the patient making an appointment after he or she has left the session will decrease. The box below provides further insight into a patient's willingness to return.

Determining Your Client's Readiness to Return

Clients are most likely to come back if they...

- are somewhat ready to change,
- know that real change happens gradually over time and in stages,
- believe that you understand their concerns and care about them,
- trust that you have the skills and knowledge to help them reach their goals, and
- are not significantly triggered to resist change in the first session.

Adapted with permission from Molly Kellogg.[26]

Patients can find it helpful to receive the follow-up appointment date and time in writing at the end of the session. Consider putting the appointment reminder on the back of your business card. Confirm patients' follow-up appointments with a phone call, an email, or a text message based on their preferred form of communication. Generally, patients who receive a reminder message or detailed information in a behavioral contract are less likely to be a no-show.

Bundling sessions as a package and giving patients discounts for multiple sessions may also encourage follow-up. If you use this technique, it is advisable to require payment up front. By using this technique to encourage follow-up, you can also give patients a preview of topics that may be covered in subsequent sessions. Patients may focus on the need to cover specific topics in the sequence that best meets their needs. This ensures that the sessions' goals are the patient's goals, not the RDN's goals for the patient.

Evaluating Private Practice Success

Success. How does one determine whether he or she is succeeding in private practice? According to the Merriam-Webster website, success is defined as "the fact of getting or achieving wealth, respect, or fame," "the correct or desired result of an attempt," or "someone or something that is successful; a person or thing that succeeds."[27] Measuring the success of your private practice will depend on you and what is important to you.

Is it about...

- the number of appointments on your calendar?
- how much money you are earning?
- patients and referral sources valuing your service and work?
- patients improving their health and achieving their goals?
- your patientss satisfaction?
- needing to hire another RDN?
- outgrowing your space?

Success will be different for different RDNs. Read in the Words of Wisdom box on the next page how other RDNs define success. May you be bestowed with success in your private practice, however you define it!

How Do RDNs in Private Practice Define Success?

Penny Wilson, RDN, CSSD, LD
"Profit. Profit. Profit."

Joey Gochnour, MEd, RDN, CSSD, LD, NASM-CPT
"Actually helping people in my own way and making a living doing what I want."

Digna Irizarry Cassens, MHA, RDN, CLT
"When my clients get better and their health improves, even just a smidgen."

Lisa Young, PhD, RD
"Making a difference AND a living!"

Judy Simon, MS, RDN, CDE, CHES, of Mind Body Nutrition, PLLC
"I measure success by the outcomes and feedback I receive from my patients and providers."

Aarti Batavia, MS, RD, CLT, CFSP, IFMCP
"Emotional: Sense of gratification that I am an instrument to help an individual achieve their health goals.

Mental: Intellectual ability to synthesize information, read studies, and translate [information] into practical solutions.

Financial: Numbers speak for themselves."

The Future of Your Practice

You may decide that you want to run your practice as a part-time business. You may be happy to keep it small and manageable, knowing that in the future if you change your mind you can expand your practice. On the other hand, you may envision having a full-time practice with the goal of having a staff of support employees and other RDNs plus multiple locations. Whatever your dream is for your practice, small or large, with time you will be evaluating the status of your practice, tweaking it as you go along. Remember: This is *your* business. It is your vision and your dream. It is about what works for you and what you want. It can be personally satisfying to be your own boss and to be able to mold your practice to fit your life.

Initially, you might enjoy working alone and doing everything yourself. But when you begin to find yourself meeting with patients during the day and working in the evening and on weekends to return phone calls and do paperwork for your practice, it is time to make a change. You need balance in your life the same way we tell our patients to balance their meals. We have to practice what we preach. Explore what you can do to lighten your workload. Would hiring a support staff person or another RDN help lighten the burden? Information about hiring staff, such as a virtual assistant and other RDNs, is included in chapter 5.

To learn more about the future potential of your practice, read chapter 10, which includes other RDNs' success stories, and refer to chapter 11 for additional resources. The successful future of your practice can be a reality. Good luck!

Running a Successful Practice: A Summary

Having a flourishing private practice may require a change in your approach. To encourage follow-up visits, you must position yourself as a nutrition therapist. Successful patients are your best form of advertising. Success can be defined in many ways, but one absolute measure will be your patients' satisfaction. It may also be necessary to educate referral sources as well as patients on more acceptable measures of success. Keep the following key points in mind:

- Developing a routine when seeing patients will keep you organized.
- Staying in business means developing a practice where the need for repeat business, or follow-up sessions, is a reality.
- You will be more successful with your patients when you learn how to transition your approach to a counseling style appropriate for long-term relationships.
- Through course work, individual work, and specialized training, you will gradually become more comfortable with your role as a nutrition therapist. There are numerous resources available to RDNs, but implementing counseling techniques into your practice is the most useful way to make the transition.
- Certain techniques related to scheduling, running, and concluding appointments can encourage patients to return.
- Communicating your counseling approach to your referral sources and potential patients is necessary to avoid misunderstandings and to set expectations about what nutrition counseling will achieve.

References

1. Reiff D, Reiff K. *Eating Disorders: Nutrition Therapy in the Recovery Process.* Gaithersburg, MD: Aspen Publishers; 1992.

2. Hollis JK, William LT, Collins CE, Morgan PJ. Does motivational interviewing align with international scope of practice, professional competency standards, and best practice guidelines in dietetics practice? *J Acad Nutr Diet.* 2014;114(5):676-686.

3. Maillet JO. Dietetics in 2017: what does the future hold? *J Am Diet Assoc.* 2002;102(10):1404-1406.

4. Setnick J. *Academy of Nutrition and Dietetics Pocket Guide to Eating Disorders.* 2nd ed. Chicago, IL: Academy of Nutrition and Dietetics; 2016.

5. Greenberg KF, Bitzer R, Magee D. *Welcome to the REBELution: Seven Steps to the Nutrition Counseling Practice of Your Dreams.* Greenbelt, MD: Empowered Enterprises; 2014.

6. Saloff-Coste CJ, Hamburg P, Herzog DB. Nutrition and psychotherapy: collaborative treatment of patients with eating disorders. *Bull Menninger Clin.* 1993;57(4):504-516.

7. Smart H, Clifford D, Morris MN. Nutrition students gain skills from motivational interviewing curriculum. *J Acad Nutr Diet.* 2014;114(11):1712-1713.

8. McCaffree J. Client satisfaction: turning referrals into regulars. *J Am Diet Assoc.* 2002;102(3):340-341.

9. Kellogg M. *Counseling Tips for Nutrition Therapists: Practice Workbook, Volume 1.* Philadelphia, PA: Kg Press; 2006.

10. Hancock RE, Bonner G, Hollingdale R, Madden A. "If you listen to me properly, I feel good": a qualitative examination of patient experiences of dietetic consultations. *J Hum Nutr Diet.* 2012;25(3):275-284.

11. Herrin M, Larkin M. *Nutrition Counseling in the Treatment of Eating Disorders.* 2nd ed. New York, NY: Routledge; 2013.

12. Ozier AD, Henry BW. Position of the American Dietetic Association: nutrition intervention in the treatment of eating disorders. *J Am Diet Assoc.* 2011;111(8):1236-1241.

13. Raynor HA, Champagne CM. Position of the Academy of Nutrition and Dietetics: interventions for the treatment of overweight and obesity in adults. *J Acad Nutr Diet.* 2016;116(1):129-147.

14. Brug J, Spikmans F, Aartsen C, Breedveld B, Bes R, Fereira I. Training dietitians in basic motivational interviewing skills results in changes in their counseling style and in lower saturated fat intakes in their patients. *J Nutr Educ Behav.* 2007;39 (1):8-12.

15. What is the evidence that motivational interviewing, used as an adjunct to a cognitive-behavioral program, results in health/food behavior change in adults counseled in an outpatient/clinic setting? Evidence Analysis Library website. www.andeal.org/topic.cfm?evidence_summary_.

16. Motivational Interviewing Network of Trainers website. www.motivational interviewing.org. Accessed May 11, 2017.

17. Glovsky E, Rose G. Motivational interviewing: a unique approach to behavior change counseling. Today's Dietitian. May 2007;9(5):50. www.todaysdietitian.com/newarchives/tdmay2007pg50.shtml. Accessed March 24, 2017.

18. Clifford D. Motivational interviewing—learn about MI's place in nutrition counseling and essential tools for enhancing client motivation. *Today's Dietitian.* July 2016;18(7):48. www.todaysdietitian.com/newarchives/0716p48.shtml. Accessed May 11, 2017.

19. Sauter C, Constance A. *Inspiring and Supporting Behavior Change: A Food, Nutrition, and Health Professional's Counseling Guide.* 2nd ed. Chicago, IL: Academy of Nutrition and Dietetics; 2017.

20. Miller WR, Rose GS. Toward a theory of motivational interviewing. *Am Psychol.* 2009;64(6):527-537.

21. Spahn JM, Reeves RS, Keim KS, et al. State of the evidence regarding behavior change theories and strategies in nutrition counseling to facilitate health and food behavior change. *J Am Diet Assoc.* 2010;110(6):879-891.

22. Kellogg M. *Counseling Tips for Nutrition Therapists: Practice Workbook,* Volume 3. Philadelphia, PA: Kg Press; 2014.

23. The Academy Quality Management Committee and Scope of Practice Subcommittee of the Quality Management Committee. Academy of Nutrition and Dietetics: Revised 2012 Standards of Practice in Nutrition Care and Standards of Professional Performance for Registered Dietitians. *J Acad Nutr Diet.* 2013;113(6)(suppl):S29-S45.

24. Kohn JB. How can registered dietitian nutritionists use health coaching techniques? *J Acad Nutr Diet.* 2014;114(5):824.

25. American Dietetic Association. Code of ethics for the profession of dietetics. *J Am Diet Assoc.* 2009;109(8):1461-1467.

26. Kellogg M. *Counseling Tips for Nutrition Therapists: Practice Workbook,* Volume 2. Philadelphia, PA: Kg Press; 2009.

27. Success. Merriam-Webster website. www.merriam-webster.com/dictionary/success. Accessed May 29, 2016.

10 RDNs Pay It Forward: Profiles of Successful Private Practitioners

In this book, you have read about the fundamental tools and information you have to take into account before you start seeing your first patient and to succeed in private practice. There is a lot! Please, do not be overwhelmed. You are not the first to set out on this exciting venture of starting a private practice. Registered dietitian nutritionists (RDNs), sometimes preferring to go by RD (registered dietitian), have been working in private practice for years, and many have been pioneers in paving the path for others, like you, to follow. When they started, there were limited resources for starting a private practice. Insurance reimbursement for nutrition was in its infancy. Tremendous strides have been made for private practice RDNs—as RDNs are now recognized as the most reputable source for nutrition information and counseling.

You are fortunate to be able to read the following stories of these seasoned and accomplished private practice RDNs. They have different specialties and different approaches to their private practices. You will get a sense of how they started in private practice and how their practices have evolved over the years. They also share their recommendations to help you with your private practice.

Susan Allen, RD, CCN

How and when did you start your practice?
When I graduated high school, I decided against college because I wanted to be a professional dancer. I soon learned that dancing doesn't pay

the bills, so I became certified as a fitness instructor/personal trainer to augment my income. As I worked in health clubs, it dawned on me [that] I [could] run these clubs. I decided to go to college for a degree in fitness management and matriculated at the University of Illinois. I enrolled in an elective basic nutrition class that was about vitamins and minerals. I thought "This is very cool!" The scientist in me came out. Here was my calling! I immediately switched my major to nutrition. It was a perfect complement to fitness and dance.

Upon graduation in the early 1990s, I went right into private practice, against all advice to either go on for a master's degree or at least work in a hospital for a year. Neither were options for me! I was now teaching fitness in the same health clubs but with each client having separate sessions exclusively on nutrition.

One year after I graduated, I had twin boys, and my career became part time. When I returned to work from my maternity leave, I transitioned my focus from fitness to mainly nutrition. I was fortunate to obtain space in my obstetrician-gynecologist's office at no charge. With his referrals, I now had a new clientele. At the same time, I started [working] in my home office in Chicago.

I was fortunate to be interviewed by the health writer for a major newspaper, the *Chicago Tribune*. I became a frequent contributor to the newspaper's health column. One day a chiropractor contacted me because of the *Tribune* articles. He wanted me to work with his patients, and he inquired if I used testing such as organic acids and gastrointestinal function tests in my practice. I had to admit I did not. He handed me a book by Jeffrey Bland, PhD, on nutritional biochemistry and said, "Susan, there's a whole other world of nutrition out there—read this." I read the book and attended a conference by Bland a few months later. There were 500 attendees and I was one of only two dietitians, but this conference was my motivation. I was angry that I didn't learn this in college, and yet I was told I was the "nutrition expert." This motivated me to learn about what was then called "integrative" or "complementary" (now often referred to as "functional") nutrition. This was the beginning of an exciting journey.

I became a certified clinical nutritionist (CCN) with the International & American Associations of Clinical Nutritionists. This was training more specific to the functional nutrition approach. With newfound passion, my practice started thriving. [With this, and] with my new credential, I attracted the interest of a newly opened integrative medicine clinic that bought out my private practice and hired me as a salaried employee. Initially, services were reimbursed by insurance. As insurance started questioning the different testing approach, it became increasingly difficult to get timely reimbursement and, as a result, the clinic had to close.

I subsequently worked for the Center for Integrative Medicine affiliated with Northwestern Memorial Hospital's Physicians' Group but didn't have the freedom to practice at the deepest level I was familiar with. At that time, integrative medicine concepts were challenged by the conventional medicine sector much more than today. Being frustrated, I went back into private practice and worked mainly with an integrative doctor I [had] previously worked with. Insurance was reimbursing some and when it didn't, clients were happy to pay for my specialty expertise. I had a four-week waiting list!

Many of my colleagues inquired about my practice and wanted to learn what I knew, so I started a mentoring program. As interest eventually surpassed capacity, I clearly saw a need for more dietitians to be trained in functional medicine and in 2012 I started an online training program. Soon after, I moved to Florida, where I attempted an in-person private practice, though it became apparent that Florida's poor insurance reimbursement for nutrition would be a hindrance. I broadened my availability in a virtual practice while focusing on the expansion of my integrative and functional nutrition training program for dietitians.

Briefly describe your practice.

Now my part-time private practice is exclusively integrative and functional medicine based. I use Skype to consult my clients. I see complicated cases where my functional nutrition approach gives results my clients weren't getting with other practitioners. I have an all-cash practice and do not accept third-party payments. I [believe] that [because] the global shift of health consciousness [has expanded], my patients are willing to pay out of pocket.

I have a full-time assistant who manages details related to my private practice and my training program. I see a wide range of diagnoses. My intake forms are 12 pages long, and I review these prior to a client's appointment, after which I spend as much as two hours in an initial consult. I obtain standard and specialty laboratory tests, including genomics, to find the imbalances, deficiencies, or insufficiencies underlying these diseases and conditions. I recommend personalized diet, nutritional supplements, and mind-body practices that contribute to very successful outcomes. I also consult other dietitians on their cases. It is my passion that functional nutrition become mainstream and that our profession become revitalized as a result.

What effective marketing tools do you recommend or have you used?

My referrals now are strictly word of mouth. In the past, I found brochures describing my approach and video interviews with testimonials from clients posted on my website very effective marketing as well. In the past, I would also place all these accolades in letters I received from patients into a notebook placed in the waiting room of my office.

What is your one invaluable gem for RDNs starting out in private practice?

If you are starting a private practice, go as deeply as you can to understand all aspects of any client's health. Functional nutrition offers a very comprehensive and personalized approach. Do not allow fear to get in your way; get the extra training you need to feel confident. Fear can also dictate your fee schedule. Value your expertise. Dietitians who find their worth in a specialty and claim their value do the best!

Jill Castle, MS, RD, LDN

How and when did you start your practice?

I knew I wanted to open a practice in 2007 when my youngest child entered preschool, but I had trepidation (and fear!) after being out of the workforce for an almost eight-year span while raising four kids. After our family moved to Nashville, Tennessee, in 2008, it was clear that the timing was right. All four kids were in school, and I had spent the better part of a year researching, reading, preparing, and planning. The first week I had one client, and by a month, I had three or four and it just kept growing! I initially started in a little office in my home in Nashville and stayed there for two years. Although I said I was part time, I was seeing about 20 to 25 clients a week over four days. I knew I needed more space and needed to hire another registered dietitian to help me, so I moved to a rented space and hired a consultant RDN. My new space had two offices, a waiting area, a bathroom, a kitchenette, and a general meeting area. I operated a self-pay practice and offered detailed receipts for insurance reimbursement (at the time, Tennessee was pursuing RDN reimbursement). My family relocated from Nashville to Connecticut in 2012, during which I coauthored the highly recommended book *Fearless Feeding: How to Raise Healthy Eaters from High Chair to High School* (Jossey-Bass, 2013) and also wrote the book *Eat Like a Champion* (AMACOM, 2015).

Briefly describe your practice.

In 2016, I reopened my practice after many referrals and requests to start seeing clients again. I see clients one day per week, and I only accept self-pay [clients]. My private practice focuses on pediatric nutrition, so my clientele are limited to children aged 0 to 18 years and their parents.

What effective marketing tools do you recommend or have you used?

The most effective marketing tool I have used outside of the usual website (www.jillcastle.com), brochures, business cards, etc, is sending a letter to the pediatrician after seeing their patient. This effort has been a great relationship and trust builder and has been integral for future referrals.

I use the term *childhood nutrition expert* on my website and [in my] search engine optimization (SEO) efforts, and this has brought many opportunities my way, including invitations for international consulting.

Word of mouth is extremely powerful. I am seeing my current, yet small, practice get many referrals from my patients of record. Facebook advertisements are very effective as well—so effective I haven't used them yet for my private practice because I want to contain my practice at this time.

What is your one invaluable gem for RDNs starting out in private practice?

Do excellent work! You have to be effective (meaning your clients need to see results—either in more knowledge, better numbers, motivation, etc)—in order to sustain the success of your practice. My goal is that each person who walks out of my office understands nutrition better, is motivated to make a positive change, and sees value in coming to my office.

Another piece of advice is to diversify your practice. I started blogging, which turned into book deals, consulting opportunities, and speaking engagements. I conducted parent workshops, developed materials for other RDs, and have found ways to make passive income on my website. All these diversifications add to your bottom line—your reputation, your opportunities, and your income.

Nancy Clark, MS, RD, CSSD

How and when did you start your practice?

SportsMedicine Brookline, a new sports medicine clinic, hired me in 1980 to be their sports nutritionist. After about 10 years, the management decided to change the financial agreement. Instead of them paying me a salary, they switched to having me be a consultant—and I had to pay them rent for use of the office space. Yikes, that was a big change within a five-minute conversation! I coughed up the rent until it became obvious that the doctors really needed my office space for their booming business. I started looking for a new professional "home" and found a wonderful spot just down the street at a new fitness center for women called Healthworks. They welcomed me (rent-free), knowing that I would bring credibility and visibility to their center. I enjoyed my office there and saw the same clients as at the sports medicine clinic. (The doctors had not been a major source of referrals to me; most of my clients tracked me down via word of mouth.) As the health club's membership grew, space became an issue and they wanted my office to take care of their business needs. I then decided to find my very own office.

Briefly describe your practice.

I now see my clients in a remodeled historical building in the same vicinity as my first two offices. I do not have any office staff; I am able to handle my 12 to 20 clients per week by myself. I want to keep my life simple! I recently became a provider for three health insurance companies. When athletes do not have to pay out of pocket, they are more likely to come see me and continue for follow-up visits! I submit the insurance claims using Office Ally and have not had problems or overwhelming hassles. Yes, there is a learning curve, but it's good information to learn. Plus insurance payments contribute to a stronger income stream.

What effective marketing tools do you recommend or have you used?

My best marketing has been writing a monthly sports nutrition article that includes a credit line filled with important information about my business:

> Sports nutritionist Nancy Clark, MS, RD, CSSD, has a private practice in the Boston area (Newton, Massachusetts, 617-795-1875), where she helps both fitness exercisers and competitive athletes create winning food plans. Her best-selling book, *Nancy Clark's Sports Nutrition Guidebook*; food guides for marathoners, cyclists, and soccer players; and teaching materials are available at www.nancyclarkrd.com. For online and live workshops, visit www.NutritionSportsExerciseCEUs.com.

My monthly article goes to over 100 sports and fitness publications. The readership is large, and I am honored that a wide range of fitness exercisers and competitive athletes enjoy the information. This article has helped me market my best-selling book, *Nancy Clark's Sports Nutrition Guidebook*, now in its fifth edition.

What is your one invaluable gem for RDNs starting out in private practice?

My gem for RDNs starting [a private] practice is to find your niche, figure out how you can make yourself visible in the (social) media, write profusely, never stop advertising your services, and enjoy the ride.

Marci Evans, MS, CEDRD, LDN, cPT

How and when did you start your practice?

In 2009 I was finishing my master's degree with a dual emphasis in business/entrepreneurship and eating disorders counseling. At this time, I was also working a full-time job as a dietitian and personal trainer at a gym and covering for a maternity leave at a local eating disorders facility. Two jobs and graduate school, sounds like the perfect time to start your business. Right? Turns out it was! My degree from Northeastern University provided me with the practical academic knowledge and accountability to develop a thorough business plan. My two jobs were flexible so I could start my practice and eventually work full-time hours as my practice grew. I didn't know it at the time, but it was an ideal situation to take the risk and venture into business ownership!

Briefly describe your practice.

I am incredibly fortunate to live around the corner from my beautiful office in Harvard Square, which is situated in Cambridge, Massachusetts. I lease three offices, and I also sublease one office to two therapists for an additional income stream. Currently, in addition to myself, I have two RDNs on staff. I also have an absolutely phenomenal biller, who happens to be my mom, and an administrative assistant to help me with all new referrals who is one of my very best friends. I know general business advice is to steer clear of mixing business and personal relationships, but my current arrangement has been nothing but positive. My mom and my friend are professional, highly organized, attuned to detail, and—perhaps most importantly—trustworthy and care immensely about my success. Currently, my practice is dual focused. The first specialty is treating people with eating disorders, disordered eating, and chronic histories of dieting. I am grateful that insurance reimburses quite well in the state of Massachusetts, so about 70% of my clients use their insurance for treatment and the other 30% self-pay. Given the long-term nature of the work with eating disorders, I personally believe in the value of accepting insurance to provide access to treatment. The second specialty is training RDNs in the art and science of counseling people with eating disorders. This service is self-pay, and I accept cash, check, and credit cards as forms of payment.

What effective marketing tools do you recommend or have you used?

I do very little "traditional" marketing—no visits to primary care physician offices, no mailers, next to no mass emails, and no lunch and learn[s]. I can summarize my marketing efforts in three key points:

1. Be visible—join committees, write articles, ask for interviews, submit proposals to speak at conferences, attend networking events, socialize, and work your social media. I HIGHLY recommend hiring someone to help you with your social media strategy.

2. Establish relationships with your referral sources rather than marketing to potential clients. These people are easy to identify if you are clear about your niche and expertise. Make coffee dates and become an expert communicator about the work you are doing with your clients. As you illustrate the work you do via email, fax, or phone, they will be so impressed and [will] WANT to send more clients your way!

3. Invest up front in a beautiful and highly professional website. In the eyes of potential clients and colleagues, your site reflects the caliber of work you do. I believe so firmly that anything you put out on the internet is a reflection of YOU that you must take seriously. If anything is worth doing, it is worth doing well.

What is your one invaluable gem for RDNs starting out in private practice?

Some clinicians experience private practice as lonely and isolating. Assess your tolerance for working independently and use that information to decide the type of practice you want and whether it would work best for you to integrate one or two other jobs while maintaining a part-time practice. Be creative! Also, build communities of colleagues around you through mastermind groups, supervision groups, online forums, Academy of Nutrition and Dietetics dietetic practice groups (DPGs), and like-minded colleagues so you feel supported, challenged, and inspired! I have done all of the above and over time [have] created other avenues of work, including adjunct teaching at three universities and developing online trainings for dietitians. It has helped me stay energized and prevent burnout. I have built myself a dream job and wish you all the best as you do the same!

Jan Patenaude, RD, CLT

How and when did you start your practice?

As an RD since 1982, I've started three private practices. In 1986, as the only RD in town, working at a small hospital, I was responsible for food service, nutrition services both inpatient and outpatient, a community wellness/weight loss program, and a biweekly radio program. With great name recognition in this small community, but added job duties, I asked for and was denied a 50-cent per-hour raise. That was the motivation [I] needed to start a private practice. I worked from my home office combined with some consulting positions and taught weight management classes and have never returned to full-time employment.

In 1989 I moved to New Jersey and started my second combined consulting/private practice. There, I was asked to write a monthly nutrition column in a large suburban newspaper, so again, the name recognition helped draw clients. Even though it was not a paid position, the size of the article, if it had been paid advertising, would have cost over $1,000 per month.

By 2001, now living in the middle of the Colorado Rockies, 30 miles from the nearest gas station or supermarket and not wanting a long winter commute, online seemed [like] the place to search for work. I ended up being hired very part time to post on a medical message board online, for very small pay—but this was a way to get my foot in the door. Through this board, I met the now-president of Oxford Biomedical Technologies and was hired to work with Lifestyle Eating and Performance commonly referred to as LEAP (www.nowleap.com) clients [virtually]. My responsibility was to provide anti-inflammatory personalized elimination diet counseling based on the client's non-IgE, non-IgG mediatory release test (MRT) food sensitivity blood test.

Briefly describe your practice.

Currently, my private practice remains small, as I'm also a consultant, mentoring other RDNs [who] want to use LEAP protocols in their private practices.

What effective marketing tools do you recommend or have you used?

Having a profile on HealthProfs (www.HealthProfs.com) is the best marketing tool out there. But word of mouth from happy clients has been equally effective. I am blessed to be able to continue to travel and work from the Colorado Rockies and the Hawaiian rain forest.

What is your one invaluable gem for RDNs starting out in private practice?

Learn negotiating skills! Get your hands on articles or recordings by Roger Dawson, master negotiator and author of the revered book and audio program *Secrets of Power Negotiating*.

Dee Pratt, RDN, LDN

How and when did you start your practice?

My journey to private practice started out more in the consulting side of dietetics and has developed more into the private practice world over the past 21 years. In 1995, after confiding to one of my colleagues, Linda Pennington, that I was going to leave the hospital to start a practice, she asked if I would consider a partner. I must admit I hadn't thought much about it up to that moment, but we discussed it and we both agreed to a partnership. This was a very big step because it changed a lot of things from working from home to having an office for two people. It changed the focus from just consulting to providing more clinical services since Linda was a very strong clinical dietitian.

We found a small office, which needed cleaning and painting, which we did ourselves to save money. We quickly grew out of that office after hiring our first full-time employee three months after starting our company. Our business rapidly grew as we provided consulting to small hospitals, cancer centers, developmental disabilities, diabetes [centers], long-term care and assisted living [centers], restaurants, and many other companies. We also found ourselves in high demand doing staff relief for all the major hospitals in town. We were affectionately known by some as the "rent a dietitians." In addition to consulting and staffing, we did see some outpatients in our offices, but since there was no reimbursement at that time, our numbers were very small.

We had 14 full-time RDNs for about the first 10 to 12 years, and we were busy as could be, but there was something missing for Linda and myself; we were missing getting to practice dietetics. We were spending most of our time scheduling and doing paperwork. There was no time for anything else, and we were spending long hours at the office. We decided at that point to downsize, and so, by attrition, we were able to meet our goals. We learned a valuable lesson that bigger is not necessarily better. Instead of us controlling the business, it seemed to be controlling us.

About this same time, Medicare was starting to reimburse for medical nutrition therapy (MNT). Once we became comfortable with the process for billing, I started contacting Cigna, Blue Cross Blue Shield, and other insurance companies in Tennessee to get them to see the value of our services; it took some of them a couple of years, but finally they started to reimburse as well. At this point, our focus became more on private practice, which we have continued for about the past seven to nine years.

Briefly describe your practice.

We now have a staff of four full-time RDNs and one part-time RDN along with support staff, which has allowed Linda and myself to once again actually do hands-on practice. Probably 75% of our practice is from insurance reimbursement for outpatients in our offices and telenutrition, 20% from facility consulting, and 5% from other sources such as self-pay customers.

We have always tried to stay on the cutting edge of what is going on in the field of nutrition. Our company, Dietitian Associates, Inc, is not only the longest-running nutrition company in Tennessee but [was] also the first to file for reimbursement from insurance companies. We have worked for reimbursement from all the insurance companies in our area, which has helped other dietitians to be reimbursed. We provide a full range of services, including metabolic testing, mediator release testing for food sensitivities, and in 2014, we started [providing] telenutrition. We provide telenutrition to federally qualified clinics across the state of Tennessee as well as to clinics in Mississippi and Arkansas.

What effective marketing tools do you recommend or have you used?

Having a quality service has helped others to recommend us to their friends and colleagues. Our dietitians are highly qualified, and we make sure we are available for follow-up questions to our customers. We volunteer a lot with other organizations as well as with our professional organizations at various levels, which helps keep our company's name and dietitians' names out in the public. Our website and marketing brochures help. We have used many marketing strategies over the past 21-plus years and have learned that you have to adjust your marketing to what group you are targeting.

What is your one invaluable gem for RDNs starting out in private practice?

Advice I would give to someone just starting out: Get experience in a hospital for a couple of years to develop a good knowledge base and always be honest and ethical in all your dealings with people. In private practice, you often have to go above and beyond for your customers. Be willing to pay it forward; none of us got to where we are without someone behind us.

I have truly enjoyed private practice and consulting over the past 21 years, and I wouldn't change anything about this experience.

Ann Silver, MS, RDN, CDE, CDN

How and when did you start your practice?

It was August 1991, with only three weeks left to my maternity leave before returning to work, that I received a phone call. The call came just as I was walking out of my house for the ocean beach with my family and friends. The facility's administrator informed me [that] my consulting contract as a dietitian was being terminated immediately. My services were no longer needed. I was devastated and angry! Since having moved to the eastern end of Long Island [also known as the Hamptons] in the late 1980s, there was limited employment for a chief dietitian, my previous position. So instead, I had been working as a consultant. At the same time, I had been dabbling in private practice, seeing my obstetrician's patients with gestational diabetes and weight management [issues]. I can vividly remember that day sitting on the beach deciding to make this situation a positive one by starting a new chapter. And it was a new chapter! My plan of action was to go full steam ahead with my private practice. The first two most important decisions I had to make [were] where I would see patients and how [I would] market myself. I started out in my husband's office and sent out letters to all the health care providers in the area introducing myself and asking to meet them. I was pleasantly surprised by the overwhelming receptive response. Within a short time, I was counseling patients and my practice was taking off.

Briefly describe your practice.

I have three office locations. My main office is in East Hampton, New York, and then I rent space by the hour at a primary care office also in East Hampton and also at an endocrinologist's office in Riverhead, New York. I found [that] making my services geographically convenient for [patients] increased my patient load. My areas of specialty are diabetes, eating disorders, and weight management. I am a solo practitioner with an amazing virtual assistant who has been running my practice since 2005. Although many may think of the Hamptons as an area of the rich and famous, those who live in the area year-round are hardworking people. We have a saying here: "You feast in the season and starve when it's not season." I knew to have a thriving year-round practice I had to accept insurance and gear myself to the year-round residents. Back in the "dark ages," third-party payers did not recognize dietitians as in-network providers. It took a couple of years of repeated targeting, cultivating, and marketing to become a participating provider. Once I became a provider of one insurance company, I used it as leverage to become a provider of other insurance companies. Because I practice in a smaller community, I have found it extremely important and helpful to develop a relationship with my patients. I pride myself on understanding each individual's life situation and the impact it has on their nutrition and food choice[s]. At times, I feel I am [a] detective trying to figure out what is going on and how I can best help the person.

What effective marketing tools do you recommend or have you used?

Marketing needs to be approached from different angles. We have to remind people we are out there. To the health care providers who send me referrals, I fax my chart note[s] for each new patient (with the patient's permission). At holiday time, I send a subscription to a monthly nutrition newsletter to my top 20 referral sources as a thank you and a year-round reminder I'm here to help. For each new patient, I send an email expressing my appreciation [for] meeting them and informing him or her I am available to answer questions between appointments via email. All my patients who want can subscribe to my monthly email newsletter. Otherwise, in the community I stay involved in different activities of interest to me that will continue to nourish my practice. Word of mouth has certainly been my BEST form of marketing.

What is your one invaluable gem for RDNs starting out in private practice?

Be kind and understanding. Show you really care. Go out of your way, but within limits. Always have business cards on you. Make sure you love what you do. Enjoy!

Lisa Stollman, MA, RDN, CDE, CDN

How and when did you start your private practice?

Crazy as it seems, I've known I wanted to have my own nutrition practice even before I started college. My love for food and nutrition began in high school when I discovered through various books the enormous impact optimal nutrition has on long-term health. I knew I wanted to help people improve their lives, and after having way too many jobs in high school (!), I knew I wanted to use my creativity, coupled with my entrepreneurial spirit, and work for myself. I started my first private practice in 1984 in New York City while I was working in a hospital when one of the physicians had patients to refer to me. From there, my practice took off as my referral base grew. I continued with my full-time clinical hospital position and part-time practice until I moved to Florida for my husband to complete his fellowship. In Florida, I took a part-time position in a small psychiatric hospital as a nutrition consultant and started my second private practice seeing a variety of patients with an emphasis on weight management and diabetes. After two years, I sold my private practice, and we moved north to Boston. Within a month I had a great part-time position as a clinical nutritionist teaching dietetic interns and medical students at the Frances Stern Nutrition Center. And I found a great office space in Brookline and opened my third private practice. And once again, after two years, we moved (I should have been a professional mover!)—this time to Long Island, New York. I was seven months pregnant when we arrived. When my son was a couple months old, I found an office (my fourth practice!) and started to promote my services to all the local physicians who I felt would have patients for me, such as internists, endocrinologists, and obstetricians. I sent out an introductory letter along with a brochure and business cards.

Briefly describe your practice.

My practice slowly grew, and I'm pleased to say that my Long Island practice is now 26 years old. I'm the nutrition consultant for a large medical group practice [and] receive a lot of referrals from surrounding physicians. My specialties include weight management, diabetes, and gastrointestinal issues. Three years ago I hung up my shingle in New York City and work there part of the week as well. I LOVE being my own boss and using my strong clinical nutrition background to help my patients live healthier lives.

What effective marketing tools do you recommend or have you used?

I do very little marketing, with the exception of social media, as I have many referring physicians as well as patients who refer their friends and family. You can't beat word of mouth! Being kind, asking patients what they want from you, and meeting their needs help to make happy and satisfied patients.

Several years ago, I wrote a book on healthy eating for teens (*The Teen Eating Manifesto: The Ten Steps to Losing Weight, Looking Great and Getting Healthy* [Nirvana Press, 2012]), which has brought a lot of teens into my practice. In addition, I published an ebook on healthy eating while traveling (*The Trim Traveler: How to Eat Healthy and Stay Fit while Traveling Abroad* [Nirvana Press, 2014]) that has also generated more referrals for my practice. Networking on social media with other nutrition professionals and prospective clients also helps to promote my expertise as well as introduce me to new business contacts.

What is your one invaluable gem for RDNs starting out in private practice?

Working in private practice can be isolating, so you need to build your network. Get out there and network with local people in your community. Let them know what you do. And always have business cards on hand. Find additional revenue streams to make your work and life more stimulating. Give presentations. Write a blog. If you have a great idea for a book, get writing. Get involved. One of the best things I ever did to meet new friends and enhance my career was to join the board of Nutrition Entrepreneurs (NE) DPG. Being the NE Chair was such a great experience and to this day, 20 years later, the NEDPG continues to enhance my work as a nutrition entrepreneur.

Evelyn Tribole, MS, RD

How and when did you start your private practice?

I have been in private practice since 1985. At first, I worked in a doctor's office. There were two advantages of this for me. [First], it afforded me the opportunity to see if I would even like being a private practice dietitian, and second the office staff took care of everything—scheduling patients, billing, and paying me. I moved around a bit renting offices until I leased my office from Elyse Resch. Whoever knew that with my leasing from Elyse would be the creation of intuitive eating, including a book, *Intuitive Eating: A Revolutionary Program That Works* (St Martin's Griffin, 2003), which is in its third edition. I also train other health professionals on this topic.

Briefly describe your practice.

Ten years ago, I made a great business decision by purchasing an office condominium in Newport Beach, California. To help with the expenses of property ownership, I subdivided the space, and I rent it out to another dietitian. My office literally looks like a living room. The decor is homey and makes my patients/clients feel comfortable. I am a solo practitioner specializing in eating disorders and intuitive eating. All my patients are self-pay.

Five years ago, I participated in a program with graduate students who performed business assessments. They analyzed all aspects of my practice. They recommended [that I hire an] assistant. For years, I was debating back and forth about hiring an assistant. It was the best decision I ever made! I am more productive and less stressed since I hired my assistant. I have never been a full-time private practice dietitian, even though I work full time. I divide my time between counseling and training [other] health professionals on intuitive eating.

What effective marketing tools do you recommend or have you used?

Anything you do or write, always include your practice information. It can be a [one-line] bio. I suggest inviting allied health professionals to meet for coffee to get to know each other. I did this initially when I started my practice and still do it today. It's win-win.

What is your one invaluable gem for RDNs starting out in private practice?

I have more than one gem. Do something you love! I highly, highly recommend writing great consultation reports. My reports are like brief research papers. This has generated many new referral sources in my practice. I think DPGs like Nutrition Entrepreneurs and Sports, Cardiovascular, and Wellness Nutrition, also known as SCAN, are great, but don't only become a member—get involved!

Susan Weiner, MS, RDN, CDE, CDN

How and when did you start your practice?

My mom often talks about the first words I spoke when I was only eight months old. We were at a local park when I pointed to the sky and exclaimed, "See the birdie?" Since that infamous day, I've continued to pride myself on my communication skills, which includes asking open-ended questions and patiently waiting for responses. However, my interests have changed over time from birds to nutrition, human health, and my own thriving private nutrition practice.

Along with my inquisitive nature, I've always had an entrepreneurial spirit and interest in running my own successful business. After studying nutrition in college and completing my internship, I worked in a hospital (both as a clinical and chief dietitian), saw some private clients after work, and pursued my master's degree in applied physiology and nutrition. Over 27 years ago, I decided to follow my heart and my passion and started my private practice and consulting business: Susan Weiner Nutrition, PLLC. I absolutely love going to work every day! Those early speaking skills proved to be quite valuable over the past three decades as a private practice RDN and certified diabetes educator!

Briefly describe your practice.

My private practice specializing in diabetes is in an old Victorian house in Merrick, New York, that was converted to a professional building. It is a very comfortable setting, with a communal waiting area, large couches and chairs, and two bathrooms. My office is purposely set up to be non-threatening. I don't sit behind a desk or a computer in order to eliminate any perceived barriers, which immediately puts the client at ease. I sit directly across from my clients and let them know that my office is a "no judgment zone" so they can be honest and open during our discussions. They appreciate the respect I offer them, and it takes away a lot of the anxiety that people often feel when they are meeting with someone for the first time.

I also pride myself on staying on time with appointments. My clients appreciate that I see them at the scheduled time. Being on time for an appointment helps my clients follow through on their commitment to positive change and is very helpful for me staying on schedule throughout my busy day.

I accept a few insurances, but my practice is about 80% self-pay. I've become extremely busy with other projects and speaking engagements, so I decided to hire a biller for my insurance clients. I'm in my office usually four days a week, unless I'm traveling for speaking engagements or other related work. I also write for a number of publications [and] have my own column in an endocrinology publication. I also present webinars and podcasts, sit on a board for a health care organization as well as a number of diabetes not-for-profit advisory councils, and do other volunteer work for the Academy of Nutrition and Dietetics and the American Association of Diabetes Educators, so my schedule needs to remain flexible.

What effective marketing tools do you recommend or have you used?

A positive online presence is essential for marketing your private practice. Create an up-to-date website that is mobile friendly. I recently relaunched my website (www.susanweinernutrition.com). The site has dedicated pages to recent speaking engagements, patient and speaking testimonials, [and] an "in the news" [page] and an awards page. I'm also active on social media and participate in Twitter chats and Facebook interactions associated with the online diabetes community. I coauthored two books, *The Complete Diabetes Organizer: Your Guide to a Less Stressful and More Manageable Diabetes Life* (Spry Publishing, 2013) and *Diabetes 365: Tips for Living Well* (Demos Health, 2015), [and] that has increased my client referrals for diabetes. I strongly believe in volunteering and giving back in whatever way you can. Rather than talking about yourself and all you've accomplished, it will come naturally from others when you do your job well and share your knowledge and expertise. Your colleagues and other professionals will support you if you participate in leadership roles in your professional organization. By [volunteering] your expertise and time, you will also naturally market yourself and your business and naturally promote your business at the same time.

What is your one invaluable gem for RDNs starting out in private practice?

Learn to graciously say no. Many RDNs in private practice believe they need to say yes to every opportunity that comes [their] way. Make sure to politely say no to offerings that are unpaid (unless you choose to volunteer your services), and make sure you ask for what you're worth! Saying no will allow you to keep balance in your life so you can take care of your own needs. You'll be happier and healthier if you take care of yourself while you're operating your successful private practice.

Tanya Zuckerbrot, MS, RD

How and when did you start your practice?

When I first went into private practice, my focus was on applying nutrition intervention to make patients healthier, not skinnier. I approached endocrinologists and cardiologists in order to help cardiovascular patients and patients with diabetes. These doctors would refer their patients to me as an extension of their medical team.

My job was to help lower the cholesterol of these patients or, in the case of patients with diabetes, help manage their sugars. Because of fiber's ability to lower cholesterol and manage blood sugar levels, I prescribed high-fiber diets to both and, as expected, the patients got healthier. What I had not anticipated was weight loss. Across the board, all of these patients were losing weight. By consuming fiber for its clinical benefits, patients were feeling fuller on fewer calories, which led to weight loss without hunger. This was the birth of the F-Factor Diet and my first book, suitably named *The F-Factor Diet: Discover the Secret to Permanent Weight Loss* (G P Putnam's Sons, 2006). My practice continued to grow from there and in 2012 I published my second book, *The Miracle Carb Diet: Make Calories and Fat Disappear—with Fiber!* (Hyperion, 2012).

Briefly describe your practice.

F-Factor is a concierge private practice specializing in weight loss and weight management. Located in midtown Manhattan, my staff consists of four RDs and the necessary support staff. We are a small but dedicated team.

What makes F-Factor unique is that we deliver more than just nutrition and diet advice. F-Factor dietitians are more than just clinicians, we are life coaches. My staff is trained to ensure that every client leaves our office feeling more confident and inspired than when they walked in. That, and a strict dress code. If our doors are open, my staff [is dressed appropriately].

What effective marketing tools do you recommend or have you used?

Although social media wasn't around when I started my career, I'm an avid user now and would suggest taking full advantage of it to anyone starting out. Not only is social media free, but it also facilitates an immensely large reach and makes it conceivable to position yourself as an authority in your space.

What is your one invaluable gem for RDNs starting out in private practice?

Be consistent in your messaging, and practice what you preach, everywhere you go.

Early in my career I discovered the benefits of fiber. Fiber became my core platform: I've never wavered from it, and I wholeheartedly believe in it and the efficacy of the F-Factor Diet. I practice F-Factor every day of my life. I recommend [that] my clients eat high-fiber crackers to meet their fiber needs. Since I'm always practicing F-Factor, no matter where I go, I bring my fiber crackers. Therefore, I am constantly advertising for F-Factor. People may know me as that high-fiber lady, but I'm okay with that because I want all my clients to be fiber lovers too.

11 | Resources for Starting and Staying in Business

These resources provide additional information and support and do not constitute or imply an endorsement by the Academy of Nutrition and Dietetics and the authors. The more knowledge you have, the better prepared you will be.

Business Books

This is reading material that will supplement your business knowledge.

- Allen KR, Economy P, Edwards P, et al. *Starting a Business All-in-One for Dummies*. Hoboken, NJ: John Wiley & Sons; 2015.

- Guillebeau C. *Born for This*. New York, NY: Crown Business; 2016.

- Guillebeau C. *The $100 Startup: Reinvent the Way You Make a Living, Do What You Love, and Create a New Future*. New York, NY: Crown Business; 2012.

- Johnson K. *The Entrepreneur Mind: 100 Essential Beliefs, Characteristics, and Habits of Elite Entrepreneurs*. Atlanta, GA: Johnson Media Inc; 2013.

- Pinson L. *Steps to Small Business Start-up*. Tustin, CA: Out of Your Mind...and into the Marketplace; 2014.

- Ries E. *The Lean Startup*. New York, NY: Crown Business; 2011.

- Staff of Entrepreneur Media Inc. *Start Your Own Business*. 6th ed. Irvine, CA: Entrepreneur Press; 2015.

- Strauss SD. *The Small Business Bible: Everything You Need to Know to Succeed in Your Small Business*. 3rd ed. Hoboken, NJ: John Wiley & Sons; 2012.

- Tyson E, Schell J. *Small Business for Dummies*. 4th ed. Hoboken, NJ: John Wiley & Sons; 2012.

Business Magazines

These are publications that are commonly read by private practice registered dietitian nutritionists (RDNs).

- *Fast Company*: www.fastcompany.com
  – Provides innovative and creative ideas for businesses

- *Inc.*: www.inc.com
  – Advice, tools, and services for small businesses

- *Entrepreneur*: www.entrepreneur.com/magazine
  – Resources for small businesses

Registered Dietitian Nutritionist Private Practice Resources

These are additional publications about starting and growing a private practice written by RDNs.

- Greenberg KF, Bitzer R, Magee D. *Welcome to the REBELution: Seven Steps to the Nutrition Counseling Practice of Your Dreams*. Greenbelt, MD: Empowered Enterprises; 2014.

- McGurk J. *Pursuing Private Practice: 10 Steps to Grow Your Own Business*. Nyack, NY: Parker Press Publishing; 2016.

- Nutrition 411 website. www.nutrition411.com/categories/private-practice.

General Business Support and Resources

- All Business website: www.allbusiness.com
  – Provides numerous products and services, such as sample forms, contracts, and business plans, to small businesses

- Bplans.com: www.bplans.com
  - Provides articles and links for creating successful business plans
- Chamber of Commerce: www.2chambers.com
  - Can be helpful to small businesses in their communities (nearly every town in the United States has a Chamber of Commerce)

Personal Health Insurance Information

These are links to health insurance programs for individuals and small businesses.

- COBRA Health Plan Advice: An Employee's Guide to Health Benefits Under COBRA: www.dol.gov/sites/default/files/ebsa/laws -and-regulations/laws/cobra/COBRAemployee.pdf
- Healthcare.gov: www.healthcare.gov
  - Personal health insurance you can purchase through the marketplace or through health exchanges
- Insurance.com: www.insurance.com
  - Provides quotes on insurance

Self-Employed Tax Information

These are helpful Internal Revenue Service (IRS) links.

- IRS home page: www.irs.gov
- Tax forms: www.irs.gov/formspubs/index.html
- Specific information on small businesses: www.irs.gov/business/small
- Employee Identification Number (EIN) application: www.irs.gov/ein

Small Business Assistance

These are services for small businesses.

- FastTrac: www.fasttrac.org
  - Offers classes nationwide on starting and running a small business
- My Own Business: www.scu.edu/mobi/
  - Free online courses on starting a business

- National Association for the Self-Employed (NASE): www.nase.org
  - Provides many benefits and services, including insurance and resources, to make small businesses or "microbusinesses" successful
- Office of Small Business Development Centers (SBDC): www.sba.gov/tools/local-assistance
  - Sponsored by the US Small Business Association (SBA); joint effort of the private sector and various levels of government to help with all aspects of small business locally and nationwide
- Service Corps of Retired Executives (SCORE): www.score.org
  - Volunteers who were successful in business now provide small business counseling
- Small Business Association (SBA): www.sba.gov
  - A wealth of information for small businesses, providing assistance to help individuals start, run, and grow their businesses; local SBA chapters may offer classes on specific topics

Professional Liability Insurance

These are malpractice insurance providers that cover private practice RDNs.

- Healthcare Providers Service Organization (HPSO): www.hpso.com
- Proliability (also known as Mercer): www.proliability.com

Accounting Software Programs

Research different accounting software programs to determine the best software for your practice.

- FreshBooks: www.freshbooks.com
- GoDaddy Online Bookkeeping (formerly Outright): www.godaddy.com/email/online-bookkeeping
- Intuit QuickBooks: www.quickbooks.intuit.com
- Intuit Quicken: www.quicken.com
- Zoho: www.zoho.com

Marketing Resources

WEBSITE DEVELOPMENT

These publications provide guidance on how to build your own website.

- Hollenberg J. (2014) *Love at First Site*. (E-Reader version). Australia: Five by Five Online Marketing, Pty Ltd. Retrieved from www.fivebyfive.com.au/book/
- Rockwood ME. (2015) *Website Building: How to Build Your Own Website and Blog to Perfection!* (Kindle version). Malcolm Rockwood.
- Smith B. (2016) *Website Building Checklist*. www.mytrainingcenter.com

WEB DESIGN AND HOSTING PLATFORMS

Choose from do-it-yourself website builders with hosting and other website tools.

- GoDaddy: www.godaddy.com
- SquareSpace: www.squarespace.com
- Weebly: www.weebly.com
- Wix: www.wix.com

BUSINESS CARDS

These are some online resources for creating business cards.

- Business card design, marketing, and printing tips: www.businesscarddesign.com
  - Includes links to templates, resources, and printers
- Vistaprint: www.vistaprint.com
  - Provides business cards and other marketing materials

PATIENT NEWSLETTERS

- Customized Nutrition Newsletters: http://customizednutritionnewsletters.com
  - Develop your own newsletter from predesigned templates to send to patients

Social Media Resources

These publications provide information on using social media in your private practice.

- Kawasaki G, Fitzpatrick P. *The Art of Social Media*. New York, NY: Penguin Group; 2014.
- MacCarthy A. (2016) *500 Social Media Marketing Tips*. (Kindle version). http://andrewmacarthy.com/buy-my-e-book.
- Nutrition Entrepreneurs Dietetic Practice Group. Social media & self-promotion: what works and what doesn't (Entire Issue). *Ventures*. Summer 2016;33(1).

Nutrition Trade Tools

PRACTICE FORMS

These are essential forms for private practice RDNs.

- Academy of Nutrition and Dietetics forms: www.eatrightPRO.org
  - Sample Business Associates Agreement for Compliance with the Privacy Rule
  - Notice of Privacy Practices
  - Sample HIPAA Privacy Notice for RDs in Private Practice
  - Sample Patient Written Acknowledgment Confirming Receipt of Privacy Notice
- Customized Nutrition office forms: http://customizednutrition-newsletters.com/product-category/office-forms/
  - Private-practice forms that can be personalized and customized
- Nutrition 411 website: www.nutrition411.com/categories/blank-clinical-forms and www.nutrition411.com/categories/private-practice
  - Offers free downloadable forms

Food Models and Nutrition Education Tools

- Nasco Nutrition Teaching Aids: www.enasco.com/nutrition
  - Various nutrition education tools, including food models, to use when counseling

- Nutrition Counseling Education Services Publications (NCES):
  www.ncescatalog.com
  - Health and nutrition educational material and food models
- Total Nutrition Therapy, LLC:
  www.eatright123.com/products.php
  - Reproducible nutrition handouts

Nutrient Analysis Programs

These are programs to nutritionally analyze a patient's intake.

- Food Processor Nutrition and Fitness software: www.esha.com
  - Nutrient analysis plus fitness evaluation with the ability to plan
    meals; clients can upload their diets online
- FoodWorks (The Nutrition Company): www.nutritionco.com
  - Full-featured nutrient analysis software package
- NutriBase (Cybersoft, Inc): www.nutribase.com
  - A nutrient analysis program capable of transferring informa-
    tion from a client directly to your computer or smartphone

Electronic Health Record Platforms and Electronic Claims Submission

These are web-based electronic health record (EHR) and billing services.

- Connect and Coach: http://phrql.com/
  - EHR based on the Nutrition Care Process developed by RDNs
    for RDNs
- Healthie: https://gethealthie.com/
  - A platform for scheduling, billing, and claims submission via
    Office Ally; patient management; organizing forms and docu-
    ments; and conducting telehealth appointments
- KaiZenRD: http://kaizenrd.com
  - EMR that includes both HIPAA-compliant telehealth and elec-
    tronic billing; produces customized physician and client notes,
    meal plans, and outcomes reports
- Kalix: www.kalixhealth.com
  - An EHR incorporating the Nutrition Care Process; uses Office
    Ally for billing third-party payers

- MNT Assistant: www.mntassistant.com
  - Offers an EHR, billing, and electronic claims submission through Office Ally
- Nutrihand Inc: www.nutrihand.com
  - Electronic medical record (EMR) and nutrient analysis program
- Office Ally: www.officeally.com
  - Provides free claims submission and billing services with the option to purchase an EHR and real-time verification of insurance coverage

Billing Information

This section lists resources for compensation from self-paying patients and third-party payers.

CREDIT CARD PROCESSING

In addition to using these options, you can contact your bank and credit card processing companies for information on how to accept credit cards.

- Capital One Spark Pay: www.sparkpay.com
- PayPal: www.paypal.com
- QuickBooks GoPayment: www.quickbooks.intuit.com
- Square: www.squareup.com

REIMBURSEMENT RESOURCES

Private practitioners should stay current with all the reimbursement issues. The information is constantly changing. Fortunately, staying current is made easy by the resources available through the Academy of Nutrition and Dietetics. Resources that can help you stay informed include the following:

- The Nutrition Services Coverage Team at the Academy of Nutrition and Dietetics
  - Members of the team are extremely helpful and available if you have specific questions; email the team at reimburse@eatright.org
- The *MNT Provider* newsletter on the Academy of Nutrition and Dietetics website: www.eatrightPRO.org/resources/news-center/in-practice/mnt-provider
  - Academy of Nutrition and Dietetics free online monthly publication available to members covering topics on Medicare;

Medicaid; and private insurance billing, coding, and coverage, as well as practice and business management

- *RDN's Complete Guide to Credentialing and Billing: The Private Payer Market:* www.eatrightSTORE.org/product/7C8BA30A-CC36-4163-A7FC-31909575FECD
  - Free download for Academy of Nutrition and Dietetics members

- The Academy of Nutrition and Dietetics Reimbursement Online Community: https://adareimbursement.webauthor.com
  - Join to post and read questions and replies

- The Academy of Nutrition and Dietetics annual Public Policy Workshop and affiliate meetings
  - Participation in these meetings or online webinars transmists the latest information on policy as well as the opportunity to meet and lobby political representatives

- Your state Academy of Nutrition and Dietetics affiliate, district Academy of Nutrition and Dietetics affiliate, or dietetic practice group (DPG) reimbursement representative
  - Should be available to assist you with local issues

- DPGs, several of which offer mentoring services to Academy of Nutrition and Dietetics members.
  - Reimbursement manuals and/or materials available published by some DPGs; some sell resources while others provide them as a free service to members; consult individual DPG websites for listing of materials; link to DPG sites through the Academy of Nutrition and Dietetics website (www.eatrightPRO.org)

- Your local library and the internet (which are good places to re-search business-related information, reimbursement issues, and policy issues)

- The Centers for Medicare & Medicaid Services (CMS) and Medi-care Administrative Contractor (MAC) webpages: www.cms.gov

BECOMING A THIRD-PARTY PROVIDER

This is useful information for credentialing with third-party payers.

- Council for Affordable Quality Healthcare (CAQH) Getting Start-ed: https://proview.caqh.org/PR/Registration
  - Resource to organize and share all your professional and prac-tice information for credentialing, recredentialing, and updat-ing your records for participating third-party payers

- National Provider Identifier (NPI):
https://nppes.cms.hhs.gov/NPPES/Welcome.do
  - Obtain your unique 10-digit NPI for your superbill and/or to submit claims to third-party payers

Third-Party Payers

These are nationwide third-party payers.

- Aetna: www.aetna.com
- Blue Cross Blue Shield (BCBS): www.bcbs.com
  - Note: BCBS is a franchise system;use this website to find your local BCBS to enroll as a provider
- Cigna: www.cigna.com
- Medicare application online: https://pecos.cms.hhs.gov
- Medicare, Medicaid, and Children's Health Insurance Program: www.cms.gov
- United Healthcare: www.uhc.com

INTERNATIONAL CLASSIFICATION OF DISEASES, CLINICAL MODIFICATIONS, 10TH REVISION DIAGNOSIS CODE LOOKUP

The following are free resources to obtain an International Classification of Diseases, Clinical Modifications, 10th Revision (ICD-10) code for a diagnosis or to find the diagnosis for the ICD-10:

- Centers for Medicare & Medicaid Services ICD-10 code lookup: www.cms.gov/medicare-coverage-database/staticpages/icd-10 -code-lookup.aspx
- ICD-10-CM free lookup: www.icd10data.com/

BILLING SERVICES

Online Billing Services

Submit your claims electronically.

- Availity: www.availity.com
  - Free eligibility, benefits, and claims management for participating third-party payers
- Office Ally: www.officeally.com
  - Provides free claims submission and billing services

Billers

Contract with a biller service or biller to manage claim submission on your behalf.

- Camille DeSimone: www.dietitianbilling.com/
  - Billing service with experience working with RDNs

- Healthy Bytes: www.healthybytes.co/
  - In addition to filing claims, Healthy Bytes also assists with the paperwork to become a participating provider

- InMediata: www.inmediata.com/us/
  - Claims submission and reconciliation

HIPAA Resources

These sites provide additional information on complying with HIPAA regulations.

- Health Information Privacy—HIPAA: US Department of Health and Human Services: www.hhs.gov/hipaa/for-professionals/index.html

- HIPAA and Registered Dietitian Nutritionists, The Academy of Nutrition and Dietetics: www.eatrightPRO.org/resource/practice /getting-paid/smart-business-practice-and-management /hipaa-requirements

Becoming a Nutrition Therapist

This section lists tools to develop skills and techniques for counseling in private practice.

BOOKS

- Drago L. *15-Minute Consultation: Tips, Tools, and Activities to Make Your Nutrition Counseling More Effective*. Chicago, IL: Academy of Nutrition and Dietetics; 2017.

- Herrin M, Larkin M. *Nutrition Counseling in the Treatment of Eating Disorders*. 2nd ed. New York, NY: Routledge; 2013.

- Hoffinger R. *Hands-on Nutrition Education: Teaching Healthy Eating Skills Through Experiential Learning*. Chicago, IL: Academy of Nutrition and Dietetics; 2016.

- Setnick J. *Academy of Nutrition and Dietetics Pocket Guide to Eating Disorders*. 2nd ed. Chicago, IL: Academy of Nutrition and Dietetics; 2016.

RESOURCES FOR THE EMERGING NUTRITION THERAPIST

These are different approaches to and support for competency in counseling.

- Academy for Eating Disorders: www.aedweb.org
  - Offers the *International Journal of Eating Disorders*, a bimonthly newsletter, an annual conference, educational seminars, and publications on eating disorder topics
- Bulimia.com: www.bulimia.com
  - A comprehensive listing of books, periodicals, and resources about treatment and prevention of eating disorders and other food issues
- The Center for Mindful Eating: http://thecenterformindfuleating.org
  - Offers a newsletter, webinars, teleconferences, and professional development in mindful eating
- International Association of Eating Disorders Professional Foundation: www.iaedp.com
  - Offers courses and resources on counseling specific to eating disorders
- Intuitive Eating: www.intuitiveeating.com
  - Offers books and training on the intuitive eating approach
- The Renfrew Center Foundation: http://renfrewcenter.com/renfrew-center-foundation
  - Publishes a quarterly newsletter addressing counseling topics, holds an annual symposium, and offers clinical training

MOTIVATIONAL INTERVIEWING RESOURCES

These publications provide information on acquiring competence in motivational interviewing.

- Clifford D, Curtis L. *Motivational Interviewing in Nutrition and Fitness*. New York, NY: Guilford Press; 2016.
- Miller W, Rollnick S. *Motivational Interviewing: Helping People Change*. 3rd ed. New York, NY: Guilford Press; 2013.
- MollyKellogg.com: www.mollykellogg.com
  - Resource for supervision information and a monthly newsletter; offers three publications: *Counseling Tips for Nutrition Therapists (Vol. 1-3)*
- Motivational Interviewing (MI) Organization: www.motivationalinterviewing.org

- MI resources, information, and training through the Motivational Interviewing Network of Trainers (MINT)

- Sauter C, Constance A. *Inspiring and Supporting Behavior Change.* 2nd ed. Chicago, IL: Academy of Nutrition and Dietetics; 2017.

HEALTH COACHING

Health coach training can vary. Research coach training programs through the International Coach Federation.

Health Coaching Program Certification

- International Coach Federation: www.coachfederation.org
  - Certification agency for coach training programs

Health Coaching Training

- Coach Training Alliance (CTA): www.coachtrainingalliance.com/

- Coaches Training Institute (CTI): www.thecoaches.com/

- Duke University Integrative Health Coach Professional Program: www.dukeintegrativehealthcoach.com/

- National Society of Health Coaches: www.nshcoa.com/

- Wellcoaches: http://wellcoachesschool.com

The Academy of Nutrition and Dietetics Nutrition Education and Counseling Networking and Mentoring Opportunities

- Academy of Nutrition and Dietetics: www.eatrightPRO.org

- DPGs of the Academy of Nutrition and Dietetics
  - Members of various practice groups receive free resources, such as monthly newsletters and access to electronic mailing lists; most DPGs sell resources to both members and non-members; consult their websites for information on additional benefits (DPG sites are linked to the Academy of Nutrition and Dietetics website at www.eatrightPRO.org)
  - DPGs you may find helpful might include the following:
    - Behavioral Health Nutrition: www.bhndpg.org
    - Diabetes Care and Education: www.dce.org

- Dietitians in Business and Communications: www.dbconline.org

- Dietitians in Integrative and Functional Medicine: http://integrativerd.org

- Nutrition Entrepreneurs: www.nedpg.org

- Sports, Cardiovascular, and Wellness Nutrition: www.scandpg.org

- Weight Management: www.wmdpg.org

- eMentoring and Mentoring Resources from the Academy of Nutrition and Dietetics: www.eatrightPRO.org/resource/career/ career-development/mentoring-networking-and-volunteering/ ementoring-and-mentoring-resources

  - A free service provided to all members as mentors or protégés

Continuing Professional Education

This edition of *Making Nutrition Your Business*, Second Edition, offers readers 6 hours of Continuing Professional Education (CPE) credit.

Readers may earn credit by completing the interactive online quiz at: https://publications.webauthor.com/makingnutritionyourbusiness2nd.

Index

A

B

business
> books, 239–240
> card, 87–88, 158, 243
> consultant, 30
> contract, 29
> license, 28
> magazines, 240
> phone, 83–84, 154
> plan, 24–25

C

calorimeter, 111–112
cancellation policy, 48
CAQH, *see Council for Affordable Quality Healthcare (CAQH)*
case study
> DJ, 209–210
> SD, 211

cash payment for services, 44
Cassens, Digna Irizarry, 216
Castle, Jill, 224–225
CBT, *see cognitive behavioral therapy (CBT)*
Centers for Medicare and Medicate Services (CMS), 122, 1124, 128, 129, 134, 144, 150
check payment for services, 45
Children's Health Insurance Program (CHIP), 125
CHIP, *see Children's Health Insurance Program (CHIP)*
Chernus, Andrea, 212
Clark, Nancy, 225–226
client database, 40
CMS, *see Centers for Medicare and Medicate Services (CMS)*
CMS 1500 form, ***see Form CMS-1500***
coaching, *see health coaching*
cognitive behavioral therapy (CBT), 203
contract, for your business, 29
coleasing, office space, 68–70
collection policy, 48
Commission on Dietetic Registration, Academy of Nutrition and Dietetics, 54
communication, 8
competitor profile, 60

E

F

I

business cards, 87–88, 158, 242
conducting research, 178–179
consultant, 31
direct, 163
directories, 172
elevator speech, 63–64
email, 177
focus groups, 165–166
follow-up letter, 171
gifts, 171–172
internet, 179
logos, 56, 57
mail, 171
multimedia tools, 186–187
networking, 12, 167–170, 206–207
newspaper, 171
newsletter, 172, 241
niche, 61–62
plan, 25, 164–165
radio, 171
resources, 243
self-promotion, 5, 166–167
social media, 160–161, 167–168, 179–186, 244
target market, determining your, 58–62
television, 171
thank-you notes, 171
marketplace analysis, 58
medical nutrition therapy (MNT), 9, 52, 114–115, 122, 123, 130–131, 137, 151, 204
Medicaid, 48, 121, 122, 124–125, 129, 134
medical model of patient care, 196–197
Medicare, 48, 121, 122, 123–124, 128–129, 133, 134, 144
Medicare Access and Chip Reauthorization Act of 2015, 150
mentor, 31–32
merit-based Incentive Payment System (MIPS), 150–151
Mills, Linda Eck, 206
MIPS, *see Merit-based Incentive Payment System (MIPS)*
missed appointments, 48
mission statement, 62–63
MNT, *see medical nutrition therapy (MNT)*

Q

R